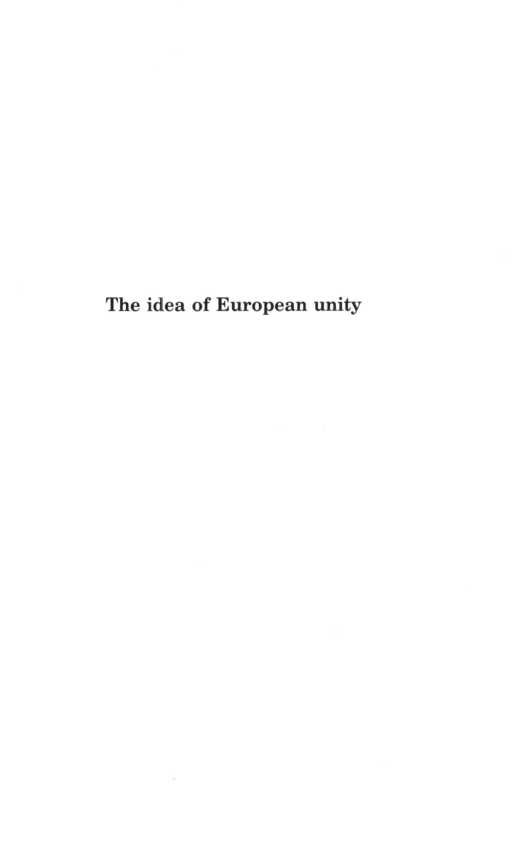

The idea of European unity

The Idea of European Unity

Derek Heater

St. Martin's Press
New York

First published in the United States of America in 1992

Printed in Great Britain

ISBN 0-312-07947-8

Library of Congress Cataloging-in-Publication Data

Heater, Derek Benjamin.
  The idea of European unity / Derek Heater.
    p.   cm.
  Includes bibliographical references and index.
  ISBN 0-312-07947-8
  1. Europe--Politics and government. 2. European federation.
  I. Title.
  D105.H43 1992
  320.94--dc20   91-44260
                                                              CIP

Contents

List of maps

Diagram

Preface

Neither the idea of a European federal union nor the problems which confront those who would bring it to fruition are entirely novel. As early as the fourteenth century plans were drafted to provide for tighter collaboration among the several states of Europe than prevailed in political practice. The urge to produce such schemes is continuous from the seventeenth century to our own day.

The purpose of this book is to present the major projects that have been drafted from the early seventeenth century to the 1950s. A detailed analysis of these texts is not, as far as I am aware, available in any other single volume. But, more than that, the schemes are set in the context of the international conditions of their time and the personal experiences and convictions of their authors. For, although the numerous schemes for European unity tackled problems that have proved persistent over the centuries, each has been coloured by the particular circumstances of its composition.

I am once again very happy to record my deep gratitude to my wife for help in so many ways in the composition of the manuscript, not least the loving and diligent labour she expended in its typing.

Derek Heater
Rottingdean

―――――――――――― CHAPTER 1 ――――――――――――

Introduction: Medieval origins

Unity and division in the Middle Ages

Europe has never been effectively united. Even in the early Middle
Ages – before the age of the nation-state – political fragmentation ran
as a vigorous counterpoint to the themes of cultural unity and dreams
of a universalist empire.

One of the recurrent dreams pictured a resuscitated Roman Empire
as a unifying force. But in truth the Roman Empire had provided the
continent of Europe with little in the way of unity. Geographically its
centre of gravity was the Mediterranean basin, thus incorporating
much territory that was African and Asian and excluding much that
was European. Culturally, the distinction between Latins and Greeks
persisted, to be virtually institutionalised ultimately by the division
of the Empire. In the fourth century Valentinian I inaugurated a
dyarchy by establishing his brother as Emperor of the Eastern Empire.
This partition was consolidated by the survival of an Eastern (Byzan-
tine) Empire, until finally extinguished eleven hundred years later,
and by the increasingly distinctive Orthodox Church. Meanwhile, in
western Europe the British, Gallic, Iberian and (with varying fortunes) Italian provinces were broken off the Empire and divided as
spoils by the barbarian invaders.

True, for a fleeting moment c.450 all Europe except the northern
and extreme western fringes were apportioned among three great
emperors; the Western Roman Empire under Valentinian III, the
Eastern Roman Empire under Marcian and the sprawling central
Hunnish Empire of Attila. However, by the end of the eighth century
the political map of the continent had resumed its more usual patchwork quality. England was divided into the heptarchy. Three-quarters
of the Iberian peninsula was under Muslim rule. The Eastern Empire
was but a shadow of its former self. Vast areas of central and eastern

Europe were populated by politically inchoate Slavs, Avars, Bulgars and Magyars.

The largest European kingdom was that of the Franks, which the eldest son of Pepin III inherited in 768. His name was Charles, later entitled 'the Great' and known therefore as Charlemagne. The ultimate geographical expanse of his dominions and his assumption of the imperial purple prompted commentators at the time and since to somewhat exaggerated views concerning the significance of the unificatory achievements of his reign. To take a few examples from recent history. An early exponent of European monetary union proposed to call his currency unit the Charlemagne (see p.111). Ominously a century later, in the view of one German historian, 'it was more than a gesture of empty ceremony when Hitler, in Nuremberg at the beginning of September [1935], accepted the presentation of a reproduction of Charlemagne's sword.' (Fest, p.731). Then, after the Second World War, those who were considered to have made a signal contribution to the unification of Europe by peaceful means were awarded the Charlemagne Prize. Finally, it may be noted that when the Europe of 'the Six' was created in the 1950s (see Chapter 7), the similarity of the geographical extent of the Community with that of the Carolingian Empire was often remarked upon.

But let us return to Charlemagne himself. What are the bases for the idea that his Empire was a kind of proto-United States of Europe? In the first place, he held sway over very extensive territories, from marchlands just south of the Pyrenees in the south-west to Holstein in the north, to a frontier along the river Drave in the south-east, to a frontier in the south in Italy, a little north of Naples. Secondly, at a time when, as we shall notice below, the very concept of Europe barely existed, Charlemagne was described as the 'father of Europe' and 'the worshipful head of Europe' (see Hay, p.51). On Christmas Day 800 the Pope crowned him as Emperor. But what did this imperial style portend? This has been one of the most vexed questions in medieval historiography. It must have vexed Charlemagne too; for not until five months after his coronation did he settle on his own, extraordinarily pompous title, namely, 'Charles, most serene Augustus, crowned by God, great and pacific emperor, governing the Roman empire' (see Barraclough, 1950, p.10).

Charlemagne's coronation was an attempt by the Church to revive the idea of the Western Roman Empire. It was not immediately very effective. On Charlemagne's death in 814 his dominions were divided among his sons and the imperial title gradually faded into disuse.

The Holy Roman Empire did, however, live as a potential, indeed, on occasions actual, force for unity in central Europe for some four centuries – from the mid-tenth to the mid-fourteenth century. During this period some Emperors attempted by propaganda and appeals to law to construct a theoretical edifice of widespread authority over Europe, or properly speaking Christendom, as a whole. In 1157 the

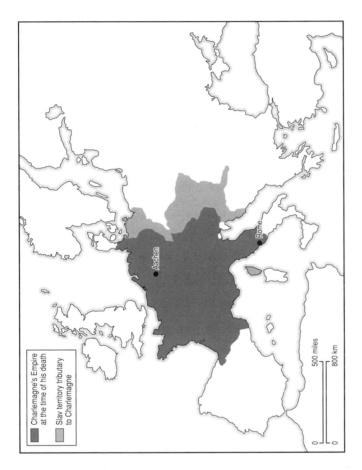

Map 1 Charlemagne's Empire

Emperor Frederick Barbarossa coined the term 'Holy Empire' to describe this institution. Frederick, the first of the Hohenstaufen line, was particularly energetic in putting himself forward as the secular champion of all Christians. As the Austrian historian Friedrich Heer has written,

Official and semi-official court poetry and imperial propaganda hailed the Holy Roman Empire, revived by the Emperor Frederick I, as the kingdom of salvation and righteousness, the terrestrial representative of the Kingdom of God, and presented it as such to 'truly believing subjects', that is subjects faithful both to God and the Empire (Heer, p.192).

On the other hand, there was much to be said for the view of Voltaire who quipped that the Holy Roman Empire 'was neither Holy, nor Roman, nor an Empire.' Any attempt to translate the *Reichsmystik* into political hegemony was fiercely resisted by states beyond the imperial domain of Germany and northern Italy. Furthermore, the Papacy was jealous of its own authority throughout Christendom. And so, fearful of imperial pretensions, Popes both clashed with some of the more ambitious Emperors and developed a policy of national or local ecclesiastical autonomy under papal leadership.

Yet the common faith of Christianity was a powerful bonding-force. Together with the persistence and revival of Latin and civil law from the old Roman Empire, it provided Europe with considerable cultural homogeneity. As Christianity spread, by the thirteenth century to the very fringes of the geographical continent, so Europe achieved religious, if not political, unity.

For much of the Middle Ages the term 'Christendom' was used rather than 'Europe' to describe the continent. As Professor Denys Hay has shown, the very word 'Europe' was rarely used until the fourteenth century (the Carolingian episode excepted). Thus 'One can count the score or so references to Europe in Dante: in Petrarch they are too frequent for enumeration.' (Hay, p.59). (Dante died in 1321; Petrarch in 1374.) The notion of Christendom gave the high Middle Ages a sense of both integration and differentiation. As the Asiatic and African Christian churches decayed, were reckoned heretical or lost their flocks by conversion to Islam, so Christendom and Europe became increasingly coterminous. The land-mass from the Arctic to the Mediterranean, from the Atlantic to the River Don (the traditional eastern boundary-mark of Europe) was peopled by Christians. The other two known continents were not.

This European feeling of Christian identity was measurably reinforced by the collision with the expanding power of Islam. Arabs and Saracens, variously termed, spilled into the Levant and along the southern Mediterranean littoral in the seventh and eighth centuries. Sicily was conquered, and Spain. Then the Muslim banner was carried across the Pyrenees, until the onrush was stemmed in the great Battle of Tours in 732. Even Rome was sacked in 846. The Islamic challenge to Christendom had revealed how hollow the Imperial claim was of being able 'to defend the holy Church of Christ with arms against the attack of pagans and devastation by infidels from without' (quoted, Davis, pp.254–5). In default, the Papacy provided leadership. It was the French Pope, Urban II, who took decisive action. At the Council of Clermont in 1095 he exhorted Christians to bear the cross and arms for the recovery of Jerusalem. And so it transpired that, in the words of Geoffrey Barraclough, 'in the First Crusade Europe, for the first time in its history, undertook a united action.' (Barraclough, 1963, p.15). In truth, it was a precarious sort of unity. Four separate armies were recruited; and the crusaders wreaked considerable havoc in the march through the 'European' Eastern Empire. Even so, a unity of purpose did impel them.

By the end of the thirteenth century the environment in which we might search for clues to a striving for European unity had once again changed. This newly emerging pattern was characterised by a strengthening of state identity and a concomitant weakening of both Imperial and Papal pretensions to overarching authority. The shapes of nation-states were already recognisable in primitive form in certain parts of Europe. To the north lay the kingdoms of Norway, Sweden and Denmark; to the west, the kingdoms of England, Scotland, France, Portugal, Castile and Aragon; and in eastern Europe Lithuania, Poland and Hungary were also gradually crystallising as centralised kingdoms.

In the very heart of the continent, however, this process of the consolidating of princely power operated against Imperial hegemony. The authority of the Emperor, first outside the Empire and then inside, was more and more challenged. To give a few examples. Pope Innocent III at the beginning of the thirteenth century declared that Philip Augustus, the King of France, 'recognises no superior *in temporalibus*' (Barraclough, 1963, p.17). Even the strong Emperor Frederick II, grandson of Barbarossa, could not retard the decay of Imperial power in Germany and Italy for long. By the time of his death in 1250 the Empire was a hollow institution. Civil war supervened. (Ironically it was only in 1254 that the full title 'Holy Roman Empire' was adopted.)

The Papacy too was showing signs of weakness as an alternative unifying force. The schism with the eastern Orthodox Church was too deep for the Papal claim to the leadership of all Christians to be at all credible. Furthermore, even in the extensive lands which recognised the primacy of the Pope, neither princes nor people were in a mood to accept Papal interference in their national affairs.

This decay in Europe's sense of unity was a cause of some concern. As a consequence, during the generation *c.*1280–1310 publications were urgently produced as outline schemes for achieving effective integration. These plans are the start of the habit of drafting blueprints for European union which has lasted to our own day and is the theme of the present book. It is important, therefore, to examine the background concerns impelling these writers who founded such a long-lasting tradition. We may distinguish four separate motives.

One was the worrying situation in the Middle East. In 1291 the fortress-city of Acre fell, the last Christian stronghold in the Holy Land. The crusading venture had failed. In the meantime, the Byzantines were being steadily pushed out of Asia Minor by the combined power of Seljuk and Ottoman Turks. These Christian reverses were interpreted by commentators in Europe either as a punishment for the disunity into which Christendom had fallen or as evidence that the crusading efforts should be revived with a greater unified strength.

Another, second consideration at this time was an attempt to revive the Empire. Arguments that it was essential to prevent the victory of anti-Christ and the forces of disorder were published to counteract the common opinion of the late thirteenth century that the Empire had proved itself to be useless. The tracts of Englebert of Admont, Alexander of Roes and Dante Alighieri were particularly notable in this campaign. They are reviewed in the next section of this chapter (pp.8–9).

A third objective was the parallel effort to revive the hegemonic ambitions of the Papacy. We shall take note of the arguments of Giles of Rome, James of Viterbo and the Bulls of Pope Boniface VIII himself below (pp.7–8). What we need to notice here is the utter determination of Boniface to exert his authority when he became Pope in 1294. He combined an autocratic personality, a well-educated legal mind and a love of ceremonial spectacle. In 1300 he organised a mass gathering of Christians in Rome to mark the Jubilee Year which he invented. It is even said that he donned the imperial purple for the occasion.

At the same time in Paris, and fourthly, pamphleteers were writing similar propaganda in defence of the national pretensions of their monarch, Philip the Fair. He became King of France in 1285. France was now the most powerful state in Europe; and Philip, conscious of his strength both internally and externally, pursued most vigorous and audacious policies. Could there not in consequence be a case for arguing a system of European unity based not on Imperial or Papal leadership but rather on that of the power of France? This historically significant concept was the core of Dubois's work, the most important of all the medieval schemes for our purpose (see pp.9–12).

The personalities and policies of Boniface and Philip were mutually combustible. When the match was applied the fiery explosion was dramatic to behold. The quarrel started in 1296 with the Pope's claim to the proceeds of taxation of the clergy and Philip's refusal. The conflict was fought with all the weapons at their disposal. Boniface discharged several Bulls of justification and threatened Philip with excommunication. Philip's ordnance proved mightier. After the casting of spells against his enemy, he eventually had Boniface kidnapped in 1303, after which the Pope soon died. Philip subsequently consolidated his influence over the Papacy by securing the election of a Frenchman as Pope Clement V. This Pontiff, by establishing the Holy See at French-controlled Avignon, inaugurated what William of Occam called 'the Babylonish captivity'.

Any claim by the Papacy to an imperial-style authority was now unthinkable. Just under half a century later, in 1356, the Emperor Charles IV discarded the final trappings of medieval temporal imperialism by issuing his Golden Bull recognising constitutional decentralisation in Germany.

The restitution of the very concept of European unity now depended on the persistence of the scholars and statesmen who published their written plans for the unification of the continent. This long and frustrating history started at the turn of the thirteenth and fourteenth centuries.

Early schemes for unity

From the late thirteenth century, for some three decades, lay and clerical pens were busy in the production of plans for enhancing the unity of the world, Christendom or Europe. The majority sought salvation in Imperial or Papal supremacy; the most prescient of the authors, Dubois, advocated French leadership.

Let us examine the Papal proposals first. The two most important are Boniface's Papal Bull, *Unam Sanctam* of 1302 and *De Potestate Ecclesiastica (On Ecclesiastical Power)* by Giles of Rome (Egidius Colonna), probably written at about the same time. Giles had been tutor to Philip the Fair some years earlier; ironically, for his book is an extreme exposition of the theory that the power of the secular prince is righteous only if grounded in ecclesiastical authority. Even private property, he argued, could be owned in any just sense only by true believers. The immediate purpose of the tract was clear: to condemn the pretensions to autonomy of his former pupil. Its relevance for us is the forthright exposition of the case for the Pope's overlordship over the whole of Christendom – and beyond. In the words of Walter Ullmann,

The aim of the book of Giles of Rome was to prove that the pope had sovereignty (here called 'supremacy') over the whole of the world, concerning everyone and everything, and that consequently princes (in no wise different from ecclesiastics) were subjects of the pope; furthermore, that all sacerdotal and regal powers were located in the pope by virtue of his plenitude of power (Ullmann, pp.124–5).

By asserting such extreme claims Giles proved himself to be more papal than the Pope. In his famous Bull Boniface contented himself with a succinct summary of previous arguments for the universality of Papal authority. He constructed a hierarchical monocephalous model of the world. As Christ's vicar on earth the Pope must, nat‑ urally, be the supreme ruler. And although he delegates the wielding of the temporal sword to the secular princes, they may exercise this power only 'at the bidding and sufferance of the pope' (quoted, Ullmann, p.115). The Bull concludes with the declaration that 'it is altogether necessary to salvation for every human creature to be sub‑ ject to the Roman Pontiff' (quoted, Morrall, p.86).

Much of the Papal case obviously related to the spiritual supremacy of the Pope over all God's creatures. As such it has little relevance for our study of European political unity. Nevertheless, given the context of the Franco-Papal 'cold war' in which these statements were written, the practical message for the continent was clear. By both explicit enunciation and implicit allusion, the Papacy was claiming an overar‑ ching political authority over all the secular rulers of Europe.

In similar fashion the Imperial claim to continental sovereignty avoided an ending with a whimper by being finally supported by the big gun of Dante's *De Monarchia*. However, before looking at Dante's book, it is fitting to notice two earlier and lesser works. These authors, writing in the early 1280s, were Englebert of Admont and Alexander of Roes. Englebert argued for persisting with the Empire because, for all its imperfections, Europe was more likely to achieve tranquillity and security with it than without it. He is also of interest to us for his argument concerning the underlying homogeneity of the continent. Despite ethnic, linguistic and cultural differences, he pointed out, all peoples lived by the precepts of natural and Roman law. The Roman Emperor should therefore be recognised as rightfully ruling over a pyramidal social and political structure held together by common Christian and legal principles.

Alexander, too, was concerned to warn against disorder. His tract, which became widely read, was written largely to defend the interests of the Germans against Papal and French ambitions to European supremacy. He sketched a kind of triumvirate of German Emperor endowed with political leadership; Italian Pope, with spiritual leader‑ ship; and French King, with intellectual leadership.

Dante is in a different category from any of the above. He was a layman, an experienced politician and a writer of genius, whose book on the subject of universal empire, *De Monarchia*, was a major contri‑ bution to political theory. It is evident that he was thinking about this problem throughout the first decade of the fourteenth century. He left an unfinished treatise in Italian before publishing *De Mon‑ archia* in 1311.

Reflecting his lay background Dante, unlike other writers of the time, is at pains to emphasise that he is concerned with *temporal* power, unencumbered with overtones of spiritual authority. He argues the utility of a universal monarch as the preserver of peace and the fount of justice. His function is to stand above and damp down the internecine strife of quarrelling states. Dante was impressed by the example of the ancient *Pax Romana* and further argues that a revived universal monarchy would derive its authority direct from God, not via the Pope as intermediary. Dante goes further: he makes a distinction between humanity and Christianity, between the universal human state and Christendom. Politics and government belong to the first sphere only.

We have already remarked that a concept of Europe was but weakly formed in Dante's mind (see p.4). Dante's theory of universal monarchy is none the less relevant to the history of European unity. He secularised European political thinking and proposed a kind of federal structure of states beneath a supreme peace-keeper. it was a framework which was readily adaptable in future centuries in ways that the heavily Christianised thought of the period from Charlemagne to Boniface could not be.

Pierre Dubois (Petrus De Bosco, in its latinised form) was also a layman – a lawyer by training and a pamphleteer by inclination. He has been described by one authority as 'one of the greatest medieval pamphleteers' (Sabine, p.233). And by another as, 'one of the boldest speculators of the Middle Ages' (Power, p.144). He was born, in about 1255, in the vicinity of the Norman town of Coutance, where he later practised law. He studied at the University of Paris under the famous and controversial philosopher, Siger of Brabant (who also taught Dante). Eventually, Dubois became an adviser to Philip the Fair and one of his most skilful propagandists. In this capacity he was centrally involved in the conflict with Boniface VIII already described (see p.6). He advised his monarch to adopt both anti-clerical and anti-Papal stances and a positive policy of personal and national aggrandisement. For example, in 1308 he counselled Philip to arrange for his own election as Emperor and to lead a crusade to liberate Jerusalem.

In 1300, in the middle of Philip's dispute with Boniface, Dubois wrote his *Treatise on the Way to shorten Wars* (its lengthy Latin title is usually truncated to *De Abbreviatione*). This work is of interest not just for its hostility to the pretensions of the Church but also for its conscious national pride. 'It would be salutary,' he wrote, 'for the whole world to submit to France, for the French make better use of the power of rational judgment than do other people' (quoted, Heer, p.340; see also Hinsley, p.16).

About five years later Dubois briefly took service with Edward I. The English king's resistance to Boniface's demands had been almost as determined as Philip's. It is also pertinent to note Edward's well-known keenness to resume the crusades. Edward's zeal was, indeed, posthumously attested by the provision in his will of thirty thousand pounds to finance a military expedition to bury his heart in the Holy

Land. It is therefore not surprising that, when Dubois came to write his major two-part work, *De Recuperatione Terrae Sanctae (On the Recovery of the Holy Land)*, he should address the first part, which was published *c*.1306, primarily to the English monarch.

It is this book which contains Dubois's plans for European union. Not that he refers to 'Europe' nor even 'Christendom', but rather 'all catholics', 'the republic of catholics' and 'the republic of Christians' – so rare was the concept of Europe at the time (see Hay, p.36n). It is none the less clear that it is the states of Europe that he has in mind in presenting his proposal.

Dubois's book is a somewhat confused compilation. The gist of his recommendations is as follows. War is abhorrent yet endemic. On the other hand, fighting has not been stopped by the lessons of 'the Holy Scripture, which detests wars, and the preachers who say this to the public . . . ' (quoted, de Rougemont, p.63). Some international disciplinary system is needed. But he rejects anything like a restoration of the Roman Empire as outdated. He explains:

I do not think that a sensible person can regard as possible, after all these centuries, that everyone should be ruled in respect of temporal things by a single monarch . . . there would be endless wars, seditions, and dissensions; . . . because of the multitude of nations, the distances and the diversity of lands, and the natural disposition of men to discord (quoted, de Rougemont, p.63).

Dubois's solution is that the princes and cities of Europe should form a confederal 'Christian Republic' overseen by a Council. This Council would establish a panel of nine judges to arbitrate in the event of an international quarrel: three each from the two litigant states and three neutral ecclesiastics. These should be 'well-to-do men and of a condition such that they could not be corrupted by love, or hatred, or fear, or greed, or anything else' (quoted, de Rougemont, p.64). If these arbitrators fail to reach an acceptable solution, the matter is to be referred to the Pope as a justice of appeal. However, since the 'Sovereign Pontiff' can threaten only the postponed and horrifying disciplinary measures of the hereafter, Dubois provides for the immediate and worldly punishment of the recalcitrant. The penal powers of the Council are two-fold: military or economic sanctions and exile. The state or city deemed to be guilty may be invaded or subjected to an economic blockade. Once the offenders have been seized they and their families are to be dispatched to the Holy Land.

It is in this part of his scheme that Dubois particularly reveals his ingenuity. A whole vista of benefits is opened to the reader's admiring gaze. Trouble-makers are 'rusticated' from Europe. And because they tend to be of a belligerent nature (they would not have caused trouble in the first place otherwise), they will be particularly efficacious in prosecuting the holy war against the infidel. Moreover, because whole families are to suffer the exile, it could be hoped that highly educated and nubile European women might seduce the Islamic peoples from their faith and convert them to Christianity. In due course of time through this process of colonisation the Mediterranean Sea would become a European lake, as it had once been a Roman, to the inestimable advantage of profitable commerce.

Meanwhile, in Europe peace and the dominant position of that continent in the world were to be consolidated by the civilising powers of education and an enhanced French state. Education was to be reorganised and largely freed from ecclesiastical control. Modern European, classical and Middle Eastern languages were to be included in the curricula. Oriental tongues were to be taught for the purpose of having interpreters available to facilitate the process of converting the infidel. Medicine and science were also to be emphasised. The neglect of women's education would be remedied. Most relevantly for our purposes Dubois proposes the creation of international schools to be funded from the 'peace dividend'. Thus Dubois was perhaps the first advocate of education for international understanding since Zeno founded his Stoic academy in Athens sixteen hundred years earlier.

Finally, it is a vital part of Dubois's scheme to cast his native France in a pivotal role. To modernise the French state he sketches out a series of reforms. Her international power was to be enhanced at the expense of others. France should hold sway over the Papal States, Lombardy, Naples, Sicily, Aragon, Hungary and England. Dubois also had plans for the French royal family to control a large eastern empire, including Constantinople. This plan was contained in the second, shorter, volume of his work, a kind of secret protocol, for the eyes of the King of France only. Furthermore, the appellant role of the Pope could be read as a further increase of French power since the Pontiff was at the time little more than a Capetian puppet: Dubois probably published his book a few months after the coronation of Clement V at Lyon (see p.7). Even the punitive exile arrangements were in French interests, for as Hinsley has written, 'His proposals for the resort to sanctions against disobedient rulers in Europe were intended to further French expansion by justifying the banishment of insubordinate royal houses to the East.' (Hinsley, p.16).

This statement raises the question of Dubois's primary objective. Commentators have been extraordinarily diverse in their judgments, which 'stretch the entire octave of praise and condemnation.' (C.C. Tansill, quoted, Hemleben, p.4). Praise derives from the acceptance of Dubois's eirenic purpose for Europe at its face value; condemnation, from the underlying ambition of French hegemony. We can illustrate something of the range of opinions even in recent authorities. Thus de Rougemont states that 'For Du Bois . . . peace is the *summum bonum*' (de Rougemont, p.63), whereas Stawell, in contrast, expresses the belief that 'He has . . . no real love of peace and no real sympathy with any country other than his own.' (Stawell, p.68). On the issue of his proposed crusade, Hinsley, despite the comment already quoted, states that 'His primary purposes . . . were the recovery of the Holy Land and the preservation of the unity of Christendom . . . ' (Hinsley, p.15). The American scholar, Sylvester Hemleben, is more sceptical, expressing the opinion that, 'It is probable that Dubois used the subject of the Holy Land as a means of popularizing his work . . . ' (Hemleben, p.2). Were, then, Dubois's proclaimed objectives of peace and crusade mere camouflage for a scheme to build France into a regional super-power? This is the unabashed realist reading of Dubois by Barra-clough. 'There were . . . those,' he writes, 'who demanded the "trans-lation" of the Empire; that is to say, its severance from Germany and its conferment on the strongest continental power, i.e. the king of France . . . its most notorious exponent was Pierre Dubois.' (Barra-clough, 1950, p.21). And, more curtly, 'His plea for European unity is a concealed plea for French hegemony.' (Barraclough, 1963, p.19).

How, then, may we characterise Dubois's plan? In brief we may say that he presented a number of current ideas about and facts of international life in an original synthesis together with some novel details. Eileen Power explained the duality in his thought very strik-ingly by declaring that 'he is so modern that he seems to be writing for a Louis XIV or a Napoleon, rather than for a Philippe le Bel and yet he is so much a man of his own day that his new ideas struggle out like a butterfly, still half enmeshed in its mediaeval chrysalis' (Power pp.140–1). He reflected the contemporary desire for renewed crusade, the current device of arbitration in disputes and the evident obsolescence of any continuing Imperial or Papal claims to continental temporal sovereignty. The notions of the transportation of trouble-makers to the colonies and education for international understanding are new, albeit subsidiary, ideas. Dubois may be marked out as a true herald of a modern style of thinking about European unity for three reasons. In the first place, he clearly has the continent and the whole continent in mind, not the whole world or a portion of Europe, as had been the contexts of previous plans. Secondly, he sees the process of co-operation undertaken by a Council, not in the hands of an indi-vidual such as an emperor. Thirdly, he provides for the wielding of power, behind the scenes of the Council, by a dominant nation-state, a form of polity just emerging. And paradoxically this very emergence of the nation-state rendered Dubois's scheme a scarcely practicable plan.

Perhaps it was the *Realpolitik* of the age – of the unremitting Hundred Years War in the west, then the egoistic Renaissance state-craft in Italy – which prevented any immediate follow-up to the bur-geoning interest in union *c*.1300. It was a neglect which persisted despite a growing consciousness of Europe's cultural identity. Then the Reformation further emphasised the political fissiparousness of the continent of Europe. Throughout the span of the fourteenth, fifteenth and sixteenth centuries we find few blueprints for European unity.

Nicholas of Cusa (or Cues), political theorist and diplomat who lived in the first half of the fifteenth century, had a vision of concord embracing all faiths and a Europe composed of states untroubled by ambitions for supremacy.

Much closer to the style of Dubois's proposal and to subsequent plans was that devised by George Poděbrad and Antoine Marini (or Marius). The former was the Hussite King of Bohemia; the latter, an industrialist who came to serve George as a diplomatist. They drafted schemes for a compact against the Turks and a confederal structure for Europe (*De Unione Christianorum Contra Turcos* and *Traité des Alliances et Confédérations*). The main institutional features of the rambling texts are an Assembly, a Court of Justice, international arbitration machinery, union armed-forces and a confederal budget.

The constitutional arrangements are drawn in some detail and have some remarkable features. The Assembly was to be convened at Basle in February 1465. It was to meet regularly and move its seat every five years. Its work would be conducted by a College of permanent members and a Council of kings and princes. What is especially significant about this plan, however, is that for the first time the rulers' sovereignty is abridged by the use of decision-making by majority:

The above-mentioned College shall have as well over us, over our subjects and those who will have prolonged its term, gracious and contentious jurisdiction, at the same time as maternal and joint empire, according as the above-mentioned Assembly or *majority thereof* [emphasis added] shall have resolved and decided (quoted, de Rougemont, p.71).

It is provided for the consistory or International Court to sit in the same city as the Assembly.

The members of the confederation would be required to renounce war with each other. Nevertheless, if conflict were to break out,

the Assembly . . . must . . . immediately send ambassadors at our common expense, even without being requested to do so by our attacked colleague, with the mission to settle the litigation and restore the peace . . . And if by deed and fault of the aggressor, peace and union cannot be achieved, . . . all the others among us, by unanimous agreement, shall aid our ally attacked or forced to defend himself by giving him tithes of our kingdom every year for his defense . . . (quoted, de Rougemont, pp.69–70).

Further economic aid is also to be provided for the welfare of the civilian population of the abused state.

The source of confederal funds is an ingenious, even if naïvely impracticable device: the Pope is to be asked to arrange for church tithes at a rate of three days' income per year to be paid into the Assembly's exchequer on the grounds that this institution is to be the new defender of the Christian faith against the Turk. For the Assembly is charged to decide, by majority vote, on the forces to be mobilised for the crusade and to fix a 'D-day' date for the invasion. Marini was sent to interest various rulers in the plan, most notably Louis XI, at whose court he arrived at the end of 1462. The assistance of France was crucial to George's plan. As a Hussite and therefore heretic he needed help against the Pope; as a Bohemian, he wanted to resist the vestigial authority of the Emperor. Lurking beneath the impressive confederal pooling of some authority lay the offer that the King of France should become Emperor in the West while George himself assumed the titles of Emperor in the East and of Germany.

We then have to wait until the seventeenth century for a general revival of an interest in drawing up blueprints for European union. The most famous of all such schemes was then produced, namely, Sully's Grand Design. Could this have been consciously built on the foundations laid in the Middle Ages? It certainly has much affinity with Dubois's proposals: the aggrandisement of France, peace in Europe, a joint army, war against the Turk, the promotion of trade, a representational central body. It is sometimes assumed that Dubois's work was lost soon after its composition, to be rediscovered only in the 1870s. In fact, a new edition appeared in 1611, soon after Sully had probably made a start on his memoirs.

The belief that medieval Europe could teach modern Europe valuable lessons concerning practical unity is a distorting overestimation of the actual political union achieved in the Middle Ages. Contrariwise, any neglect of medieval hypothetical plans for European unity results in a distorting underestimate of the very solid foundations laid in this field of work in the Middle Ages. It was c.1300 that the pioneering writing was undertaken for a tradition which was revived in the seventeenth century as a permanent feature of European propaganda, pleading and planning for unity.

CHAPTER 2

On the reputation of Henry IV

The Habsburg problem

The Duc de Sully, the subject of this chapter, lived in an age, from the mid-sixteenth to the mid-seventeenth century, of civil and international conflict exacerbated by the religious controversies which were the aftermath of the Reformation. The Netherlands rebelled against Habsburg control; Elizabeth of England helped them. Philip of Spain sought to solve the problem by launching the luckless Armada. In Germany religious schism further inflamed endemic social discontent. France distintegrated into civil war. The early seventeenth century was dominated by the terrible Thirty Years War and the machinations of the French cardinal Richelieu. For an appreciation of the particular background against which Sully worked, it is helpful to analyse the major factors dominating European politics as perceived from the vantage-point of France. These were: religious conflict; the widespread search for a peaceful solution to European quarrels; the thrust of the Habsburgs to hegemonic power provoking rivalry with the Valois-Bourbon monarchy of France; and the policy and distinguished reputation of Henry IV.

Luther and Calvin finally destroyed the medieval ideal of a unified (Catholic) Christian Europe. Religious conflict sundered the twin pillars upon which the ideal was built, namely western Christendom and the Holy Roman Empire. True, well before the Reformation both pillars were, as we have seen in Chapter 1, visibly and dangerously cracked. None the less, a strengthening of these spiritual and secular supports of the European idea was perhaps not out of the question before religious protest cut such deep and gaping fissures. The shattering of Roman Christianity – the destruction of its pretended catholicity – involved, of course, not just the political act on the part of Protestants of renouncing the leadership of the Pope. What rendered the religious divisions of western and central Europe so bitterly irreconcilable was the quarrel over dogma. The reformers could not stomach the concept of the Real Presence in the wine and wafer of the Mass; the adherents to the Roman rite abhorred the heretical simile of the Protestants' Holy Communion. For generations, each side rent Europe and each other apart in orgies of torture and slaughter. The fury, intensified and prolonged by cynical secular political motives, reached its height in the horrendous Thirty Years War. Although historians have recently shown that the horror and carnage of this conflict have been considerably exaggerated, its impact on the seventeenth-century mind was none the less very vivid. News of the terrible sufferings of the civilian population of central Europe, as troops marched and counter-marched across the German states, added up to a grim picture.

But the religious divisions did not coincide with state boundaries. They consequently occasioned or embittered civil discord, which in turn enticed foreign states to intervene in some of these domestic conflicts in aid of their co-religionists. England survived the Catholic-inspired sixteenth-century uprisings such as the Pilgrimage of Grace and the Rebellion of the Northern Earls, though succumbed to civil war a century later. In Germany the Peasants' War of 1524–25, draw-ing upon discontents from a far broader social spectrum than the conventional title suggests, terrified the ruling classes. Moreover, despite Luther's horrified denunciation of the uprisings, there can be no doubt that the Protestant challenge to ecclesiastical authority encouraged the oppressed lower orders of society to believe in the rectitude of a more generalised challenge to the status quo. The crisis soon passed, the rebels crushed with cruel savagery. The threat to political stability in France was more sustained. The generation-long civil wars from 1560 to 1589, though symptoms of the weakness of the Valois monarchy and irresponsible factionalism of certain of the leading nobility, were exacerbated by the religious cleavage between Catholic and Huguenot. Meanwhile, the same Calvinist faith nour-ished the revolt against Spanish rule in the Netherlands, even if geographical as much as theological differences explain the success of the revolt in the north and its failure in the south.

It was the Netherlands revolt more than any other civil religious conflict that tempted neighbouring states to interfere in the internal affairs of others. Elizabeth strained every financial muscle to assist the Dutch – out of strategic as well as religious considerations. Eng-land from the age of Philip II to that of Hitler consistently feared the establishment of major hostile forces in the Low Countries. But if Elizabeth felt justified in her policy, so too did Philip. He could not tolerate the resistance of the Dutch rebels being stiffened by the Tudor arch-heretic. It is no coincidence that the Spanish king started to lay plans for the Armada in May 1585 when news reached him of England's preparations for military intervention in the Low Coun-tries. Affairs in the Netherlands also intertwined with events in France. For example, the Huguenot leader Coligny was preparing to lead a force into the Netherlands in 1572. A pro-Spanish group attempted to assassinate him. This bungled plot led directly to the Massacre of St Bartholomew (see p.22). The year after the Armada fiasco Philip judged that the decisive arena in the confessional 'cold war' between Protestant and Catholic was France. The extent and outcome of his adventures are matters which will also be more aptly dealt with below in the context of the internal history of France (see p.19).

These violent conditions were naturally extremely propitious for quests for a political elixir of peace. This is the second dominant feature of the age. Many a pamphlet broadcast their authors' pet plans. More substantially Campanella produced schemes for a world empire, initially in the 1620s under Spanish control, then in a revised version, in 1635, under French. A more thoughtful and distinguished plan was compiled by Émeric Crucé and first published in 1623. Because of his likely influence on Sully (see p.27) we must pause a little longer on Crucé. He is a shadowy figure. Indeed, his very name was inaccurately thought to have been Lacroix until the present century. His book was entitled *'Le nouveau Cynée' ou discours d'estat représentant les occasions et moyens d'establir une paix générale et la liberté du commerce par tout le monde aux monarques et princes souverains de ce temps.* The title itself reveals two of his main purposes. These were to propound his belief in the symbiotic relationship between peace and free trade and to advocate a scheme embracing all rulers throughout the world. All the princes were to send ambassadors to form a permanent council of arbitration in Venice. Crucé was much exercised by protocol and interestingly accorded second place after the Pope to the Sultan of Turkey. He was at pains indeed to advocate ethnic and religious toleration. Nor must we forget, in this list of Sully's contemporaries, the most influential of all the writers in this field – the Dutchman Hugo Grotius, who laid the foundations for a generally applicable international law in *De Jure Bellis ac Pacis* (On the Law of Peace and War), published in 1625.

What was clear by the end of the sixteenth century, even if some writers like Campanella did not see it, was that any thought of integrating Europe politically by the religious means of a unified Christian Church was out of the question. Furthermore, a revivification of the Holy Roman Empire was equally impossible. This was partly because Germany, the geographical heart of the medieval Empire, was itself sundered by the Reformation. Partly, too, because the Habsburgs, in whom the Imperial crown was now vested, clearly aligned themselves with the Catholic Counter-Reformation.

Moreover, the very extent of Habsburg power in the sixteenth and seventeenth centuries, independently of its religious affiliation, was the third, and extraordinarily weighty, factor to be taken into consideration by anyone wishing to plan a closer union of European states.

Bella gerant alii; tu, felix Austria, nube,
Nam quae Mars aliis, dat tibi regna Venus.

[Let others wage war; you, happy Austria, marry,
For what Mars gives to others, Venus gives to you in sovereignty.]

The advice was well taken by the Habsburg princes in Vienna. While not exactly eschewing conflict, their marriage policies did indeed produce a most remarkably happy expansion of territory, both by planned liaisons and quite fortuitous inheritance. Most felicitous of all was the marriage of the Archduke Philip the Handsome to Joanna the Mad, daughter of Ferdinand and Isabella of Spain. The early deaths of Joanna's only brother and her husband together with the official declaration of Joanna's insanity ensured that Charles, the son of Philip and Joanna, inherited the Spanish (including some Italian) lands. His dominions also embraced vast colonial territories in the New World. What is more, by different lines of inheritance he became also the ruler of the Austrian and Burgundian (including the Netherlands) patrimonies. Although on his abdication in 1556 Charles V divided this great empire between his brother Ferdinand I (Austria) and his son Philip II (Spain), it is reckoned that a quarter of the population of Europe were ruled by Habsburgs (Kennedy, p.54). Furthermore, the family increased the lands over which they ruled yet more substantially when, in 1580, Philip became king of Portugal. The Treaty of Tordesillas, by which Spain and Portugal in 1494 had agreed to divide the non-Christian world between them, was now redundant. For two generations (until 1640 when Portugal regained her independence) the Habsburgs ruled extensive colonial possessions in three continents.

The potential for the Habsburgs to become the overwhelmingly dominant ruling house in Europe rested not merely on the size of their realm. They also commanded great riches and awesome military might. Dramatic problems such as inflation, the Dutch revolt and the failure of the Armada must not blind us to the power behind these debilitating experiences. Inflation was endemic in Europe at the time, due to several contributory causes. In the Habsburg dominions, however, it was exacerbated by the massive influx of precious metals from Peruvian and other American sources. No other European government enjoyed such accessible wealth. Without it Spain would not have been able to sustain so many military operations. No other state in Europe, for example, could possibly have contemplated mobilising such a force as the great Armada. Nor should the success of the guerrilla resistance of the United Provinces lead us to forget the incomparable quality of Spanish infantry in conventional combat.

Well before the end of the fifteenth century France was growing fearful of the burgeoning strength of the Habsburgs. This fear is the next factor for us to consider. In April 1477 Maximilian, Archduke of Austria, married Mary, daughter and partial heiress of Charles the

Bold of Burgundy. The establishment of the Habsburgs on the northern and eastern rim of France, followed rapidly by a clash of interests in northern Italy, wound up the two royal houses to a tense rivalry which was not to be relaxed until the Diplomatic Revolution and the ill-starred marriage of Marie Antoinette and the Dauphin Louis in the mid-eighteenth century. Any draftsman of a plan for European union would clearly need to address this deep-seated animosity.

By the middle of the sixteenth century no matter in which direction the French turned their gaze towards their land frontiers their eyes fell upon Habsburg lands. To the north Artois marched with Habsburg Flanders; to the east, Burgundy, with Habsburg Franche Comté; to the south, Béarn and Languedoc, with Habsburg Aragon. To the southeast lay the Republic of Genoa, with inextricable financial and economic links with both Austria and Spain, and Savoy, whose friendship with France under 'Iron Head' Emmanuel Philibert was to say the least uncertain. In any case, behind Genoa and Savoy lay Milan. After the death of the last of the Sforza line in 1535 the duchy was gradually absorbed into the Habsburg empire. Furthermore, anxious to ensure their lines of communication, the Habsburgs secured a supply route by effective local control from the Tyrol via Milan, Franche Comté and the Rhine to the Netherlands. This came to be known as the Spanish Road. Whether the Habsburgs specifically planned hegemony over western Europe or not, Frenchmen were frightened – and with good reason.

We have seen that the religious schism of the Reformation provided an excuse (or justification depending on your point of view) for some states to intervene in the internal affairs of others. The confusion in France occasioned by the civil wars provided Philip II with a heaven-sent opportunity which, as God's instrument, he could not pass by. 1589 was the critical year. The formidable queen mother, Catherine de Medici, died; and her last son, Henry III, fell to the fanatical assassin, Jacques Clément. The Huguenot, Henry of Navarre, was next in line. Philip felt impelled to act. Nor was he alone in sensing the pivotal significance of the situation. Theodore Beza, Calvin's disciple and successor in Geneva, wrote: 'It is on the outcome of the French crisis that the principal change of the whole world, for better or for worse, depends.' (quoted, Hauser, p.153). The king of Spain conceived a grand scheme to partition France. Troops were sent to Brittany and Provence, which he planned to allot to his daughter Isabella and Charles-Emmanuel of Savoy respectively. The main stroke, however, was from the north. Philip ordered his commander in the Low Countries, the Duke of Parma, to redeploy his forces and invade France. He linked up with the Catholic League, who were holding Paris against the new king, Henry IV. By tactics reminiscent of Fabius Cunctator Henry forced Parma to withdraw from France. That particular interventionist episode was at an end. And in 1598 he signed the Treaty of Vervins which concluded that phase of the Franco-Habsburg conflict.

However, when Cardinal Richelieu became chief minister in 1624 he was faced with a dilemma. The Thirty Years War was under way, in which the contestants were divided largely along religious lines. As a prince of the Church he should support the champions of the Catholic side, the Habsburgs; as a French statesman he should support their Protestant opponents. All the while Gustavus Adolphus placed the power of Sweden and his own remarkable qualities of leadership in the anti-Habsburg balance, Richelieu could afford to avoid an overt decision. But Gustavus was killed in battle in 1632 and two years later Habsburg troops destroyed the Swedish army as an effective fighting force at the Battle of Nördlingen. The danger to France could not be ignored. In May 1635 she formally declared war on Spain. Both states were to drain themselves until they signed the treaty of exhaustion known as the Peace of the Pyrenees in 1659. At least the decline of the Habsburgs was by then sufficiently evident to reduce the threat of a total Austro-Spanish imperium to little more than a menacing shadow.

In sketching the main features of the age in which Sully lived we have trespassed rather deeply into the seventeenth century, though the relevance of these events will, it is hoped, become clear in due course. Meanwhile, it is necessary to retrace our steps chronologically. We have considered the urge for greater peace, the religious wars, the power of the Habsburgs and the Franco-Habsburg rivalry. We must now, finally, reveal the reputation of Henry IV.

In the sixteenth century France was still in many ways only a loosely-knit collection of principalities. In the south, Antoine de Bourbon, himself related to the royal Valois line, became through marriage King of Navarre. His brother, the Prince de Condé, became effective leader of the Huguenots in the civil wars. Antoine died when his heir, Henry, was but ten years old. After many vicissitudes during the early phases of the Wars of Religion Henry, as we have seen, became King of France in 1589. Henry's legacy was scarcely enviable. The country was still bitterly divided by religion and economically exhausted by war, while invading Spanish forces were still in his kingdom. Henry tackled each of the problems with great vigour. In 1590 he gambled on a pitched battle near Ivry-sur-Eure against superior Spanish and French forces of the Catholic League commanded by the Duc de Mayenne, won a decisive victory, and relieved the immediate military threat to his position. Three years later, to reconcile the Catholics to his assumption of the crown and to gain effective control of his hostile capital city, Henry was converted to Catholicism. 'Paris is worth a Mass,' he is said to have declared. He brought both internal and external conflict to an end in 1598. He entrusted the task of physical and economic reconstruction to his able minister, Sully. However, Henry was still extremely nervous of the Habsburg threat. In March

1609 the death of the Duke of Cleves-Jülich, a Rhineland principality, led to a disputed succession. The Habsburg Emperor sent troops. War threatened. In August Henry started to mobilise his forces, and it has sometimes been suggested that he was preparing to smash the Habsburg encirclement. Whether he would have followed through his bellicose posturing we do not know. He had less than a year to live.

The fourteenth of May 1610 was a fine, warm day in Paris. The king, in melancholy mood with premonitions of personal disaster, decided to visit his friend and chief minister, the Duc de Sully. Sully, living in his official residence of the Arsenal, was ill. The royal carriage made its slow progress through the streets of Paris, turned from the rue St Honoré into the narrow rue Féronnerie and was brought to a halt by a traffic jam caused by a wine cart and another laden with hay. Henry had been followed by a religious fanatic, François Ravaillac, who was determined to kill the king. He now seized his chance. The day being fine, the leather blinds to the windows of the coach were not pulled down. Ravaillac plunged a knife into Henry's side. It hit a rib. He struck again. The knife penetrated the heart.

What manner of man was this Henry, dubbed already in his lifetime 'the Great'? He was a soldier, first and foremost, a man of action. He ate, drank, hunted and fornicated with immense appetite and energy. As one French historian has written, 'With women, as on the field of battle, he knew only how to be victorious.' (Pagès, p.35). He dressed simply, loathed ceremony and easily identified with the ordinary people, all of whom, he promised, should have 'a chicken in a pot every Sunday'. He became a national hero. His reputation was reflected and brought to its apogee in Voltaire's epic Virgilian poem *La Henriade*, first published in 1728. It opens thus:

> Je chante ce héros qui regna sur la France
> Et par droit de conquête et par droit de naissance;
> Qui par de longs malheurs apprit à gouverner,
> Calma les factions, sut vaincre et pardonner,
> Confondit et Mayenne, et la Ligue, et l'Ibère,
> Et fut de ses sujets le vainqueur et le père.
> (Voltaire, n.d., p.43)

> [I sing of this hero who reigned over France
> Both by right of conquest and by right of birth;
> Who by extended misfortunes learned how to govern,
> Calmed down the factions, knew how to defeat and to pardon,
> Confounded equally Mayenne, the League and Spain,
> And was to his subjects both conqueror and father.]

By a mixture of authoritative will-power, sound commonsense, religious tolerance and extrovert good nature the first Bourbon king of France won the respect and hearts of his subjects. Of course, the horrific manner of his death as well as the stern personality and unpitying religious and fiscal policies of Richelieu in the succeeding generation no doubt enhanced Henry's reputation retrospectively. Nevertheless, his accomplishments were real enough to warrant the high regard in which he has been held. And if he could be shown to have conceived a plan for the union of European states, how much would such a scheme be enhanced in the eyes of its readers!

Sully and his memoirs

The most famous of all schemes for European unity was the Grand Design. This has often been attributed to Henry IV and is described in the memoirs of the Duc de Sully. But there is much that is strange about the duke, the memoirs and the plan. To start at the beginning, we do not know when Sully was born. Perhaps December 1559, perhaps January 1560, perhaps December 1560. His parents were Huguenots of middling prosperity, his father having some claim to nobility. They lived at Rosny-sur-Seine, a small town between Paris and the Channel. The family name was Béthune; and our memoir-writer was christened Maximilien. He was sent to Paris to study and was caught up in the massacre which started on Saint Bartholomew's Day, 24 August 1572. He vividly describes in his memoirs how, while walking through the streets, he witnessed assaults and killings and believed 'the perpetrators of these cruelties had a plan and taken an oath to kill all, as far as babes at the breast, even Catholic women known to be pregnant by a Huguenot.' (Buisseret & Barbiche, p.14). The young Maximilien de Béthune took refuge with a friend. Four years later he left home to fight for Henry of Navarre in his campaigns in the civil war. He distinguished himself as a courageous soldier, most famously at the Battle of Ivry, during which he sustained seven wounds. By this time he had become the Baron de Rosny and a close associate of Henry. Henry came to use him for various diplomatic and administrative tasks, in both of which capacities he showed considerable flair.

In 1598 Rosny became Superintendant of Finances, in charge of fiscal policy. In effect he became Henry's chief minister, for, by the addition of sundry other responsibilities, he became a kind of chancellor of the exchequer, minister of transport and minister of defence rolled into one – a Bourbon Pooh-Bah. As a minister the achievements of Sully (he became Duc de Sully in 1606) were considerable. He tightened the financial administration to such an extent that by the end of Henry's reign the king had a very substantial cash surplus.

The death of Henry undermined Sully's position. He had many enemies, including the queen. Bereft of the king's support, he fled to the Bastille, the impregnable fortress of which he was governor. But his life was not in danger. He was forced to resign in 1611 and retired to an obscure private existence on his estate at Villebon, between Paris and Tours, though he was honoured with the coveted title of Marshal of France in 1634. It was in his retirement, in all probability, that he wrote his memoirs under the strange title (in its abbreviated form) of *Sages et Royales Œconomies d'Estat*. Incorporated in these memoirs was the Grand Design – a plan for the reorganisation of Europe into a confederal structure. No other scheme for the union of the continent became quite so famous nor its authorship the subject of quite so much dispute.

Despite this extended autumn of his career (he died in 1641), Sully's reputation in history almost matches that of his monarch. Voltaire, in a footnote to his *Henriade*, summed him up in the following way: 'He was a very brave warrior, and an even better minister; incapable of deceiving the king and of being deceived by the financiers . . . the courtiers . . . found in him a strictness consonant with the economic mood of Henry IV. They called him "the negative", and it was said that the word "yes" was never in his mouth.' (Voltaire, n.d. p.202). A recent French biographer has declared, perhaps somewhat hyperbolically, that, 'In the gallery of the heroes of French History, Sully occupies a select place by the side of Vercingetorix, Joan of Arc and Napoleon. All French people, ever since primary school, know about the fine minister who helped Henry IV . . . ' (Barbiche, p.11).

Sully was an exceedingly conscientious and meticulous worker with a passion for technical, cartographic and statistical detail. His sense of public duty, his rooting out of corruption in his rigorous administration of the state's finances, the dour bearded face of his portraits and his lifelong commitment to Calvinism have combined to form an impression of a forbiddingly austere character. Unlike his king, Sully remained faithful to his Huguenot upbringing. For example, when the Pope in a letter pleaded with him to embrace the true faith, Sully replied assuring the Holy Father that he prayed to God every day for *his* conversion! (see Voltaire, n.d. p.203). This whimsical tone shows that the traditional characterisation of Sully is far too simple. We also know, for example, that he organised domestic evening entertainments which would have brought a blush to the cheeks of a true puritan. He attempted, though left incomplete, a novel of doubtful propriety, entitled *Les Estranges Amours de la Reine Myrrha* (The Peculiar Love Affairs of Queen Myrrha).

Yet his religious commitment to the Reformed Church and his patriotic commitment to a restored France consistently shone through in his burning hatred of Spain. The Habsburgs were Sully's arch-enemies in both religion and power politics. In 1608 he advised Henry that ' . . . we ought to attack Spain in her heart and belly, that is to say at this time in the East and West Indies which, as they have been the main cause of her greatness, may also become the chief agent of her downfall.' (quoted, Buisseret, p.196). He continued to press for war in the crisis of 1609–10 against the more cautious counsel of the Secretary of State, Villeroy.

Sully had a peculiarly close relationship with the king, albeit punctuated by frequent rows occasioned by Henry's hot temper as much as any deep differences in policy. Indeed, on the fundamental requirements of internal rehabilitation, religious toleration and wariness of Habsburg intentions their views coincided. They also had a mutual respect for each other's abilities. Moreover, the official relationship was underpinned by a personal friendship which lasted for some twenty years. Indeed, Sully's financial and diplomatic skills, so ably displayed on the national stage, were invaluable to his monarch in such private matters as settling his quarrels with his wife and mistresses and his gambling debts. It is perfectly natural for us, therefore, to expect to read in Sully's memoirs of conversations on state matters which passed between the two men. But did these conversations include the king's expressed grandiose ambition to revamp the political map and structure of the continent along confederal lines? Was Henry the true originator of the Grand Design?

Complex problems surround the authenticity and reliability of Sully's memoirs so that a true understanding of the Grand Design, for which the memoirs are the sole source, has been no easy task for historians. The first problem, though soon dispatched, is the strange device of pretending that the material is a record of his secretaries addressing him. Thus Sully is referred to throughout in the respectful second person plural or as Rosny (his name before the conferment of his dukedom). There is no doubt about his own authorship. The device was a means of enabling him to attack his enemies in print while seeming not to be engaged in the criticisms personally. Drawing upon a substantial collection of written sources and memories, bolstered, on occasion, it has to be said, by pure invention, Sully spent his retirement drafting and constantly amending the text. But he hesitated to publish. However, he became increasingly concerned by the publication of other works throwing doubt on the wisdom and ability of Henry IV and himself. In 1635 Sully read the second edition of *Histoire de Henri le Grand, IV de nom*. The author, Scipion Dupleix, was official historiographer to Louis XIII. What Sully read enraged him. Dupleix heavily criticised Henri and virtually ignored Sully.

In 1638 he decided to publish. The first half of the manuscript was produced in two volumes in 1640. Since the title contains eighty words there is little mystery in the fact that it is usually abbreviated to two, namely, *Œconomies royales*. These words are taken from the first phrase: *Memoires des sages et royales œconomies d'Estat domestiques, politiques et militaires de Henri le Grand*, which may be rendered as 'Memoirs of the wise and royal administration of the state of Henry the Great in domestic, political and military matters'. Both Henry and Sully himself are portrayed in a favourable light. Furthermore and in particular, he made late amendments to exaggerate Henry's war-

like mood against the Habsburgs at the time of his death. This tamper-
ing with the evidence should be considered against the background of
Richelieu's prevarication and final declaration of war in 1635 outlined
on p.20. Perhaps, as some historians have speculated, Sully hoped to
influence Richelieu. The most significant changes from the early drafts
are the insertions relating to the Grand Design. Much of this material
appeared well after Sully's death: only in 1662 were volumes 3 and 4
printed.

The memoirs became famous and have been constantly reissued in
various editions over the past three and a half centuries. One of the
peculiarities of this peculiar tale is that the edition which was perhaps
one of the most influential substantially changed the originally published text. In the eighteenth century the Abbé de l'Écluse des Loges,
suffering from the strained device of Sully's use of the second person
plural and even more from the convoluted syntax of his elongated
sentences, produced a 'tidied up' version. This was published in London
in 1747. This text later appeared in English in a translation by Charlotte Lennox. The first edition was published in London in 1755, a
new edition in 1810, and yet another, in Edinburgh, in 1819.

Partly because of the existence of different versions of the memoirs
and partly because the Grand Design took on increasingly grandiose
features in Sully's mind as the years passed, as much confusion as
fame has surrounded this plan for European union. One authority on
the history of European unity has even stated, 'For three centuries
everyone has referred to it, but almost no one has read it. Can we
even be sure that it exists?' (de Rougemont, p.98). And what was
Henry IV's part in its devising? The king undoubtedly harboured
and talked about ambitions to consolidate French and curb Habsburg
power. The term 'grand design' seems to have been first used by
Aggrippa d'Aubigné in the third volume of his *Histoire Universelle*,
published in 1620. He refers to ' . . . the grand design, the King con-
tenting himself with reducing Spain to the frontiers of the Pyrenees
and the sea.' (quoted, Seward, p.186). Indeed, one French historian,
referring to the mobilisation of 1609–10, has written, ' . . . his bold
decision sustained the legend of the "Grand Design".' (Pagès, p.56).

However, the plan for the massive reorganisation of Europe, which
we shall summarise below, almost certainly did not originate in
Henry's mind. True, for generations it was consistently referred to as
'the Grand Design of Henry IV'; and in that sense Sully's judgment
concerning the propaganda value of assigning the king's name to it
revealed a sure touch. But it was fictitious. In the words of the French
co-editor of the most authentic version of the memoirs, 'In fact, all
this [i.e. the Grand Design] seems to be the fruit not of the thought
of Henry IV, but of the chimerical meditations of the ageing Sully.'
(Barbiche, p.17). The attribution of the plan to Henry was consolidated
and in large measure transmitted by Bishop Péréfixe, tutor to Louis
XIV and who held his pupil's grandfather in great esteem. In his

Histoire du Roy Henri le Grand he credited Henry with a scheme for 'a Christian Commonwealth'. The influence of Péréfixe, who was later to become Archbishop of Paris, was immense. The French historian, Charles Pfister, who undertook splendid detective work on the memoirs, revealed that the bishop saw the manuscript of Sully's final volumes before publication and decided to publicise the Grand Design himself. Writing of Péréfixe's history, he noted: 'there were innumerable editions of it, and it was translated into almost every language. Also, belief in the Grand Design became very nearly universal.' (Pfister, p.332).

Sully himself had claimed even wider royal support than just his own monarch for the Grand Design: he 'improved' his memoirs by fabricating imaginary conversations on the matter with Elizabeth I and James I of England. He invented a totally fictitious diplomatic visit for himself in 1601 and hinted at a triple authorship of the proposals. In the Lennox translation he has himself saying to Queen Elizabeth: 'I have frequently made similar propositions to the king my master, and . . . I have often found him disposed to adopt plans conformable to those your majesty has just mentioned to me.' (Béthune, vol.2, p.432n). Elsewhere we read the following passage: 'I found her deeply engaged in the means by which this great design might be successfully executed . . . A very great number of the articles, conditions, and different dispositions, is due to this queen.' (Béthune, vol. 5, p.80). On the accession of James in 1603 Sully was in truth sent by Henry to enlist his friendship against Spain. Sully, however, claims that he also pressed James to support the Grand Design but received only a lukewarm response: ' . . . nothing further could be obtained of the king of England than the same promises which were required of the other courts; namely, that he would . . . contribute towards [the anti-Habsburg alliance] in the same manner as the other powers interested therein.' (Béthune, vol.5, p.101). Unfortunately, the truth about the embassy has here been somewhat stretched to include discussion of a Grand Design which did not exist at that date – even, almost certainly, in Sully's own mind, let alone Henry's.

It is clear, then, that the Grand Design, in so far as it was an elaborate scheme to redraw the frontiers of Europe and create supranational institutions, was Sully's scheme, not his king's. It is clear, too, that, it was only in his retirement that he even started to devise the plan, probably no earlier than 1620 (see Pfister, p.326). During the compilation of the memoirs, the Grand Design became increasingly important and elaborated in Sully's mind. How, then, are we to imagine the circumstances of Europe in his lifetime affecting the manner in which he shaped his proposals?

He was, of course, only too aware of the horrors of religious conflict. He lived through the French Wars of Religion. He personally witnessed something of the cruelty of the Saint Bartholomew Massacre;

he fought and suffered wounds in battle. Although he was unwilling to compromise with his own faith, there is nothing in his character or career to suggest other than his desire for peaceful co-existence between the contending Churches.

As a diplomat and student of international affairs Sully could also hardly have been ignorant of the yearning for an end to war in Europe. We have also seen how publications with this purpose proliferated in the second and third decades of the seventeenth century at the very time Sully was composing his memoirs. For example, he may well have known Grotius, who, as a young man, frequented Henry's court, and it is quite possible that he read Crucé's work (see p.17). Pfister indeed goes so far as to say that Sully's idea of an arbitrative council was not original. He asserts that 'Sully took it, it seems to us, from a very curious book of this period, le Cinée d'Éstat, written by an author who should not be forgotten: Em. Lacroix.' (Pfister, p.330). Pfister goes further – he virtually accuses Sully of plagiarism, so commonplace were schemes for perpetual peace and Christian unity. For example, he quotes a letter from the statesman Villeroy in 1608 at the time of projected royal marriage alliances: ' . . . if the opportunities which offer themselves are handled well, as they can be, . . . we can build and maintain for our own times a universal peace in Christendom, and principally among the three great kings [i.e. France, Spain and England] . . . It would be necessary in order to achieve this for the said kings to content themselves with their present possessions, none having an advantage over any other.' (Pfister, p.329). However, he was not a man to desire peace irrespective of the political cost. His hatred of the Habsburgs and his patriotic pride were bound to make him dream of a time when, through war, the Habsburgs had been weakened and the two powers brought more nearly into balance. And if France could emerge, if anything, a trifle the stronger from this duel, so much the better.

The assumption of overwhelming power by France was not, Sully tried to suggest, part of the plan. Indeed, the key feature of the Grand Design was the concept of 'equilibrium', of a number of states co-existing in roughly equal size and power (see p.32). This notion has the stamp of Sully all over it. It is just the kind of almost mathematical formula one would expect from a man obsessed with statistics, fascinated by maps and meticulous in the storage of the mass of his own private papers. Finally, perhaps we should not be too cynical in our interpretation of Sully's motives in fathering the Grand Design on Henry IV. He undoubtedly recognised the supreme value of this fraud for publicity's sake. Yet it was a pious fraud: his respect for the memory of the late king was assuredly genuine.

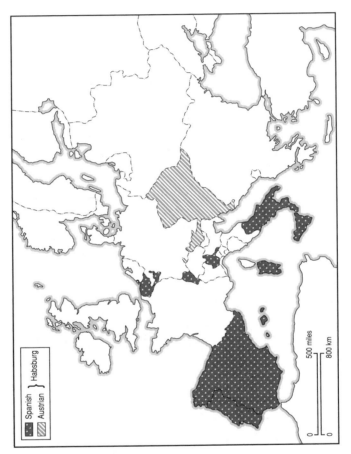

Map 2 Europe c. 1600

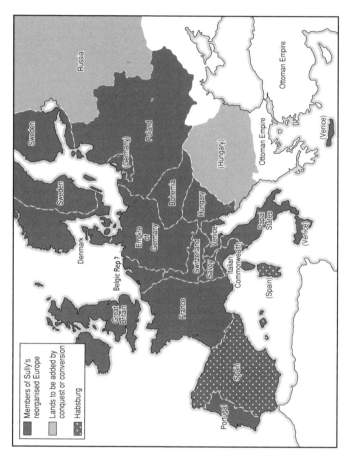

Map 3   Sully's Grand Design

The Grand Design

The English co-editor of the definitive edition of Sully's memoirs has stated that 'The Grand Design owes most of its fame to the eighteenth century edition of the memoirs.' (Buisseret, p.197). Although, as we shall notice below (pp.36–7), this statement underplays the immediate impact of the plan, it seems reasonable to use this influential version, in Charlotte Lennox's translation, in this exposition. (For the sake of simplicity we shall pass over the inconsistencies which Sully failed to correct in the text.)

The Grand Design is very evidently a product of its age and its author. In the first place, Sully recognised that, if the divisions of Europe were to be healed, the religious causes of conflict had to be addressed. He distinguishes three forms of Christianity: Roman, Reformed (Calvinist) and Protestant (Lutheran). (He dismisses the Eastern churches as too heretical to count.) He then provides a formula for combining a strong faith with sectarian co-existence:

Each of these three religions being now established in Europe, in such a manner that there is not the least appearance that any of them can be destroyed, and experience having sufficiently demonstrated the inutility and danger of such an enterprise, the best therefore that can be done, is to preserve, and even strengthen all of them in such a manner, nevertheless that this indulgence may not become an encouragement to the production of new sects or opinions, which should carefully be suppressed on their first appearance. (Béthune, vol.5, p.85)

In each country the Church adhered to by the majority should remain dominant and no restrictions should impede any dissenters who wished to do so from emigrating. A perfectly simple and practicable formula, Sully avers: after all, the Protestants have no wish to force their beliefs on others; and the Pope would acquiesce to the permanent loss of the schismatic states because of his new appointment as chief arbitrator in Sully's proposed peace-keeping structure (see p.33). Moreover, the balanced co-existence of the three major Christian churches would complement his plan for the political equilibrium of the continent.

The second basic problem was the reduction of Habsburg power, namely, to 'divest the house of Austria of the empire, and of all the possessions in Germany, Italy, and the Low-Countries: in a word, to reduce it to the sole kingdom of Spain, bounded by the ocean, the Mediterranean, and the Pyreneean mountains.' (Béthune, vol.5, pp.89–90). Nevertheless, the Habsburgs should retain their European islands and their overseas colonies (including those derived from Portuguese conquest). Indeed, they are to be encouraged to expand their colonial activities and be guaranteed a monopoly to exploit the other continents. This aspect of the plan was to be a means both of reconciling them to their losses in Europe while at the same time diverting their imperialist ambitions out of Europe. Again this uncomplicated arrangement had only to be set in train: 'all the parties would have been gainers by it, and this was what assured Henry the Great of the success of his design.' (Béthune, vol.5, pp.92–3). Other states would gain by the removal of the threat of Habsburg hegemony; by the accretions of territory from the pickings of lands dismantled from the Habsburg European realm; and by the renewed availability of the Imperial crown to other princes. The Habsburgs themselves would not dare to challenge the arrangements, faced with such a phalanx of personified self-interest. In any case, if they were realistic, they would be grateful for having their Afro-Asian-Latin American activities underwritten and for being relieved of their troublesome Italian and Netherlandish territories, which had been such a drain on their resources.

The major central European lands of the Habsburgs were to be organised as follows. Bohemia, together with Silesia and Moravia, was to become an elective kingdom. Hungary too was to become an elective kingdom, acquiring in the process the Archduchy of Austria itself and the smaller duchies stretching to the south of Austria as far as the Adriatic. Moreover, as the Hungarian kingdom, thus strengthened and indeed assisted, steadily pushed the Turks back further into the Balkans, so she was to retain these liberated provinces. Poland, a third elective kingdom, was to be privileged also and for the same reasons as Hungary: 'its power was to have been augmented, by annexing to it whatever should be conquered from the infidels adjoining to its own frontiers, and by determining in its favour those disputes which it had with all its other neighbours.' (Béthune, vol.5, p.94). It should be noted that Sully embraces within the term 'infidels' Muscovy and Tartary as well as Turkey. The tsar was to be invited to conform to one of the three 'proper' Christian churches; and in the event of his refusing, an international European force would strip him of all lands west of the Urals.

The countries to the south of Germany were to be consolidated into five enlarged states. Switzerland was to be augmented by the accretion of lands (mainly Habsburg) to the north-west and east. Venice was to be given Sicily. Savoy was to embrace Lombardy. The great cities of Genoa, Florence, Mantua, Modena and Parma were to be consolidated into a new republic. And the Pope was to be recognised as a powerful secular prince, holding sway over the whole of the central and southern provinces of the peninsula.

As to the Netherlands Sully seems to have been in considerable confusion. While on the one hand he proposes the establishment of a Belgic republic, he also scatters eighteen 'sovereign fiefs' to lords of France and England. At the same time he is at pains to emphasise that those two ancient monarchies have no greedy ambitions. In fact, Sully suggests that the selflessness of Henry IV in these, his supposed dispositions, is one of the most remarkable features of the whole Grand Design: 'Among all these dismemberings, we may observe that France received nothing for itself, but the glory of distributing them with equity. Henry had declared this to be his intention long before.' (Béthune, vol.5, p.96.) 'Besides, what is it that France wants? Will she not always be the richest and most powerful kingdom in Europe? It must be granted.' It remains to the kings of France to 'employ their power in preserving the peace of Europe; for no other enterprise can, truly, be to them either profitable or successful.' (Béthune, vol.5, p.72).

The result of all these changes would have been a revolutionary simplification of the European jigsaw of political geography so pleasing to Sully's tidy mind. Moreover, as a result of these dismemberments and reallocations we have, lo and behold!, a continent of fifteen powers of approximately equal strength. This key principle of 'equilibrium' would create a situation in which 'none of them might have cause either of envy or fear, from the possessions or power of the others.' (Béthune, vol.5, p.98). These fifteen major states are classified as six hereditary monarchies (France, Spain, Britain, Denmark, Sweden and Lombardy (or Savoy)); five elective monarchies (the Empire, the Papacy, Poland, Hungary and Bohemia); and four republics (Venetian, Italian, Swiss and Belgic).

Any difficulties which might attend these reallocations of territory Sully dismisses as 'trifling'. For one thing, 'in every attempt at new combinations . . . care must be taken to respect the natural dispositions and peculiar characteristics of peoples and races and thus guard against the folly of trying to unite in any one State . . . men whose differences of temperament or diversity of language, law and tradition are so great as to be incompatible.' (quoted, Stawell, p.110). A remarkable anticipation of the nationalist idea. In any case, problems could all be efficiently handled by 'the general council, representing all the states of Europe; the establishment of which was certainly the happiest invention that could have been conceived, to prevent those innovations which time often introduces in the wisest and most useful institutions.' (Béthune, vol.5, p.98). Here we have the political/institutional nub of the Grand Design. The all-wise Henry had produced a most excellent geopolitical confection. But lest it disintegrate, it had to be set in the cohering aspic of a pan-European council. Sully was quite frank in admitting as his model the Amphyctionic Leagues – those experiments in co-operation among ancient Greek city-states which have so often been seized upon by European and world federalists to furnish their own schemes with credibility and respectability.

Representatives from all the Christian European states were to form a senate in permanent session in a city to be chosen for its geographical convenience in the heart of the continent. Their function was 'to discuss the different interests, pacify the quarrels, clear up and determine all the civil, political, and religious affairs of Europe, whether within itself or with its neighbours.' (Béthune, vol.5, p.99).

The representatives were to serve three-year periods of office, and they were to number sixty-six in total. Provision is also made for subordinate regional councils. None the less, all ultimate power is to be vested in the senate or great central council, 'whose decisions, when considered as proceeding from the united authority of all the sovereigns pronounced in a manner equally free and absolute, must have been regarded as so many final and irrevocable decrees.' (Béthune, vol.5, p.100).

How, then, to sum up this Grand Design in military, political and economic terms? Sully drew up quite detailed lists of forces – infantry, cavalry, artillery and warships – which each of the constituent states were to supply for two operations. One represented the power he considered necessary to quell any initial resistance of the Habsburgs to the scheme. Indeed, he leads the reader to believe that Henry was already well under way in negotiating the mobilisation of these forces when he met his death. The other planned use of military means to achieve his ends was for crusade-type operations against the tsar and sultan. Sully did not foresee any need for military power to underpin his reorganised Europe once the changes had been implemented. The Grand Design was essentially a political solution to political problems.

The optimism (or conceit) with which Sully viewed the practicability of the plan derived from his placing it firmly on a platform of four political principles: authority, balance, union and self-interest. The political authority which was to keep the redesigned Europe in peaceful continuity was an interesting mix of old and new. Sully sought to revive the medieval authority of Pope and Holy Roman Emperor. The Pope's was to be restored by an expansion of his temporal power in Italy and by his moral leadership in the central council or senate. The Emperor's was to be restored by liberating the Imperial crown from the monopoly of its use which the Habsburgs had acquired. By rotating the honour round the royal houses the impartiality of the Imperial authority could be ensured. Furthermore, the dignity of the Emperor would be enhanced by a declaration that he was the first and chief magistrate of the new European union. Balance of power, a political concept which dominated eighteenth-century diplomacy, was understood in Sully's time in only a primitive sense. His notion of reallocating territory to achieve an 'equilibrium' of power is therefore something of a novelty. The principle of equilibrium, he seems to believe, would hold the system in place much as Newton was later to show how the force of gravity holds the component celestial bodies of the universe in their relative positions to each other. His central institution of unification therefore needs to perform only a limited function of detailed arbitration.

If the institutional framework for European unity is thus somewhat frail, Sully has in addition a vision of what we might term social unity. For he suggests that one of Henry's purposes was to convince 'all his neighbours' that the design would 'unite them all in an indissoluble bond of security and friendship, after which they might live together like brethren, and reciprocally visit like good neighbours.' (Béthune, vol.5, p.83). And the beauty of it all is that everyone would gain from the peace and security which Europe would then enjoy.

Self-interest is also served by the economic benefits of the Grand Design. These seem to be threefold. One is basic to the whole plan, namely, to save 'those immense sums which the maintenance of so many thousand soldiers, so many fortified places, and so many military expenses require.' (Béthune, vol.5, p.83). Secondly, there were to be mutual agreements on free trade. The third advantage is the expansion of trade, which he foresees to be forthcoming from the intensification of Habsburg overseas colonisation; since free commercial access for all European states was to be a condition for supporting that diversion of Habsburg hunger for power.

All in all, his tone tells us, it is so commonsensical and so unlike other plans for European collaboration. Sully fears that the Grand Design might be confused with these other, faulty schemes: 'I must confess I am under some apprehensions, lest this scheme should at first be considered as one of those darling chimeras, or idle speculations, in which a mind susceptible of strange and singular ideas, may be so easily engaged.' Such people 'confound the wisest and noblest enterprises that have ever been formed, with those chimerical projects which princes, intoxicated with their power, have in all ages amused themselves in forming.' (Béthune, vol.5, pp.73–5).

But was the Grand Design really such a splendid proposition? What have been the judgments of recent historians? We may distinguish four different interpretations. The first is the idealistic, supporting Sully's own self-acclaim. This can be exemplified by one American authority who wrote in 1916. 'The project is in very truth the classical project of international organization, and it has been both the inspiration and the foundation upon which well-wishers of their kind have, consciously or unconsciously, raised their humbler structures.' (James Brown Scott, quoted, Hemleben, p.31). Melian Stawell, the Cambridge historian, wrote in similar vein, assured of the practicability of the Grand Design: 'In the long and chequered history of Europe there are few examples of a lost opportunity more poignant than the neglected advice of Sully, the great minister of Henry IV.' (Stawell, p.97).

The reverse of this view may be illustrated by the dismissive attitude of Sully's recent biographer and editor, David Buisseret, who has declared that 'Many schemes for a new political organization in Europe were in the air on the eve of the Thirty Years' War; his ideas on this were neither coherent nor original.' (Buisseret, p.197). Similarly critical though not quite so unflattering is the judgment of the American scholar Hemleben, who has pointed out the impracticability of the scheme: Sully was too optimistic about defeating Russia and Turkey and too naïve about the ease with which he proposed to redraw the state boundaries and keep them permanent (Hemleben, p.33).

Then there are the cynical commentators: the belief that what really lay behind the proposition was the replacement of the Habsburgs by France as the dominant power in Europe, but that France lacked the strength to achieve this objective at the time. This is the view of the American diplomatic historian, René Albrecht-Carrié in his book *The Unity of Europe*. Sir George Clark, in a brief reference to Sully's Grand Design, is also quite blunt about the Duke's motive, stating that 'it may be regarded as a reply to some of his French contemporaries who were writing that a State which does not expand must perish.' (Clark, p.15). It must be admitted that, for all the paraded altruism of Henry IV in Sully's memoirs, he does rather let the cat out of the bag, as several contemporaries noticed. In the very process of denying any avarice on the part of France, Sully boasts, as we have seen (p.32), that she will always be the richest and most powerful. France was obviously destined to be less in equilibrium than the rest!

Finally, we may discern the approach of scholars like Sir Harry Hinsley of Cambridge, who seek to analyse Sully's work in its historical context, a process which, admittedly, aligns him with the cynical: 'Essentially, this remains a plan for the weakening of the Habsburgs and the establishment of French hegemony in Europe.' (Hinsley, p.25). Rather more interesting is Hinsley's emphasis on the way Sully straddled old and new ways of thinking – between the medieval ideas of Empire and Christendom and the modern idea of the sovereign state, and between the concept of equilibrium and his ambitions for France. The contradictions in his thought, Hinsley argues, are the outcome of this uncomfortable intellectual posture. He nevertheless warms towards the Grand Design and concludes that, 'When all has been said it remains the case that Sully did attempt to reconcile his two positions . . . If he was still attached to an old conception of the European order he also recognised the vitality of the independent state and the extent to which the European order must be based on it: that the domination of Europe was at least having to become indirect, the Empire a delegated power.' (Hinsley, p.29).

'The Grand Design was never executed, never even attempted, and need not be discussed.' (Acton, p.171). That was the brusque dismissal by Lord Acton. But some ideas, even if not given the vitality of living implementation, do not in consequence of that kind of failure, necessarily succumb to the utter oblivion of death. Sully's Grand Design, however 'elucidated' in various editions, however impractical, however ignored by hard-nosed statesmen in the real harsh world, nevertheless persisted for generations in fascinating the more idealistic, who kept alive the dream of an orderly, pacified continent of Europe.

We shall see in the next two chapters how the seemingly interminable wars of Louis XIV concentrated men's minds again on the problems of reorganising Europe to reduce this persistent fratricidal con-

flict. Three of the most notable schemes all refer to the Grand Design
– those of William Penn (1693), John Bellers (1710) and Saint-Pierre
(1713–17).

William Penn took Sully's exposition of the provenance of the Grand
Design quite literally and justified his own essay by reference to it,
explaining that ' . . . something of the nature of our expedient was, in
design and preparation, [owing] to the wisdom, justice, and valour of
Henry the Fourth of France . . . For he was upon obliging the princes
and estates of Europe to a political balance when the Spanish faction
for that reason contrived and accomplished his murder by the hands
of Ravilliac [sic]. I will not then fear to be censured for proposing an
expedient for the present and future peace of Europe when it was not
only the design but glory of one of the greatest princes that ever
reigned in it.' (Penn, p.21; see also Chapter 3 below).

Bellers draws even more heavily on the Grand Design. He provides
a lucid summary of the main proposals at the same time interestingly
revealing his source. His prefatory heading is: 'An Abstract of a Model,
for the good, and perpetual repose of Christendom; by that Great
Prince, King Henry the 4th of France; as in the Memoirs of the Duke
of Sully, and published by the Bishop of Rodez, (once Tutor to the
present King, Lewis the 14th), in his Life of Henry the 4th.' (reprinted,
Fry, p.99; see also Chapter 3 below). This bishop was the M. de Péréfixe
whose influential work we have had occasion to mention (p.25) and
which appeared in an English translation forty-seven years before
Bellers's brief essay.

At much the same time as Bellers was writing his pamphlet the
attention of the Abbé de Saint-Pierre was drawn to the Grand Design.
' . . . what greatly persuaded me,' he wrote, 'that this project [i.e. for
a European governmental body] was no Chimera, was the Information
I received from one of my Friends, soon after I had shewn him the
first Sketch of this Work: He told me that *Henry IV* had form'd a
Project, which, in the main, was much the same; and so I found in the
Memoirs of the Duke of Sully, his Prime Minister.' (reprinted, de
Rougemont, p.115; see also Chapter 4 below). He later wrote of Henry
IV, in his *Discours sur le Grande Homme*, that 'if . . . he had been so
happy as to have executed this great design, it would have rendered
him, beyond all compárison, the greatest man the world has ever, or
probably ever will produce'; and described the Grand Design as 'the
most important invention, the most useful discovery, for the benefit
of mankind, that has yet appeared in the world.' (quoted, Béthune,
vol.5 p.75n). Further, when Rousseau came to write a commentary on
Saint-Pierre's work, much of it turned into a panegyric of what he
supposed was Henry's plan (for Saint-Pierre and Rousseau, see Chapter 4).

The original editions attracted both praise and cynicism. For example, the l'Écluse version of the memoirs has a footnote to explain that
' . . . among all those who have considered it ever since about the

middle of the seventeenth century, I find scarce any who have questioned the possibility of executing it.' (Béthune, vol.5, p.73n). On the other hand, doubts about Henry's authorship of the scheme, its practicability and the altruism of Sully's motives were quickly expressed. The earliest detailed criticism came from the pen of Vittorio Siri in his *Mémorie Récondite* of 1677. Indeed, so incensed was l'Écluse at his hostility that he dismisses him as a serious commentator on the Grand Design by recording the opinion: 'This writer seems indeed to have been in the pay of the house of Austria'! (Béthune, vol.5, p.96n). Then in 1715, in his *Observations sur le projet d'une paix perpétuelle, de M. l'abbé de Saint-Pierre* Leibniz also reveals a judicious scepticism.

This evidence of early influence must surely lead us to temper the forthright statement of one of Sully's most distinguished recent biographers and editors, David Buisseret, partially quoted already (p.30). He has written: 'The Grand Design owes most of its fame to the eighteenth century edition of the memoirs, where what had been a self-contradictory mass of different schemes was welded into a relatively neat whole by the abbé de l'Écluse des Loges, and caught the attention of Europe at a time when Sully was popular for other equally misconceived reasons.' (Buisseret, p.197. The final phrase refers to the way Sully's economic theories were misconstrued.) One may notice too the comment made by Saint-Pierre that 'nine or ten years' before his abridged version of his *Project for Perpetual Peace* the public had become conscious of the Grand Design (see p.70). This was well before the l'Écluse edition. While not wishing to discount the widespread interest in the Grand Design in the second half of the eighteenth century and thereafter, it is surely clear that a number of important writers, including Péréfixe, and perhaps largely through his work, Penn, Bellers and Saint-Pierre, knew about the Grand Design and that its proposals influenced their own work, as we shall see in subsequent chapters. All this interest and literary activity, it should be noted, was sustained well before the presentation of the Grand Design in the 'tidy' version by l'Écluse.

In whatever form, the plan has been constantly reviewed, amended, rejected and honoured by men from many parts of Europe. It naturally seemed especially pertinent in times of war. In the mid-eighteenth century Eobald Toze wrote *Die allgemeine Christliche Republik in Europa* (The Universal Christian Republic in Europe) in which he surveyed, inter alia, the contribution of Henry IV to the ideal. Rousseau recalled Sully's plan while reflecting on Saint-Pierre's work against the background of the Seven Years War. Then, during the French Revolutionary wars when Kant published his *Perpetual Peace*, in the opinion of one modern authority, 'The extensive and lively discussions that Kant's project provoked in Germany are accounted for by the recent interest among the Prussian elite in the plans of Sully and the Abbé de Saint-Pierre.' (de Rougemont, p.191). As the Napoleonic War ended Saint-Simon recalled the Grand Design in his own plan. The Crimean War prompted the Belgian economist Molinari to review a number of schemes, including Sully's, in order to advocate a more pacific conduct of international affairs. The nineteenth century witnessed the creation of peace societies and visions of a United States of Europe. The debt owed by these movements to Sully is epitomised by the action of the Comte de Sellon, founder of the Geneva Peace Society, in establishing an essay prize for suggestions for the practical implementation of the Grand Design.

In our own century, the founder of the Pan-Europe movement, Count Coudenhove-Kalergi, was conscious of the Grand Design. And then in 1948, speaking at the Hague Congress which led to the creation of the Council of Europe, Winston Churchill said, 'There are many famous names associated with the revival and presentation of this idea [of United Europe], but we may all, I think, yield our pretensions to Henry of Navarre, King of France, who, with his great Minister Sully, between the years 1600 and 1607, belaboured to set up . . . "The Grand Design". After this long passage of time we are the servants of The Grand Design'. (de la Mahotière, p.7). Furthermore, in two wartime statements, although not mentioning Sully by name, he had seemed to echo some of the Frenchman's basic ideas. In a secret War Cabinet memorandum Churchill wrote of the need to unite after the War to protect Europe against 'Russian barbarism' and of his hope of seeing 'a Council of perhaps ten units' (quoted, Schuman, pp.725–6n). Six months later, in a broadcast he spoke of his putative Council of Europe having 'a High Court to adjust disputes, and with forces . . . held ready to enforce these decisions and to prevent renewed aggression.' (quoted, Wistrich, p.23).

Through both the myth and reality of provenance and content the Grand Design was thus kept alive in the minds of generations of men as a noble, albeit unsuccessful, attempt to bring peace to a war-torn Europe through a plan of quasi-unification. In that sense historical fiction became historical reality as the Grand Design remained for centuries continuously relevant.

CHAPTER 3

Two Friends

The wars of Louis XIV

If Henry IV's reputation rests on his mythical dream of a united Europe and his real gift of peace to France, his grandson, Louis XIV, became the very personification of the discrete sovereign state and a veritable Mars, the bringer of war.

Although Yorkist and Tudor monarchs achieved a considerable centralisation of power in England, political theory lagged behind. It was the European experience of religiously aggravated strife from the mid-sixteenth to the mid-seventeenth centuries that finally consolidated the sovereign state. The theory was propounded by Bodin in the context of the French civil wars and by Hobbes in the context of the English Civil War. The practice further evolved from the example set by the centralising policies of French ministers and monarchs from Richelieu to Louis XIV. The anarchic barbarism of the Thirty Years War stimulated the process. The Treaties of Westphalia, which finally brought this terrible conflict to a conclusion, emphasised the sovereign independence of states. Moreover, rulers were henceforth determined to exercise much tighter discipline over military forces. In pursuit of this aim they developed the practice of standing armies, which in turn underpinned the sovereignty of the prince and consequently the state in whose name he acted. Thus, paradoxically, the nightmare of war, which might well have taught Europe and need to realise the dream of unification, in fact led to the awakening of differentiated state power.

Barely two decades from the end of the Thirty Years War Louis XIV plunged Europe into a series of conflicts which were to last, intermittently, for nearly half a century. He started his reign with a consuming ambition to achieve military glory. On his deathbed, in 1715, he confessed to his successor, the little five-year-old boy, soon to be Louis XV: 'Do not imitate me in my passion for building, nor in my liking for war; try, on the contrary, to live in peace with your neighbours.' (quoted, Mousnier, p.4). Whatever his motives and justification (which have been endlessly debated and do not concern us here), the chronicle is a depressing record in the eyes of anyone who abhors war: War of Devolution, 1667–68; Dutch War, 1672–79; Spanish War, 1683–84; Nine Years War, 1688–97; War of the Spanish Succession, 1702–13/14.

By the time of Louis's campaigns land warfare had changed substantially in nature from the style of the early seventeenth century. Armies were bigger, siege warfare was more common, commissariats were better organised and (with the exception noted on pp.41–2) armies tended to terrorise the civilian population and live off the land much less. Although violent international conflict had become more civilised in comparison with the era of religious wars, one should not conclude that it had lost the capacity to inflict widespread misery and opposition. The new-style warfare was immensely costly in both financial and human terms.

By sixteenth-century standards the armies of the age of Louis XIV were exceedingly large, those of France herself, enormous. Although accurate figures are difficult to compute, towards the end of the War of the Spanish Succession three states alone – France, the Dutch Republic and the Habsburg Empire – had together just short of 600,000 men under arms. This was equivalent to a little under one in fifty of their combined total populations. After subtracting women, children and elderly men from this proportion, it is clear that the percentage of the able-bodied men recruited for warfare must have been crippling to the productive economies of those states. What is more, these troops had to be paid, equipped and fed.

The expense of war rose with vertiginous speed. In a futile attempt to keep pace, finance ministers tightened the screw of taxation. The wealth of the Dutch and English stood the anti-French alliances after 1688 in good stead. France showed her remarkable resilience in sustaining war for so long with few allies and even managed an armed force of nigh on half a million at the height of her power. But by 1709 she was in a state of utter exhaustion, the peasantry ground down to the depths of despair by military service, taxation and famine.

Keeping armies up to strength was a constant problem. Both siege warfare and set battles had become extremely prodigal in casualties, partly because of the large size of the forces engaged, partly because of the increased fire-power of weapons, and partly because of the lack of subtlety in tactics. The allied seizure of Lille in 1708 cost perhaps as many as 16,000 men. The pitched battles fought by Marlborough were especially bloody. At Blenheim, it is estimated, of a total of 108,000 men engaged some 30,000 were killed or wounded. This compares with a casualty rate of just under one in twenty of the previous 'record'. But it was the Battle of Malplaquet that became especially notorious for its sheer butchery. The scene was described with vivid economy by Voltaire in his *Le Siècle de Louis XIV*: 'One could hardly walk, save on piled-up corpses, which were thickest where the Dutch had fought. France lost hardly more than eight thousand men in the battle. Her enemies left about twenty-one thousand dead and wounded, but as the centre had been broken through and the two wings cut off, it was the defeated side which had inflicted the heaviest slaughter.' (Voltaire, 1756, p.231).

So the new large-scale disciplined armies suffered appalling losses in battle. But did they at least spare the civilian populations the kind of purgatory they had suffered in the Thirty Years War? Generally speaking, yes. Some areas were cruelly taxed and Marlborough won a nasty reputation for razing villages inconveniently sited for his strategic purposes. The French also acted brutally in some campaigns. Such incidences were, however, not the norm. What was a most shocking throwback to the inhumanity of the Thirty Years War was the horror visited on the wretched populace of the Palatinate by the French.

The Palatinate was the area of Germany between Alsace and Frankfurt. A relatively wealthy area, it boasted several fine cities, such as Mannheim, the seat of the local prince, the Elector Palatine. Much of the population of the region was Protestant, of both Lutheran and Calvinist persuasions. It also lay in the path of any French army striking eastwards towards Austria or any assembled Imperial or allied forces.

In 1675 the great Marshal Turenne, with uncharacteristic cruelty, set fire to two Palatine towns and a score of villages. The Elector sought to avenge the crime by appealing to the traditions of more chivalrous times: he forlornly challenged Turenne to a duel. But far worse was to come.

At the end of 1688, some months after the start of the Nine Years War, it became evident to the French government that the Netherlands would soon become the main theatre of operations. Troops, which had already invaded Germany, needed to be drawn back. How, then, was France to protect her eastern flank? The Marquis de Louvois issued an order: destroy the Palatinate. Beyond the Rhine the French army was to create a wilderness, denying fortifications, shelter and food to any advancing enemy. In the depth of winter, villagers, the inhabitants of towns, the occupants of châteaux fled before the French terror. Over a thousand villages and small towns were put to the torch, crops and livestock taken or destroyed. The devastation spread beyond the Electorate proper – to Württemberg and various Rhineland principalities. The whole region burned. Nearly a dozen cities and major towns suffered serious damage. At Heidelberg the magnificent Renaissance palace was shattered by explosives. Then, as the army finally drew back behind the Rhine in the early summer of 1689, they meted out the same fate to the cathedral cities of Trier, Worms and Speyer. As some of the homeless became refugees and the full horror of the episode was made known, civilised opinion, particularly in Germany, was shocked by the wanton incendiarism. Shock turned to fury and the fury bonded more tightly the anti-French coalition then forming.

Nor was the agony of the Palatines even now at an end. When the French returned in the mid-1690s they shamefully persecuted the Protestants. Furthermore, the Elector was Catholic. Supported by Jesuit advisers, he pursued a policy of undermining the Protestant churches. And so, over the following decades, fear of religious persecution added to the exodus of people from this unhappy region.

The extent and intensity of religious persecution and its contribution to international conflict were much abated in the age of Louis XIV compared with the previous century. The following examples of persecution may nevertheless be cited to reveal its persistence: legislation in Hungary, civil war in Switzerland and the expulsion of Protestants from Salzburg. However, it is France again which provides the most unpleasant illustration of intolerance.

One of Henry IV's most attractive achievements was the Edict of Nantes. One of his grandson's most despicable acts was to revoke it eighty-seven years later, in 1685. The Edict, in brief, guaranteed Huguenots equality of civic rights with their Catholic co-nationals. Louis's formal withdrawal of these rights, it is true, did not come suddenly. Throughout the seventeenth century some were gradually chipped away by a succession of royal ministers from Richelieu to Le Tellier. In Louis's reign, for example, an edict of 1666 (temporarily) codified sixty ways in which Huguenots could be legitimately harried; and in 1681 a proclamation required Huguenot children to renounce their faith at the age of seven. The flight of Huguenots from France started, despite the penalty of being consigned to the galleys if caught. What impelled many to seek sanctuary in other lands were the *dragonnades*. This was a system of billeting troops (dragoons) on Huguenot families, with a dreadful licence of behaviour to 'encourage' them to convert to Catholicism. The government, in turn, did all in its power to prevent their emigration. In the graphic words of Voltaire, 'It was in the nature of a hunt made in a vast enclosure.' (Voltaire, 1926, p.406).

Under pressure at court, Louis took the ultimate step. In October 1685 he issued the edict rescinding his grandfather's act of tolerance. The Huguenots became desperate. Despite the draconian laws against emigration, some 50,000 families succeeded in fleeing. The word 'refugee' entered into the English language. Many of those who would or could not escape maintained a rugged resistance in Languedoc for two decades.

Active, merciless harassment of religious minorities was discordant with the times. By the 1680s a mood of toleration pervaded much of Europe. Indeed, the very diaspora of Huguenot refugees helped to reinforce the distaste for religious hatred which had been stimulated by the post-Reformation blood-letting. This emotional reaction was reinforced by the new scientific emphasis on rational enquiry. The dogmatic detail of life, death and salvation shrivelled to a petty significance. The new, tolerant mentality found its first powerful expression in England, Holland and Brandenburg.

The great English philosopher, John Locke, set the scene with his *Letter concerning Toleration*, published in 1689, rapidly followed by translations from the original Latin into English, Dutch and French. He argued that true conversion cannot be achieved by force and that the imposition of a religion lies outside the proper function of the state: 'I cannot be saved by a religion that I distrust, and by a worship that I abhor . . . The care of each man's soul, and of the things of heaven, which neither does belong to the commonwealth nor can be subjected to it, is left entirely to every man's self.' (quoted, Cobban, 1960, p.59). Elsewhere, he described the appropriation of orthodoxy by anyone for his own particular faith as 'ridiculous' and a 'vanity' (quoted, Cobban, 1960 p.62). Locke's *Letter* was followed by works in a similar vein in the 1690s, the most radical of which was Pierre Bayle's *Dictionnaire historique et critique*, published in exile in Amsterdam in 1697.

Bayle was a Huguenot, who had fled to Holland, which, since the mid-century had become a byword for its religious tolerance. Commercial interests were perceived as being so much more important than doctrinal squabbling. In any case, the inhabitants were so doctrinally mongrel that intellectual discourse in this extraordinarily active little state was necessarily conducted in a climate conducive to religious indulgence. Furthermore, William III *qua* stadtholder of the United Provinces, provided governmental encouragement for this attitude and behaviour.

Since William was the lynchpin of alliances resisting the aggressive policy of Louis XIV, we may be tempted to interpret west-central European international relations in Manichean terms. William could thus be portrayed as the benevolent defender of the new, progressive but beleaguered principles of religious and political liberty. These principles were in peril from Louis XIV, the very epitome of religious intolerance and monarchical absolutism. Holland and England, both led after 1688 by William of Orange, were again resisting political and religious arrogance as William the Silent and Elizabeth had resisted the overbearing Habsburgs a century earlier. But this explanation depends on our ability to interpret international relations in this far more secular age in religious terms. This may be seriously questioned.

Wars were broadly speaking fought in the age of Louis XIV for overtly worldly motives: for territorial, commercial or dynastic advantage. In so far as religious differences were thought to have political implications, they were generally considered to be internal matters to be resolved between the prince and his subjects. As a rule of thumb it was little more than the acceptance of the guideline set down in 1555 of 'cuius regio, eius religio' (the ruler of a territory should determine its religion).

And yet there were still occasions when rulers felt impelled to take religion into account. At the most general level, as Professor Lossky has pointed out, the terms 'Europe' and 'Christendom' were still used almost interchangeably – almost, for there were some areas of uncertainty which cast an interesting light on the particular proposals for European unity we shall be discussing in this chapter. He explains that for diplomatic purposes, 'Balkan Christians under Ottoman rule were generally excluded from both "Europe" and "Christendom". On the other hand, Russia . . . was usually included in "Christendom" but often excluded from "Europe".' (Bromley, pp.167–8). Religious matters were still capable of becoming diplomatic issues too. When the French maltreated the Palatines several Protestant German princes threatened similar treatment of their Catholic subjects as a means of exerting pressure upon Louis. A number of rulers, most notably the Elector of Brandenburg, protested vehemently about the treatment of the Huguenots. Both Queen Christina and Charles XII of Sweden expressed concern for the fate of the Huguenots. When, at the end of the Nine Years War, Louis surrendered some captured German territory, the peace treaty (of Ryswick) required the Catholic Church to be maintained as the prime religious influence.

However, of all the major rulers of this period who felt driven in their conduct of foreign policy by an inner religious impulse, it was William III who expressed the most zealous conviction. A dour, unfriendly man, wracked by asthma and tuberculosis, the Prince of Orange was filled with a passionate hatred of Louis XIV's threat to the European equilibrium. He devoted his considerable diplomatic skills to the task of dimming the arrogant power of the Sun King. These were political motives. Even so, he was sustained at times in this demanding work by the certainty lodged in his own mind that he was God's chosen instrument for this undertaking. He was therefore happy to accept the Whig offer to share the crown of England with his wife, Mary. When he landed at Torbay in November 1688, some six weeks after the start of what was to become the Nine Years War, he knew full well that he was considerably strengthening his chances in his appointed crusade against Catholic France. England was now rescued from the francophile policies deviously established by Charles II and from the manoeuvrings of James II to afford the Catholic Church a much more central role in the land.

It has been necessary to sketch in this religious background to the period because our two subjects for consideration in this chapter held the deep religious commitment of Quakers; and their schemes for continental integration were bound to reflect this religious influence. They were also both Englishmen. We therefore need to know a little of the national as well as the broader European context in which they were writing.

The basic fact is that the Revolution of 1688 produced as radical a change in British foreign policy as in constitutional practice. William thrust Britain into the centre of the European martial and diplomatic mêlée. Henry VIII had participated at the Field of the Cloth of Gold: and there had been sundry involvements with the Dutch – Elizabeth rendering assistance and Cromwell and Charles II warring with them. However, despite these occasional forays into continental affairs, generally speaking England had stayed on the political periphery of Europe for nearly two and a half centuries.

This virtual isolationist policy may be said to have started after the Hundred Years War was effectively concluded by the French artillery's destruction of the English army at the disastrous Battle of Castillon in 1453. With the involvement of British contingents in such bloody engagements as Steenkerke (1692) and Neerwinden (1693) the human cost of the revived full participation in European affairs became painfully evident. Marlborough's campaigns were to produce even higher casualty figures. This unprecedented outlay in men was paralleled by a similarly unheard-of expenditure of money – for the expansion of the navy and army and in the form of subsidies to maintain the armies of less affluent allies in the field. The cost for Britain of the Nine Years War caused sufficient concern, yet it was cheap compared with the War of the Spanish Succession. The former cost £49m., little more than half the later eleven-year conflict (£93m.) (Kennedy, p.105). These figures compare with a public expenditure of about £2m. per annum immediately prior to 1688.

Great ingenuity was needed to raise these funds: a window tax, a more effective land tax, a national lottery and, foremost of all, the creation of the Bank of England and the formalisation of the National Debt. Little wonder that, as the wars with France continued, some people began to question whether Britain's commitment to the struggle was truly in the national interest.

By the turn of the century it seemed to many observers that the very source of the funds which had enabled Britain so successfully to resist Louis XIV – namely commercial enterprise – was being jeopardised by the priorities of continental war. This was the age when political journalism reached maturity in England – the age of Addison, Steele, Defoe, Dryden and Swift. At the end of his life Dryden pleaded:

Enough for Europe has our Albion fought;
Let us enjoy the peace our blood has bought (quoted, Ashley, p. 189).

But nothing articulated and magnified the feeling of war-weariness more effectively than the brilliant pamphlet written by Dean Swift in 1711, *The Conduct of the Allies*. By now the conduct and continuation of the war and what were considered the desirable terms of peace had become issues of bitter party political contention. Grub Street was recruited in the battle for the peace during the years 1710–13. While Addison and Steele joined the war-party of the Whigs, Defoe and Swift campaigned for the Tory policy of bringing the war to a conclusion. Swift indeed outflanked the chief Tory minister, Robert Harley, in demanding peace at any price. In his characteristic acerbic tone he questioned the honesty of conduct of both Britain's allies and her own war-profiteers.

The thrust of the argument was for Britain to enjoy the fruits of peace by disengagement from continental imbroglios: to revert to a virtually isolationist policy. And yet this was not the only conclusion to be drawn from the agonised need for peace. Britain could, alternatively, lead Europe out of these fratricidal conflicts by promoting a scheme of political integration.

The Quakers, Penn and Bellers

Of all people in England who would have deplored the French wars it was the Quakers who could be expected to hold to this view most tenaciously. The Society of Friends emerged as a coherent fraternity from the radical political and religious turmoil of the mid-seventeenth century. Only gradually did they come to define their beliefs and principles. They had also been realistic enough to recognise that not all mankind, not all Christians, not all Friends even, are capable of living strictly in full accord with their beliefs and principles. These ideals of conscience and conduct were called 'testimonies'. One of these testimonies, only gradually being confirmed at the turn of the seventeenth century, was the testimony against war. Members of the Society have perhaps become more vilified and more respected for adherence to this testimony than to any others. However, during the period in which we are here interested the potential of this moral stand had not become entirely clear.

The person who emerged as the leader of the Society of Friends in the 1650s was George Fox. He was guided in defining his yardsticks of behaviour by the sixteenth- and seventeenth-century religious reformers who emphasised the cardinal significance of love in human relationships. In the words of an American authority on the Society, 'In the early stages of the movement Quakerism was not so much a "testimony" against war as the proclamation and exhibition of a kind of Christianity that risked everything on the venture of the conquering power of love. It was a type of life which eliminated war because it eliminated hate, and it was clear that if the world came to this way of living wars were forever done.' (Jones, p.157). As the 1650s drew to a close the Stuart Restoration was clearly so much more imminent than Christ's Second Coming. Fox, who had already made his pacifist views clear to Cromwell, started to reassess his attitude towards the state. In November 1660 he and eleven other Quakers presented a pacifist declaration to Charles II. Though the pragmatic motive of defending Quakers in the face of accusations of sedition against the restored Stuart government may have been as compelling as the moral principle.

None the less, Fox could be looked to as the founder of the Society who defined themselves as partakers of a 'life and power that took away the occasion of all wars.' (quoted, Braithwaite, p.609). Robert Barclay, of Scottish ancestry and deep theological understanding, drew a distinction important for Quakers at the time. In 1676 he wrote of the imperfect, so-called Christian statesmen, that 'while they are in that condition, we shall not say that war, undertaken upon a just occasion, is altogether unlawful to them.' On the other hand, for those who have been blessed with a truly perfect Christian 'patient, suffering spirit', 'it is not lawful to defend themselves by arms, but they ought over all to trust to the Lord.' (quoted, Braithwaite, p.612). The political lesson to draw from this doctrine was a kind of belt of belief backed up by braces of weaponry: that a government should arm the state with both a spiritual armoury and war *matériel* according to the strength of faith and confidence of security it could call upon.

Consequently, when England engaged in her bloody conflicts with *louis-quatorzienne* France, members of the Society of Friends could be expected to regret the recourse to war; avoid personal involvement in it; but recognise that European man was, by and large and sadly, like that. For example, in 1697, following the Treaty of Ryswick and the ending of the Nine Years War, one John Crook published *The Way to a Lasting Peace*. In this pamphlet he argued that now the physical fighting was concluded, war must be launched on man's inner lusts and corruption.

Staunch adherence to the testimony against war required personal courage – physical courage in the face of imprisonment in dire conditions; moral courage in the face of ridicule and deprivation of civil rights. But Quakers became schooled in courage through their experience of persecution for their religious beliefs generally. This suffering would inevitably have coloured their view of international conflict in the age of Louis XIV. For, although, as we have already noted, sectarian differences were no longer the significant factor in international conflict that they had been in the period surveyed in Chapter 2, religious intolerance and persecution were still widespread.

The Quakers were particularly sensitive to these problems for two distinct reasons. One was the history of their own persecution from the time of the creation of the Society. Even during the Puritan regime of the Commonwealth, Parliament reversed Cromwell's initial tolerant policy and launched a campaign against the Society in 1654. After the Restoration Charles II's programme of rehabilitating the Church of England led to the enactment of many civil disabilities against

Dissenters. Quakers tended to suffer more than other Puritan sects from these official expressions of intolerance because of their refusal to compromise with their own principles. They scorned the defensive device of holding meetings in secret; and they drew attention to themselves by their peculiarities of conduct such as the refusal of the men to remove their hats as a mark of honour. The second interest of the Quakers in religious toleration was that they positively believed in it in any case. Tolerance was an integral part of their very gentleness and meekness of demeanour. Consequently in England members of the Society were foremost in the struggles against Dissenter disabilities. In Pennsylvania, their own settlement, Penn's views prevailed. Consequently, although his friend Locke thought the *moral* code too oppressive, tolerance of different Christian liturgical practices was fundamental to the way of life in the settlement. This benevolence was codified by the Provincial Assembly in the following words:

No person, now or at any time hereafter, living in the Province, who shall confess and acknowledge one Almighty God to be the Creator, Upholder and Ruler of the world, And who profess him or herself, Obliged in Conscience to Live peaceably and quietly under the civil government, shall in any case be molested or prejudiced for his or her Conscientious persuasion or practice (quoted, Nye & Morpurgo, pp.85–6).

And so it happened in reality, to the encouragement of waves of immigrants of most diverse sects from sundry states of Europe.

Penn's own life was a splendid exemplification of the Quaker testimonies. To live so proximately to the Friends' ideal was all the more remarkable in the light of his background – a family far removed from Quaker radical simplicity. His father, a sailor, reached senior naval rank, was knighted by Charles II, became a personal friend of the Lord High Admiral, the Duke of York (subsequently James II), and owned considerable property in London and Cork. At the impressionable age of twelve, in 1656, young William was much affected by the Quaker, Thomas Loe. When he went up to Oxford three years later he consorted with nonconformists and was sent down for this unacceptable behaviour. However, it was not until 1667 that he came to embrace Quaker beliefs, was imprisoned for the first time for them and consequently caused his father considerable distress. Penn was indeed to be arrested on several occasions. His trial at the Old Bailey under the Second Conventicle Act of 1670 became a milestone in the struggle for religious and civil liberty. The authorities exerted pressure upon the jury by outrageous threats to bring in a guilty verdict, which, with great audacity, they refused to do. Penn himself came to argue consistently in his pamphlets and later writings the integral relationship between civil and religious harmony and freedom.

Furthermore, he had the good fortune to be able to practise politically what he had preached theologically. The foundation of the

Quaker colony of Pennsylvania was the outcome of Penn's unique, and often uneasy, straddling of the Stuart Establishment and Quaker radicalism. Sir William Penn had asked the Duke of York to keep a tutelary eye on his son. It was the Duke who in 1681 arranged for his brother, Charles II, in payment of debts, to grant Penn the land, which the king himself then dubbed 'Pennsylvania' in honour of the late Admiral. In his adolescent years young William had dreamt of creating a utopia. Six weeks after the issue of the Royal Patent he wrote a letter in which he showed clearly his appreciation of the opportunity which now lay before him. He revealed that, 'as my understanding and inclination have been much directed to observe and reprove mischiefs in government, so it is now put into my power to settle one.' (quoted, Braithwaite, p.404). He arrived in the New World in October 1682 to oversee his 'Holy Experiment'.

Penn sought settlers and at the same time peaceful accommodation with the indigenous population whose lands they were invading. Hence the famous Treaty of Shackamaxon with the Indians. Quarrels and difficulties arose, it is true, for, as Penn understood, 'Let men be good, and the government cannot be bad. But, if men be bad, let the government be ever so good, they will endeavour to warp and spoil it in their turn.' (quoted, Braithwaite, p.405). And yet, the 'Holy Experiment' remained a significant lesson in the potential to build a society based upon the principles of liberty and tolerance as well as peaceable relations with neighbours even though of an alien culture.

Penn's close association with James II cast a shadow of doubt over his loyalty to the government of William III and Mary after the 1688 Revolution. He was in fact arrested on suspicion of high treason and questioned by the king personally. Although released, he was justifiably nervous. James's invasion of Ireland in 1690 rendered suspect anyone with Jacobite connections; the war with France caused William to worry that Pennsylvania might be a weak link in the chain of American defence. Penn prudently lay low for a few years.

1692–93 was a wretched time for Penn. The war was going badly for William III. In the spring of 1692 Louis XIV even made plans, admittedly of a desultory kind, to invade England. The French capture of Namur and the failure of William's counter-attack in June 1692 was a serious military setback. In this critical phase the king, in October, withdrew Pennsylvania from Penn's personal control. To add to his personal miseries his wife fell mortally ill. He turned to writing, producing half a dozen significant works during this period – more substantial and perhaps more deeply felt than his tracts of the 1670s. It was in 1693 that he wrote *An Essay Towards the Present Peace of Europe*. Perhaps because he was in hiding he did not follow the usual procedure and submit the text to the Monthly Meeting, the Society's committee for publications. Also, he published it anonymously.

Nor were Penn's last years happy. Although Pennsylvania was, conditionally, restored to him, the conduct of its affairs plunged him deeply into debt, for which condition he was consigned to the Fleet prison in 1707. In 1712 he suffered siezures which deprived him increasingly of his mental faculties for the last six years of his life. The state of Europe in the early 1690s, when Penn wrote his *Essay*, turned numerous minds to thoughts of peace. So many European states were locked in conflict with France that the idea that they might all, including France, instead embrace each other in friendship was a welcome message. Penn himself was well fitted to contemplate a scheme for the pacification and unification of Europe. In the first place he was somewhat exceptional among Quakers in wishing to take positive action to preserve peace rather than adopting the Friends' usual negative posture of simply avoiding engagement in conflict.

Secondly, he was no closet scribbler. He was experienced in state-craft and diplomacy. The liberalism and sagacity he displayed in draft-ing the Pennsylvanian constitution so impressed Montesquieu that he dubbed him 'the modern Lycurgus'. He also had some practical understanding of European affairs. He was a confidant of James II, who even sent him on a mission to Holland for a meeting with William of Orange in 1686. True, the subject of most, if not all, of these discussions was the matter of religious toleration. But Penn knew the minds and policies of princes. He became convinced that religious toleration was a necessary condition both for international peace and national greatness.

Thirdly, of course, there were his Quaker principles – of love and tolerance and peace. His religious objection to war must have been reinforced, if that were needed, by the horrific actions of the French in the Palatinate and beyond in 1688–89 (see p.41) and the uprecedent-edly bloody battle of Steenkerke (see p.45). A year after writing his essay on Europe he summed up the Quaker doctrines in *A Brief Account of the Rise and Progress of the People Called Quakers*. 'Not fighting, but suffering,' he wrote, 'is another testimony peculiar to this people: they affirm that Christianity teacheth people to beat their swords into ploughshares . . . all wars and fightings come of men's own hearts' lusts, according to the apostle James, and not of the meek spirit of Christ Jesus . . . And, Christianity set aside, if the costs and fruits of war were well considered, peace with all its inconveniences is generally preferable.' (Penn, pp.185–6).

Such a man could hardly sit in his hiding-place and idly ignore the blood being shed on the continent. He knew that he had valuable advice to proffer – even if there was little likelihood of its immediate acceptance.

In fact, the fury of Louis XIV's wars was not to abate while Penn remained deeply aware of public affairs. And so, some seventeen years after Penn's *Essay*, a friend ten years his junior, was constrained to put forward another proposal in Quaker style. John Bellers was born in London in 1654, probably in Philpot Lane. Unlike Penn, Bellers inherited Quakerism – his father, a wealthy grocer, became a Friend about the time of John's birth. John too entered business, as a cloth merchant, but acquired something of a literary education by a wide reading of the classics. However, what really shaped his thinking was his observation, as a young man, of the effects of poverty and religious persecution.

Bellers engaged in diverse activities of a philanthropic kind and wrote, as far as we know, a score of essays and pamphlets. His interest in poverty led him into economic and statistical studies. For instance, in 1695 he calculated that England's per capita GDP (to use an anachronistic term) was £40. His erudition brought him election to the Royal Society.

Poverty and unemployment were serious problems in England at this time, being especially acute in the years 1693–99. The studies which Bellers made and the practical proposals he recommended were, albeit brief, extraordinarily advanced for his day. In the fields of poor relief, education and health he proposed a veritable welfare state. He indeed emphasised the interconnections between poverty, illness, ignorance and crime. He was always concerned about people. He worried about the loss to the country that unemployment represented and the need to make all work personally satisfying. He also insisted that the wealth of the rich derived from the labours of the poor. Is it any wonder, then, that Karl Marx made several references in *Das Kapital* to two of his works? These were: *Essays about the Poor, Manufactures, Trade, Plantations and Immorality* and *Proposals for Raising a Colledge of Industry of All Useful Trades and Husbandry*. Marx described the Quaker as 'a veritable phenomenon in the history of political economy.' (Marx, p.619, n.32). Bellers's fame rests indeed much more on his analysis of social conditions than his proposal for European unity. His writings found a deep resonance in the heart of Robert Owen, from whose work Marx learned of him. And later in the nineteenth century Bernstein, the German Social Democrat, was to say of him, 'We find in him the most daring and clearest thoughts of the religious and social revolutionaries of the age.' (quoted, Braithwaite, p.594).

We must not forget the religious dimension of Bellers's thought. If Friends are noted for their social consciences and determination to soothe the ills that prick them, then Bellers had the most sensitive of consciences and the most firm determination. He had faith, too, that, by holding to true Christian principles, improvement was possible. His philanthropic campaigning and religious convictions were but two sides of the same medal. Bellers was deeply involved in the activities of the Society of Friends and was in fact arrested three times in 1684–85.

His concern to combat poverty and support the religiously persecuted fused in his compassion for refugees fleeing Louis XIV's campaign against the Protestants. In 1685 Bellers gave financial support to some Huguenots to travel on to Pennsylvania. We find Penn writing in July of that year to the governing Council there: 'The French come on John Bellers account, who has bought half of R. Marshes 10.000 acres . . . pray be kind to the people and let them be forthwith settled.' (quoted, Clarke, 1987, p.5). Bellers's recent editor is, however, mistaken in attributing this emigration to the Revocation of the Edict of Nantes, for Louis issued his revising edict only in the October of that year. They were, rather, escaping from the dreadful policy of *dragonnades* well established by that year (see p.42).

By 1709 areas of western Europe were in a desperate condition, exhausted by war and famine. In the Rhineland, Protestants particularly were in jeopardy. In that year another wave of refugees, generically referred to as 'Palatines', arrived in England. By July 10,000 had set up camps in 'canvas hutches' on the south-east fringes of London. They were received with some coolness. High-Church Tories objected to their presence on doctrinal grounds, thus exacerbating their differences with the Whigs. Many believed that they were not refugees in the proper sense of the term (a pre-echo of the objection to 'economic migrants' expressed in Britain in the 1980s!) It was indeed evident that many were attracted by the higher standard of living in England and the expectation of sympathetic treatment from Queen Anne, widow of a Lutheran prince. Furthermore, the English parishes, their resources already stretched by domestic poverty caused by high corn prices, could not cope with this influx. Nevertheless, the Palatines did enjoy many acts of generosity. For example, John Bellers, recognising their plight, wrote a memorandum *To the Lords and others Commissioners, appointed by the Queen to take Care of the Poor Palatines*. In this he proposed a revamp of his favourite 'College of Industry' scheme for economically self-contained work-colonies.

It was in the following year, his mind still mulling over the effects of war and persecution on the continent, that Bellers wrote his *Some Reasons for an European State*. The war-weariness in England was also, no doubt, a significant factor conducive to publication. The peace negotiations conducted at The Hague during the summer of 1709 broke down because of Marlborough's arrogantly impossible demands of the French. In the autumn came Malplaquet, the 'murdering' battle as Marlborough called it. Bellers's was not the only voice crying for the end of a war which benefited no one but the financiers and merchants who enjoyed some rich pickings. It is something of an exaggeration, therefore, to describe Bellers's essay as 'an act of courage', as his editor declares (Clarke, 1987, p.132). That is not to belittle the argument of the essay, of course.

Bellers briefly returned to the issue of European peace and unity. He wrote an essay in 1712 pleading with the politicians to end their party bickering and concentrate on the real problems facing the country. These included an attempt 'to find out the utmost Extent that Foreign Treaties may be brought to, for the settling of an Universal and Lasting Peace among the Powers of *Europe*, to prevent the

Effusion of Christian Blood for the future, beyond what the Common Guarantees and Treaties have hitherto produced.' (reprinted, Clarke, 1987, p.168). That was the year in which was published the Abbé de Saint-Pierre's *Mémoire pour rendre la Paix perpétuelle en Europe* (see Chapter 4). Two years later, soon after the appearance of an English translation of Saint-Pierre's Project, we find Bellers somewhat strangely tucking in some comments on this work at the end of *An Essay towards the Improvement of Physick*! The relevance is the plea, not entirely unheard today, that resources he diverted from war-preparation to health-care. While generally welcoming the recommendations of 'the Abbot St. Pierre', Bellers regrets his neglect of the religious causes of conflict. For, in Bellers's view, '... until Persecutions and Violences about Religion are prevented or stopt; they will so long make all Arguments for a General Peace ineffectual, however valuable and demonstrable those Reasons may be.' (reprinted, Clarke, 1987, p.212). He speculates that the French author has passed over this issue because of the dependence of the clergy of that land on the state for their ecclesiastical preferments. He feels that it is so obvious that religious as well as political harmony are essential: 'Without which Liberty of Conscience, an *European* Senate may turn all future War into a Religious one; but so far as any of the Clergy shall encourage Persecutions that may occasion such an endless War, and prevent so great a good as an Universal Peace, they will fall into that Crime, which the Abbot Writes, is of the Number of those which are punished with Everlasting Damnation, in the Opinion of all the Casuists of *Europe*.' (reprinted, Clarke, 1987, p.212).

The schemes of Penn and Bellers

A few years after Penn's death, a fellow Quaker, Joseph Besse wrote a biography of him. Of his essay on Europe he wrote: 'A work so adapted to the unsettled condition of the times, and so well received, that it was reprinted the same year.' (Penn, p.xxxiii). What were Penn's recommendations and how did they reflect his religious beliefs and the current international scene?

The full title of the pamphlet reveals Penn's concern to emphasise the constitutional structure of his scheme. It is: *An Essay Towards the Present and Future Peace of Europe by the Establishment of an European Diet, Parliament, or Estates*. After an introduction, in which he justifies his presentation of the project by referring to 'the groaning state of Europe' (Penn, p.3), he subdivides his essay into ten brief sections. In the first sections he argues the advantage of peace over a condition of war with particular reference to the current conflict (i.e. the Nine Years War). He declares with some passion that,

He must not be a man but a statue of brass or stone whose bowels do not melt when he beholds the bloody tragedies of this war, in Hungary, Germany, Flanders, Ireland, and at sea, the mortality of sickly and languishing camps and navies, and the mighty prey the devouring winds and waves have made upon ships and men since '88 (Penn, pp.3–4).

He continues by contrasting the beneficent features of peace with the evil side-effects of war when 'The rich draw in their stock, the poor turn soldiers, or thieves, or starve: no industry, no building, no manufactory, little hospitality or charity.' (Penn, p.4). He asserts that 'justice is the means to peace' (Penn, p.6), a principle which needs to be extended from internal to international politics. He concludes these contextual remarks by emphasising how government is essential for purposes of law and order, again a truism extensible from the domestic to the European context.

In his fourth section Penn seeks to show how the interrelated desiderata of peace, justice and government could be realised in Europe. It is at this point that he introduces his plan for a European diet. He envisages a parliament composed of the representatives of the rulers to 'establish rules of justice for sovereign princes to observe one to another; and thus to meet yearly, or once in two or three years at farthest.' If any ruler refuses to abide by a judgment of arbitration, then 'all the other sovereignties, united as one strength, shall compel the submission and performance of the sentence, with damages to the suffering party, and charges to the sovereignties that obliged their submission.' (Penn, p.8). No state, he claims, could withstand this united pressure for a peaceful resolution of disputes.

Penn foresees the parliament settling potential conflicts arising from a desire to retain current territorial possessions or recover former territory and restraining aggressors from their planned seizure of others' lands (Section V). The trouble is, he recognises in Section VI, that there is some difficulty in defining what constitutes a moral right to territory. He is inclined to disallow the ownership of lands acquired by conquest, but is forced to concede that such additions are often accorded legal sanctity by treaties. This is a very practical issue for him because he wishes to base his scheme for permanent peace on a freezing of frontiers. These should be either as determined by the Treaty of Nimeguen (1678) or as they had been at the start of the current war (1688) or as to be determined by the peace treaty at its end.

Penn then turns his attention, in the seventh section, to the composition of his proposed assembly. He addresses particularly the difficulty of apportioning the number of seats. He recommends that they be calculated on the basis of a kind of estimate of GNP. He denies that such a method might be impracticable: 'Now that England, France, Spain, the Empire, etc., may be pretty exactly estimated is so plain a case, by considering the revenue of lands, the exports and entries at the custom houses, the books of rates, and surveys that are in all governments, to proportion taxes for the support of them, that the least inclination to the peace of Europe will not stand or halt at this objection.' (Penn, p.10). He provides the following rough 'guesstimate' of a proportional allocation of seats:

Empire of Germany	12
France, Spain, Muscovites, Turks	10 each
Italy	8
England	6
Sweedland, Poland, the seven provinces	
(i.e. the Dutch Republic)	4 each
Portugal, Denmark, Venice	3 each
The thirteen cantons (i.e. Switzerland)	2
Dukedoms of Holstein & Courland	1
	90

For the Turks and Muscovites he adds the rider, 'if [they] are taken in, as seems but fit and just'. This would be a parliament of the 'best and wealthiest [quarter] of the known world'; and the most civilised, to boot, in Penn's estimation (Penn, p.11). He does not insist on a full attendance, though he would prefer it: irrespective of the number of representatives, votes in deliberations would be weighted according to the above table.

Penn is also at great pains to ensure that the proceedings are conducted in an impartial and honest manner (Section VIII). Thus, ingeniously, 'To avoid quarrel for precedency, the room may be round, and have divers doors to come in and go out at, to prevent exceptions [i.e. exclusions].' (This system may be compared with the careful insistence on precedence in some other schemes.) Voting 'should be by ballot after the prudent and commendable method of the Venetians: which, in a great degree, prevents the ill effects of corruption.' (Penn, pp.11–12). To guard further against corruption Penn insists that decisions must be reached by the vote of three-quarters of the assembly: and he would not allow abstentions.

He accepts in Section IX that four main objections might be advanced against his proposed league or confederacy (Penn, pp.13–15). The first is that the strongest and richest state would either refuse to enter or, once a member, bribe others to support its interests. The second is 'that it will endanger an effeminacy by such a disuse of the trade of soldiery' and render the confederation defenceless. The third objection is that demobilisation would increase the level of unemployment. We may note in passing that, characteristically, Penn is the first of the devisers of schemes for European unity to emphasise disarmament as a significant feature of his plan. He counters each of these arguments. However, he has some difficulty with the fourth, crucial objection, which we have heard so often is modern guise. This is 'that sovereign princes and states will hereby become not sovereign: a thing they will never endure.' His solution is to distinguish between the internal and external sovereignty of princes. The former would be unimpaired: 'Neither their power over their people, nor the usual revenue they pay them, is diminished,' he asserts. What is to be lost is the freedom to exercise 'any sovereignty over one another.' He translates this as meaning that 'the great fish can no longer eat up the little ones'. And so state sovereignty is mutually defended and restrained.

Penn leaves the catalogue of benefits to be derived from his scheme to the tenth section. His overriding concern is to prevent 'the spilling of so much human and Christian blood'; and he lectures those in government that 'it is a duty incumbent upon them to be tender of the lives of their people; since without all doubt, they are accountable to God for the blood that is spilt in their service.' (Penn, p.15). The second benefit is the redemption of the reputation of Christianity so sullied in the eyes of infidels by the propensity of Christians to slaughter one another. Christ, he reminds his readers, is the Prince of Peace. The third benefit relates to the European economy. Instead of spending money on international conflict (and he is especially concerned to emphasise the cost of espionage), 'learning, charity, manufactures, etc.' would flourish (Penn, p.16). Fourthly, the physical damage of war would no longer be perpetrated. The fifth advantage derives not so much from peace as from the confederal relationships he would establish between states. Travel could be undertaken throughout the continent with ease and security, uninterrupted by 'the many stops and examinations' (Penn, p.17) that were so irksome especially in the political patchwork of Germany at the time. Sixthly, the Turkish threat to Christendom would disappear, since Europe was vulnerable only because of its disunity. The seventh consideration is that, by meeting in the European Imperial Diet, the princes and representatives would strike up personal friendships tending to amicable rather than bellicose behaviour. And finally, the system would allow princes to marry for love and not dynastic advantage. Both personal and international happiness alike would derive from this change of habit, for 'What hatred, feuds, wars, and desolations have in divers ages flown from unkindness between princes and their wives?' (Penn, p.20).

Penn concludes by appealing to the small-scale example of the United Provinces to show that his confederal plan 'may be done' and to the Grand Design of the illustrious Henry IV to show that 'it is fit to be done.' (Penn, p.22). He also confesses to 'the passion to wish heartily that the honour of proposing and effecting so great and good a design might be owing to England, of all the countries in Europe.' (Penn, p.21).

Penn was a personal friend of Bellers, who acknowledged at the end of his pamphlet the essay 'what hath been Writ by the Eminent and

accomplished Gentleman, William Penn Esq., Governour of Pensil-
vania' (reprinted, Clarke, 1987, p.15). Bellers's brief work, published
in 1710, is entitled *Some Reasons for an European State*, and subtitled
*Proposed to the Powers of Europe by an Universal Guarantee, and an
Annual Congress, Senate, Dyet, or Parliament To Settle any Disputes
about the Bounds and Rights of Princes and States Hereafter*. The
essay opens with a dedication to Queen Anne. Here Bellers draws the
parallel between the unification and consequent pacification of the
United Kingdom and the need for a similar political achievement for
Europe as a whole. In particular, he suggests that 'it will be a great
Acquirement to the Glory of the Queen, if to the Union of *Scotland*
[i.e. the Act of Union, 1707] . . . She will Please to Use Her endeavours
for Uniting the Powers of *Europe* in one peaceable Settlement.'
(reprinted, Clarke, 1987, p.135).

In the body of the work Bellers addresses successively the Lords
and Commons of Great Britain, the Powers of Europe, the Councellors
(sic) and Ministers of State, and the Bishops, Confessors, Chaplains
and other Clergy. He sets the scene by immediately referring to 'The
Deluge of Christian Blood, and the vast Treasure which have been
spent to procure the expected Peace' (reprinted, Clarke, 1987, p.136).

A scheme for European unity is perfectly practicable, he insists. He
cites in evidence both the experiences of the United Provinces and
Switzerland and Henry IV's Grand Design:

The several Provinces of Holland as well as the Cantons of Switzerland were
the easier and firmer Settled and Strengthened, by being United in Perilous
Times. If the present Confederates [i.e. allies against France] begin among
themselves, and then Invite into all the Neutral Powers, it will draw on the
Peace the faster (if not made before) and the more incline France it Self to
come into it, by which that Kingdom will reap the Blessing of a lasting Peace,
which their present King's Grandfather had formerly proposed (reprinted,
Clarke, 1987, p.137).

The plan involves the consolidation and defence of the European
state boundaries however they were to emerge at the end of the war
(for he considered no peace settlement any more or less arbitrary than
any other). An annual congress or senate of representatives would be
instituted so that 'all the Princes and States of Europe' would be
'joyned as one State' and 'a standing European Law' would be codified
(reprinted, Clarke, 1987, p.140). Bellers is at pains to balance the
guarantee of territorial possessions, the preservation of internal sovereignty and the growth of a more uniform and unified political system.
He is realist enough to recognise the need for an evolutionary
approach to the problem: 'Europe being under several Forms of
Government, and every Country being apt to Esteem their own Form
best: It will require Time and Consideration among the Powers concerned, to draw such a Scheme as will suit the Dispositions and Circumstances of them all' (reprinted, Clarke, 1987, p.140).

Bellers incorporates a particularly novel element in his provision for cantonal devolution and representation. This idea deserves to be quoted at some length:

... Europe should be divided into 100 equal Cantons or Provinces, or so many, that every Sovereign Prince and State may send one Member to the Senate at least: and that every each Canton should be appointed to raise a Thousand Men or Money, or Ships of equal Value or Charge upon any Public Occasion . . . And for every Thousand Men etc., that each Kingdom or State is to raise, such Kingdom or State shall have a Right to send so many Members to this European Senate . . . (reprinted, Clarke, 1987, p.140).

Peace would ensue from such an arrangement for several reasons. Every state would know how foolhardy it would be to defy the will of the assembly since the forces of all the others would be arrayed against any recalcitrant. Secondly, the majority of states, having no personal interest in any given dispute, would support the side whose case was the more just. And thirdly, all states would, in any case, be required to disarm to a modest level of forces.

Bellers then turns to address 'the Counsellors and Ministers of State, of the Kingdoms and States of Europe' in an attempt to persuade them that their reputations would be enhanced, both in this world and for entry into the world to come, if they supported such a scheme for European peace. He paints a grim picture of the future if peace is not secured in Europe: ' . . . in a Thousand, or Two Thousand Years or less, there may be as many People destroyed by War in Europe, as are now living in it.' Furthermore, 'at the Great Day of Judgment' there will be no 'Crime so aggravated, as that of having been an Enemy to Settling and Establishing the Peace of Europe.' (reprinted, Clarke, 1987, p.144).

The religious tone of this section, in which he also contrasts the evil reputation of 'Heathen Heroes' such as Alexander and Caesar with the eirenic purpose of Christ, should occasion little surprise. Bellers was a devout Friend. He also allocates a sizeable portion of his pamphlet to explicitly religious matters. He is also sufficiently realistic in his assessment of human nature to recognise that man's propensity to violence, when blocked from expression in international political conflict, is likely to find renewed outlet in religious strife. He tackles this problem by an appeal to the clergy and a proposal for a European Christian Council.

Bellers urges 'the Bishops, Confessors, Chaplains, Presbyters, Ministers, and Teachers in the Kingdoms and States of Europe' to work for peace. He seeks to shame them: 'How shall the Rays of Christianity, Influence Turks and Infidels? when they shall see, that under the pretence of that Religion, it's Professors shall have the hottest Animosities and Hatred, there having been far more Christian Blood spilt, by one another, than ever was spilt, by the greatest of their Heathen

Persecutors' (reprinted, Clarke, 1987, p.145). He supplies a plethora of examples of Protestants and Roman Catholics in fact living and co-operating harmoniously. He also asserts that 'Persecution, to force conformity in Religion, as it's useless, is also as directly against the Intent of Christianity, as the worst of the Heathen Principles, and Practices.' 'Men will not be Sav'd against their own wills: Neither can a Man firmly believe what he is not convinc'd of.' It is interesting, parenthetically, to compare this argument with Locke's (p.43). More-over, 'War is usually the Consequence of Persecutions for Religion.' (reprinted, Clarke, 1987, pp.146–7).

In order to prevent future outbreaks of religious conflict he proposes 'a General Council, of all the several Christian Perswasions in Europe. To Meet together with a Disposition of Loving their Neighbours, and doing good to each other, more than to contend about what they Differ in' (reprinted, Clarke, 1987, p.148). By agreeing to and expounding a kind of highest common factor of Christian principles, he believed that open wars for religious motives could be brought to an end.

Bellers then proceeds to outline Sully's Grand Design, which he interprets as Henry IV's scheme to extend his religious pacification of France to the continent as a whole. Although he applauds Henry's association of peace with Christianity, he would extend the hand of peace and union to the Muscovites and Ottomans, expressly excluded from (indeed proposed victims of) the Grand Design. Bellers was a man of a tolerant and open mind; for he asserts that 'The Muscovites are Christians and the Mahometans Men, and have the same faculties, and reason as other Men, they only want the same Opportunities and Applications of their Understandings to be the same Men; But to beat their Brains out, to put sense into them, is a great Mistake, and would leave Europe, too much in a State of War; whereas, the farther this Civil Union is Possible to be Extended, the greater will be the Peace on Earth, and good Will among Men.' (reprinted, Clarke, 1987, p.152). He concludes with a prayer for peace.

How, then, can we compare and assess these two projects for Euro-pean unity? Both essays are short – Penn's about 8,000 words, Bellers's 7,000. Both were published as responses to war and to the senseless carnage of war – the Nine Years War and the War of the Spanish Succession respectively. They are both led to a generalised denunci-ation of war which one would expect of members of the Society of Friends. It is this urgent desire for peace which provides the motive for their constitutional proposals for bringing the states of Europe more closely together. However, when we look behind this prime motive we notice a difference. Where Bellers sticks to his religious convictions, Penn reveals that he is also a hard-nosed man of the world. Bellers harps on the guiding principle that bloodshed is con-trary to a true interpretation of Christianity; Penn reiterates the ways in which warfare interrupts the production of wealth.

Penn's essay is also more logically argued and presented than Bellers's and penetrates rather more shrewdly to the heart of the political problems. True, Bellers shows a sound appreciation of the need for a gradual harmonisation of political systems. But he gives little thought to the central issue of sovereignty, which at least Penn tries to resolve. Both tend to support the feasibility of their projects by reference to Sully's Grand Design and to small-scale examples. Penn was particularly influenced by the success of the Dutch union, while Bellers adds to that case Switzerland and the United Kingdom itself.

Both, of course, place their faith in the arbitrative power of a continental assembly and demilitarisation. Yet here again Penn perhaps shows a more practical sense in proposing financial penalties of fines and damages. On the other hand, perhaps Bellers got near to the nub of the problem in his idealised devolutionary cantonal proposal. Where Penn relied on dissuasion, Bellers backed this up by a partial emasculation of state armed power (though, true, it is not clear who would control the cantonal levies). Penn's alertness to financial considerations leads him also to worry about nefarious political habits such as espionage and bribery and corruption.

In contrast, Bellers is clearly much more concerned to promote religious toleration than to guard against murky politicking, as his provision for a clerical as well as a political European assembly reveals. Bellers's comments about the incorporation of Russians and Turks also expresses a much more positively tolerant attitude than Penn's brief passing remark. Both, nevertheless, voice a justifiable belief that internecine conflict was harmful to the reputation of Christianity.

Bellers's proposal was, however, forgotten – at least until the interwar period of our own century; and even then interest was largely confined, one suspects, to the Society of Friends. Compared with Penn, he was, of course, less famous personally. And perhaps his emphasis on the religious cause of conflict already had a somewhat obsolescent ring.

Even Penn's influence was limited. Admittedly the text was available through the publication of his collected works in 1726. Then interest in Quakerism in the USA ensured its separate republication in 1896 as an 'Old South Leaflet' and in 1912 by the American Peace Society. But it was not until the shock of the First World War that a considerable interest in his *Essay* was revived, it being reprinted in three separate collections in 1914, 1916 and 1917 (see, Hinsley, pp.370, n.1 & 380, n.91).

In fact, the succinct responses of the gentle and virtuous English Quaker to the wars of Louis XIV had an insignificant impact compared with the vast rambling memoir of the boring French rationalist, the Abbé de Saint-Pierre, inspired by a contemplation of those same conflicts.

Saint-Pierre and Jean-Jacques

Wars in a cosmopolitan age

We turn now to an age of ironic paradox. The eighteenth century, the era of revived cosmopolitanism and new-found humanitarianism, was a century of continual international conflict; France, the metropolis of the *philosophes'* world state, deployed the largest European army and was engaged in most of the major wars.

The idea that man should feel an allegiance to the cosmopolis and natural law as much as, even more than, to the polis and its human laws was a powerful thread in the Cynic and Stoic thinking of the ancient world. Steeped in classical scholarship, the men of the Enlightenment found the notion most congenial. Thus did the Encyclopedist Diderot take Diogenes as his model; and Voltaire, Marcus Aurelius. 'My country is the world,' wrote Tom Paine, 'and my religion is to do good.' (Paine, p.250). Such political thinkers took as much pride in their self-declared status of world citizen as a patriot did in his identity with his state.

The focus of this sense of cosmopolitanism, the capital city of this spiritual world state, was Paris. There, in the salons of learned discourse, the idea was shared and disseminated. And not just because of the intellectual vitality of that metropolis; but also because of the common currency of the French language and French culture. A Sussex landowner wrote to his son that 'A man who understands French may travel all the World over without hesitation of making himself perfectly agreeable to all Good Company.' (quoted, Hampson, p.53). The French scholar, Paul Hazard, goes so far as to assert that 'the cosmopolitan, though he may not have recognised as much, had come to signify someone who thought *à la française.*' (Hazard, p.445).

Among the aristocratic and educated classes, as a consequence, travel became an attractive and commonplace undertaking. The English gentleman made the Grand Tour. The Italian legal theorist

Beccaria visited d'Holbach, the French *philosophe*, in Paris. Voltaire journeyed to Potsdam to converse with Frederick the Great. Political frontiers meant little to men of letters and science. In so far as they were interested in social and political matters they were seeking policies and practices of a humanitarian kind. Belief in the worth and happiness of the human individual underlay much of Enlightenment thinking. It is a pity that the fanatical supporter of the policy of Terror in the French Revolution, Saint-Just, should have been the one to have stated memorably that 'Happiness is a new idea in Europe.' (quoted, Arendt, p.75). It was none the less true. The eighteenth century was marked by a revulsion against religious intolerance and persecution, judicial torture, war – in short, against 'man's inhumanity to man,' which as Robert Burns wrote at the time, 'makes countless thousands mourn.'

Locke set the tone with his four *Letters on Toleration* published in 1689 (see p.43). In 1762 Voltaire devised, in a letter to d'Alembert, one of the great slogans of the age: '*écrasez l'infame*'. Two years later Beccaria produced his *On Crimes and Punishments*, denouncing the cruelties and injustices of European penal codes. Slowly and patchily policy followed the wise recommendations and passionate appeals of the philosophers. Edicts relating to religious toleration and the abolition of investigative torture afford some justification for the title of 'enlightened despots' which used to be attached to the reforming rulers of this era.

Not only did cruelty offend the sensibilities of the enlightened generations, it was also held to offend against human reason. Moreover, belief in the power of this human faculty gave rise to the optimistic conviction that mankind could effect progress in its own condition. How, then, did war, the begetter of so much human misery, fit into the *philosophes'* scheme? Theirs was an anti-militarist mentality. Read the bitter and scornful sarcasm of Voltaire in his article on War in his *Philosophical Dictionary*: 'It is certainly a very fine art that desolates the countryside, destroys dwellings, and brings death to [40,000–100,000] men in an average year.' (Voltaire, 1764, pp.231–2. The figures have been placed in square brackets because Voltaire's meaning is unclear: the figures here are not a strict translation, but rather what he in all probability meant.) But if sarcasm was one weapon, reason was another, which came more naturally to most thinkers of the age. If all evil in human affairs was the result of a want of true understanding, then war, the greatest evil of all, could be expunged by cool appraisal of true state interests. When rulers rationally gauged the expenditure of human resources and treasure which their fratricidal conflicts cause, they would cease them and settle to a life of peace. War, it was perceived, did not have to be – it was neither an inevitable nor a natural characteristic of human social behaviour.

The horrors of the Thirty Years War had persuaded scholars and statesmen alike that some rules of conduct were essential to prevent a recurrence of the anarchic barbarism that was such a shocking feature of that conflict. The attempt to draft laws to regulate international relations in both peace and war was first significantly made by Grotius (see p.17). It was an ideal that appealed to the Enlightenment mentality and was eagerly propounded by the Swiss diplomat and international lawyer, Emmerich Vattel in *The Law of Nations*, published in 1758. The basic principle from which Grotius and Vattel argued was that human rights, which derive from natural law, should allow, for instance, for the humane treatment of prisoners of war and respect for non-combatants, whether individual civilians or neutral states.

Although this theoretical desire to humanise war scarcely percolated into the practical operation of the nascent international law of the eighteenth century, a number of practical considerations were tending in that direction. International conflict had been largely drained of the religious passion which had so aggravated the wars of the post-Reformation era. In the eighteenth century wars were fought for limited objectives, whether dynastic, territorial or commercial.

But it was the change in the style of recruiting and using armies that perhaps best explains the relative abatement of the horrors of war. Discipline and costs were the key considerations. Ad hoc levying of raw troops was replaced by the maintenance of standing armies. Many of these soldiers were foreign mercenaries with no sense of allegiance to the prince or country for whom they fought. Fierce discipline was essential to hold them together in efficient fighting units. It was also necessary for ensuring steadiness under fire in the stylised parade-ground mode of fighting by now in vogue. And the more disciplined an army, the less the civilian population in the theatre of war suffers from rape, theft and wanton destruction. A certain amateur and cosmopolitan gentility among the officer class also helped to keep warlike hatreds in check. There is, of course, the famous scene during the Battle of Fontenoy in 1745. 14,000 English and Hanoverian troops marched with drill-like precision through the French artillery barrage and halted before the French guards regiments. The officers of the opposing armies doffed their hats in salutation to each other. Then the English commander, Lord Charles Hay, cried out, 'Gentlemen of the French guards, fire!' His opponent, the Comte d'Auteroches replied, 'No, no, my lord, we never fire first.' Let us be clear that the motive was cunning not chivalry; for the infantry formation which fired first would be virtually defenceless while they reloaded their cumbersome muskets. On the other hand, such ease and formality would be difficult to find in other eras outside the practice of single combat.

Recruiting, training and maintaining large standing armies was an exceedingly costly business. The favoured policy therefore came to be their conservation through tactics of defence, siege and manoeuvre rather than the prodigal waste of mass slaughter in pitched battle à la Marlborough (see p.40). During the period 1713–40 especially, some of the leading statesmen were reluctant to risk the costs of war – Walpole in England, Fleury in France, Frederick William I in Prussia pursued pacific policies. It was a period, too, remarkable for a brief interlude of Anglo-French détente in the long history of their mutual antagonism.

Yet we must not be misled. The eighteenth century was scarcely an era devoid of wars. Europeans were constantly at each others' throats, both on their own continent and in conflicts for imperial and commercial advantage in the Americas, in Asia and on the high seas. Let us take the span of time covered by the texts to be analysed in this chapter. Saint-Pierre started thinking about his project in 1706; Rousseau's *Judgment* on it was published posthumously in 1782. Leaving aside wars with the Ottoman Turk, we may record the following: the Great Northern War, 1700–21; the War of the Spanish Succession, 1702–13; the Spanish-Habsburg crisis in the western Mediterranean, 1717–19; the War of the Polish Succession, 1733–35; the War of the Austrian Succession, 1740–48; the Seven Years War, 1756–63; the War of the Bavarian Succession, 1778–79; and the American War of Independence, 1775–83.

The War of the Spanish Succession was the most vivid influence on Saint-Pierre; the Seven Years War, on Rousseau. We have already had occasion to notice the influence of the wars of Louis XIV on the Quaker schemes for European unity (see Chapter 3). Let us now look at the situation as Saint-Pierre would have viewed it. From 1704 to 1708 French armies reeled under a series of defeats: Blenheim, Ramillies, Turin, Malplaquet, Oudenarde. In a desperate effort to fight back, Louis XIV exhausted his country. On 26 August 1709 the Controller-General wrote to the king:

The armies cannot be properly paid, it has not been possible to assure supplies and provisions for the troops in such unfortunate times . . . For four months not a week has passed without some uprising. It is possible to find remedies for all the troubles only by a prompt peace (quoted, Sagnac & Saint-Léger, p.488).

The Seven Years War, the background to Rousseau's work on European unity, wrought a similar state of exhaustion on Prussia. Frederick the Great wrote:

Prussia's population has diminished by 500,000 during the Seven Years War. In a population of 4,500,000 that decrease was considerable. The nobility and the peasants had been pillaged and ransomed by so many armies that they had nothing left except the miserable rags which covered their nakedness . . . The appearance of the provinces resembled that of Brandenburg after the Thirty Years War (quoted, Lindsay, pp.484–5).

Such testimony should make us pause before concluding too readily that the eighteenth century experienced an entirely effective interruption in the utter barbarity of war.

In political terms engagement in the Seven Years War brought humiliation for France: a further decline in influence in Europe and loss of an empire to her arch-rival, England.

Even so, behind this constantly recurring warfare there was developing a widespread feeling of a common 'Europeanness'. This was partly a function of the cosmopolitanism already referred to (see p.61), partly also a specific sense that Europeans had common experiences which both gave them a sense of homogeneity and distinguished them from the peoples of other continents. Montesquieu and Voltaire used almost identical language, the one declaring that 'Europe is no more than a nation composed of several provinces' (quoted, de Rougemont, p.141 n.17); the other, that ' . . . one could regard Christian Europe (except Russia) as a sort of great republic divided into several states.' (Voltaire, 1756, p.5). Writing in German, Johannes Christian Adelung declared, 'Europe is superior in every way to all other quarters of the globe . . . Uncertain its limits doubtless were, . . . but it formed none the less *ein bewunderswürtiges Ganze*, a marvellous whole.' (quoted, Hazard, p.437).

Vattel also, examining Europe through his diplomatic lens, asserted:

Europe forms a political system in which the Nations inhabiting this part of the world are bound together by their relations and various interests into a single body. It is no longer, as in former times, a confused heap of detached parts . . . [Diplomatic practices] make modern Europe a sort of republic, whose members . . . unite for the maintenance of order and the preservation of liberty (quoted, Linklater, p.90).

What of specific blueprints for political integration? Leibniz, that most fertile and versatile mind of his age, thought about the issue in the 1670s and produced two schemes. One, which he wrote pseudonymously as Caesarius Furtenarius, argued for a restoration of imperial and papal power in ways reminiscent of the Middle Ages: ' . . . if one acts in accordance with the law, the Emperor must be invested with power in a large part of Europe, as well as with a kind of supreme sovereignty corresponding to that of the Church' (quoted, de Rougemont, p.129).

In 1712 the Abbé de Saint-Pierre published the first version of his plan which we shall be discussing in the next section of this chapter. At the same time Leibniz returned to the subject in correspondence, including a letter to Saint-Pierre himself (see p.88). Schemes proliferated in the 1730s and 1740s. In 1735 Cardinal Alberoni, who had provoked the crisis of 1717–19 (see p.64), produced a plan which included 'a scheme of perpetual dyet for establishing the public tranquility' of Europe (quoted, Hinsley, p.32). Later projects included a plan by von Loen for a European Congress and a project to secure perpetual peace by Gargaz. These, like Rousseau's essays in the field, were prompted by the work of Saint-Pierre. Whether admired or scorned, the abbé's project was certainly not ignored.

Saint-Pierre's Project

Do-gooders often undermine support for their chosen causes by the tediousness of that very enthusiasm which is the motive-force of their benevolence. The great bore of eighteenth-century France was the Abbé de Saint-Pierre. A century later, the distinguished literary critic, Sainte-Beuve, was to comment on his writings in the following way:

> He expands a sound idea, he proposes a useful reform. You approve of it, he is not content; in order to establish it more firmly, he goes on to amuse himself by listing the most futile objections, giving himself the pleasure of refuting them one by one: firstly, secondly . . . twenty-eighthly . . . He will stop only after he has overwhelmed you. He is anxious to remain victorious on paper right to the end and to sleep on the battlefield. To sleep is indeed the word, above all for the reader (quoted, Drouet, p.340).

As a consequence, whereas the Quakers required only small pamphlets for the exposition of their recommendations on European unity, the French abbé felt the need of a book format – in three large volumes for good measure.

Saint-Pierre clearly felt the urge to work for human reconciliation early in his life. On the occasion of his confirmation he changed his Christian names from Charles-François to Charles-Irénée – Charles the eirenic, the pacifier. And in his teens he was already undertaking the self-imposed task of arbitrating in the quarrels among neighbours in the locality. This was the town of Saint-Pierre-Église in Normandy. His father, whose family name was Castel, was a baron and took his title from the town.

Charles-Irénée was born in 1658, received a conventional Catholic education and took minor orders, though his Christian faith was exceedingly shallow. At the age of twenty-two, as a young man of independent means, he left Normandy for Paris. There he was initially caught up in the contemporary enthusiasm for scientific study, but soon discovered his most satisfying mentors to be Plutarch (for Politics) and Descartes (for the Philosophy of Science). He was later to be described by an English publisher of his work in the following words: 'He is said to be extremely studious, though of a very tender Constitution of Body.' (quoted, Hemleben, p.57 n.56).

Saint-Pierre gained an entrée into Parisian intellectual circles through membership of the Académie Française, from which he was expelled; the Club de L'Entresol, which closed down partly because of his introduction of politically controversial issues; and the various salons, which were presided over by bluestocking hostesses, who at least tolerated him. It was the company of such as Mme Lambert, and, above all, Mme Dupin that he found most congenial. Only the ladies had the patience and courtesy to listen to endless expositions of his schemes for the betterment of mankind. Many of the men found him insufferable. La Bruyère, in his famous and avidly read *Caractères*, drew a sharp picture of the abbé's extraordinary social insensitivity:

He asks people he does not know to take him to visit others whom he does not know . . . He sidles into a circle of respectable persons who know nothing about him, and there, without waiting to be asked nor any realisation that he is interrupting, he talks both frequently and ridiculously (quoted, Vaucher, p.106).

Just as ladies were more tolerant than men of his social gaucherie, so it was a lady who provided him with satisfactory employment: he became Chaplain to the Duchess of Orleans, mother to the Duke who was Regent during the minority of Louis XV.

Saint-Pierre lived to a great age: he died in 1743; and his acceptance into the society of Parisian salons in his more mature years perhaps owed a little to a certain mellowing of manner.

He seems not to have suffered personally from the pachidermous zeal with which he propounded in minutest detail his views, judgments and projects. He was expelled from the Academy because of his criticisms in print of Louis XIV and the Regent. Yet the unjust manner of his ejection rallied sympathy. He was mocked and ridiculed in company and in print; even Grimm, who had a soft spot for him, despaired of 'his eternal chattering' (quoted, Drouet, p.335). However, no one doubted the sincere philanthropy of his intentions.

His heart was in the right place. He was determined to devote his life to bettering the lot of mankind. So important was this service that he felt the need to invent a special word: 'bienfaisance', beneficence. He described the way he devised it:

Ever since I came to see that Christians did not know what the word charity really meant, since they persecuted their opponents . . . I have been looking out for a word which would clearly remind us that it was our duty to do good to others, and I have found nothing that better conveys what I have in mind than the word beneficence. People may do as they like about using it. I find it clear and unequivocal (quoted, Hazard, pp.170–1).

Nor were his motives marred by considerations of self. When the Encyclopedist d'Alembert incorporated his Eulogy of Saint-Pierre in his biographical sketches of former members of the Académie Française, he wrote, 'Never was any author, even among those who profess themselves most indifferent to fame, less occupied with his own glory, or less susceptible to the most secret illusions of self-love.' (quoted, Cobban, 1960, p.128). Indeed, he actively sought criticism – it was the way to diminish the faults in his work. He was accused of being a dreamer, a chaser of chimeras. But he knew, and he had an unshakeable faith in the knowledge, that untold human progress was possible – if only people like himself could be sufficiently inventive and persistent to show the way. This faith buoyed him up above the dismissive laughter that would have crushed the spirit of prouder men.

In the fundamentals of his thought Saint-Pierre epitomised the Enlightenment. His nineteenth-century biographer asserted this. 'The whole of the eighteenth century,' wrote Edouard Goumy, 'may be found in the Abbé de Saint-Pierre, ideas, beliefs, hopes, illusions. Sincere love of mankind, faith that good will prevail and progress be enjoyed, that was the basis of this philosophy.' (Goumy, pp.324–5). Saint-Pierre was a Deist who believed that Christian theological controversies had been positively harmful. He was a Rationalist who believed in the power of human thought. He was an Optimist who believed in the prospect of indefinite human progress. He was a Utilitarian who foreshadowed the Benthamite principles of shaping policy and society to provide for the greatest happiness of the greatest number and of fearlessly questioning institutions and practices which hindered the achievement of this ideal.

Saint-Pierre's compassionate soul blended well with his fertile mind. Ideas for improvements tumbled forth. In the last ten years of his life alone he produced sixteen volumes of political and moral works. No topic escaped his eager desire for betterment and progress. He wrote treatises for perfecting (sic) spelling in European languages, for rendering roads passable in winter, for reforming the French system of government, for a graduated form of land tax. This last had much to commend it. The scheme was accorded an experimental trial by the Controller-General Orry. But resistance to reform and administrative problems of implementation defeated the project – even in Limoges where the admirable intendant Turgot wrestled with the task into the 1760s.

On a lighter note, in his mid-seventies he also invented an oscillating armchair. Impressed by the opinion of a court physician that riding in a carriage was good for one's health by jogging up various vital parts, Saint-Pierre realised what a benefit it would be to pursue good health in the comfort of one's home. The armchair, which the engineer Duguet produced with both vertical and lateral movements, became all the rage. Its use, declared Saint-Pierre, was crucial for people who lived a sedentary mode of existence. Such unpleasant recompenses for the body like hunting, walking and bleeding could be replaced by regular shakings in the familiar seated posture. For a while Duguet even enjoyed a brisk export trade. But the fad proved to be but a phase and the *'fauteuil de poste'* joined the rest of Saint-Pierre's dust-covered schemes.

Rather less dust accumulated on the work which consumed a great deal of his time in his mature years and appeared in several editions, namely his project to afford Europe perpetual peace. Although Saint-Pierre acquired a little diplomatic experience by attending as a secretary the peace conference at Utrecht in 1712, this circumstance was not, as some would have it, the origin of his scheme.

In order to understand the true genesis of Saint-Pierre's project we must remember that many roads at this time were a great hazard to the traveller – hard-rutted in hot weather and mud-bound in wet. On a winter's day in 1706 the forty-seven-year-old Abbé de Saint-Pierre was travelling on such a treacherous road. His carriage met with so jolting an accident that it decanted him into the mud. Some little time later, being of an inventive and philanthropic disposition, the abbé wrote a paper on the improvement of roads. As he finished his recommendations a totally unrelated thought suddenly entered his mind. He should invent something incomparably more beneficial to mankind: a scheme to ensure everlasting peace. It was to be a work in harmony with the character of the new century – an age of cosmopolitan ideals vying with the reality of persistent warfare. And of all his schemes, as Rousseau noted, it was the one 'over which he brooded the longest and followed up with the greatest obstinacy' (trans., Forsyth et al., p.157). He described how there came into his mind the notion of a project

... which by its great beauty struck me with wonder. It drew the whole of my attention for a fortnight. I felt so much the more the inclination to investigate it that the more I considered it, and from different sides, the more I found it advantageous to sovereign rulers (quoted, Drouet, p.108).

And when the text was ready, with his tiresome pertinacity he bombarded ministers and monarchs with copies. It was said that he would even have sent a copy to Attila the Hun if he had been alive!

The scheme was first published in Cologne in 1712 under the title *Mémoire pour rendre la paix perpétuelle en Europe*. Then, much changed and expanded in the light of criticisms, a two-volume version was published in Utrecht in 1713 and entitled *Projet pour rendre la paix perpétuelle en Europe*. An English translation of the first volume appeared the following year: *A project for Settling an Everlasting Peace in Europe*. Saint-Pierre completed the whole work with a third volume, published in 1717. The full title of this book was, in translation: 'Project for a treaty to restore perpetual peace in Europe among the Christian sovereigns, to maintain free trade for ever between nations, to strengthen even more the sovereign houses on their thrones. Proposed formerly by Henry the Great, King of France, agreed by Queen Elizabeth, by James I, King of England, her successor and by the majority of the other potentates of Europe. Elucidated by M. the Abbé de Saint-Pierre'. In 1729 he produced an abridged version (*Abrégé du projet de paix perpétuelle*) and in 1738 a revised edition of the Abridgement. It is this last version which forms the basis of our analysis here. The Abridgement is not simply a précis of the larger work. Saint-Pierre omits some important matter because he makes the assumption that the reader of the Abridgement is already familiar with the original three volumes! But in any case Europe had experienced a number of changes in the intervening years and Saint-Pierre changed his views on some issues.

Saint-Pierre's approach is to present five propositions to prove the inestimable benefits of the princes of Europe agreeing to a system to ensure everlasting peace. The first proposition contains the core of the work, namely the draft text of a treaty. This is divided into a number of articles: twelve fundamental, eight important and eight useful in the full work, all conflated into five fundamental articles in the Abridgement. This exposition of his project is followed by a listing of a series of objections to the scheme, which the abbé helpfully and logically knocks down like a line of Aunt Sallys.

At the start of the Abridgement we are afforded an illuminating example of Saint-Pierre's logical and irritating mode of discourse:

I ask the reader, as he does in geometry, not to pass from one proposition to another if the proofs of that which he read do not appear to him sufficient. In this case he should re-read them, lest the failure of conviction should arise from lack of attention on his part, and not by the fault of the Author (Castel de Saint-Pierre, p.17).

In the Abridgement the first proposition to be proved is as follows:

It is very unwise to assume that treaties, made or to be made, will always be observed, and that there will be for any length of time no foreign wars, so long as the Sovereigns of Europe shall have failed to sign the five fundamental articles of general alliance which are absolutely necessary to render peace durable (Castel de Saint-Pierre, p.17).

Saint-Pierre explains that so-called peace treaties are always in fact no more than temporary truces. However, it is becoming increasingly accepted that a permanent peace is possible, not least because 'for the last nine or ten years people in Europe have begun to read the great Design of Henry the Great' (Castel de Saint-Pierre, p.18).

It is appropriate to pause a little here to comment on Saint-Pierre's emphasis on the Grand Design. He is very evidently just as anxious as Sully himself had been to capitalise on the reputation of Henry IV. We have already noticed his emphasis on the relationship of the two schemes in the title of the 1717 volume. In the first volume he was positively obsequious to the memory of the king:

It falls out happily for this Project, that I am not the Author of it; 'twas *Henry the Great* was the first Inventor of it; 'twas the *European Solon* whom God first inspired with the means to make the Sovereigns of Europe desirous to establish among them an equitable Polity . . . my having hit upon it too, does not in any wise diminish the Glory of Invention due to him (English trans., quoted, Hemleben, p.56).

To continue with the first proposition: Saint-Pierre outlines the analogy of the peaceful resolution of disputes by recourse to law in the internal affairs of states. The fundamental articles he is about to list will, he asserts, provide a similar system on the international plane. Moreover, as these articles are so transparently beneficial, any prince who refuses to adhere to them will provoke the pacifically-intentioned to form both 'a strict and firm union' and 'a proper distrust' of the recalcitrant (Castel de Saint-Pierre, p.20). The articles thus provide an infallible indicator of the true attitudes of rulers.

He then lists a dozen reasons why wars have been endemic. All that is required to turn the minds of princes away from war is to show them that peace is possible and more beneficial than conflict. When so convinced, they will sign Saint-Pierre's 'invaluable treaty', whose five articles 'contain everything which is absolutely necessary for the formation of an alliance, of a permanent and lasting society' (Castel de Saint-Pierre, p.24). He concludes his general remarks in the first proposition in the Abridgement by noting that his proposal for a European Diet 'will secure the peoples of Europe from war, as the Germanic Diet has actually secured the Peoples of Germany for so many centuries.' (Castel de Saint-Pierre, p.24).

And so to the articles of Saint-Pierre's treaty. We shall refer to them, in the main, in their conflated form as they appear in the Abridgement. We must, however, note differences in the list of members as between 1713 and 1738:

Projet	*Abrégé*
France	France
Spain	Emperor of Germany
England	Spain
Holland	Russia
Savoy	England
Portugal	Holland
Bavaria & associates	Denmark
Venice	Sweden
Genoa & associates	Poland
Florence & associates	Portugal
Switzerland & associates	'Sovereign of Rome'
Lorraine & associates	Prussia
Sweden	Bavaria & associates
Denmark	Palatine & associates

Poland	Switzerland & associates
Pope	Ecclesiastical electors &
Muscovy	associates
Austria	Venice & associates
Courland & associates	Naples
Prussia	Sardinia
Saxony	
Palatine & associates	19
Hanover & associates	+ Genoa, Modena & Parma to be
Ecclesiastical electors &	encouraged to combine and be
associates	represented by one delegate

24

Some of the differences are easily explained; others are more interesting. Hanover is missing from the abridged version because by then the Elector was also King of England (George II). Courland had been absorbed by Poland. Lorraine was virtually part of France from 1736. Florence was ruled by the Habsburgs from 1738, whereas Naples was not. The Saxon monarchy was more firmly entrenched in Poland in 1738 than in 1713 and therefore a separate Saxon representation would seem inappropriate. The order of listing of states and rulers is not haphazard. France is in prime position in both. The inclusion of 'the Emperor of Germany' in the abridged version restores the Holy Roman Empire to the community of princes.

Saint-Pierre's treatment of the problem countries of Russia and Turkey requires fuller commentary. Whereas in 1713 Muscovy is allocated a most inferior position, by 1738 'the Emperor or Empress of Russia' is accorded fourth place. Given the hesitation of some proponents of European unity about the desirability of including Russia at all, this promotion, due no doubt to the success of Peter the Great's policies, is of considerable interest. The other country with large areas of European territory and which has often been excluded from plans for European unity has been Turkey. Saint-Pierre seems to have been very uncertain about how to cope with this difficulty. In the first two volumes of the full *Projet* he proposes treaties of alliance and commerce with 'the Mohommedan sovereigns' and would even accord them the status of associates of the European union. In the third volume he proposes the expulsion of the Turks from Europe. The *Abrégé* refers merely to a defensive posture, strengthening the forces of the alliance on the frontiers with the Turk (see Drouet, p.128, n.1).

The first fundamental article of the treaty which these states would be invited to sign is the commitment to 'a perpetual alliance' (Castel de Saint-Pierre, pp.24–6). The list of benefits, beside the primary purpose of banishing war, includes two others of particular note. One is the range of economic advantages from 'a very considerable dimin-

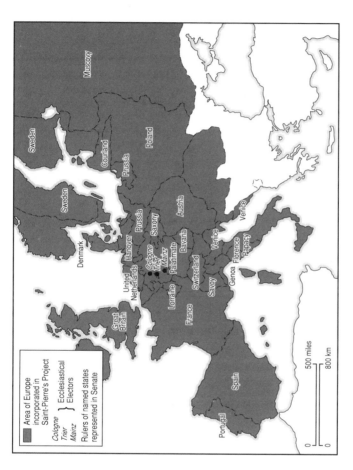

Map 4   Saint-Pierre's Project

Area of Europe
incorporated in
Saint-Pierre's Project

Cologne
Trier   } Ecclesiastical
Mainz   Electors

Rulers of named states
represented in Senate

500 miles

800 km

ution of their military expenses' and 'a very considerable increase of annual profit, which will accrue from the continuity and security of commerce'. The other is his insistence on the status quo in both domestic and international politics. Thus he writes:

[The Sovereigns of Europe] agree to take for a fundamental condition *actual possession and the execution of the latest treaties*, and they are mutually bound to guarantee, one to another, that each Sovereign who shall have signed this fundamental treaty shall be preserved for all time, him and his house, in all the territory and in all the rights which he possesses at present.

On the matter of membership, 'all Christian Sovereigns shall be invited', and every effort was to be made to recruit as many as possible to the alliance.

The confederation, once formed, would be financed according to arrangements outlined in the second article (Castel de Saint-Pierre, pp.26–7). The contributions are 'to be proportioned to the revenues of the Subjects of each Nation' with due regard to the fact that 'some Nations are more heavily burdened with public debt than others'.

The third article (Castel de Saint-Pierre, pp.27–8) deals with the peaceful resolution of quarrels by mediation or arbitration. Provided that 'the number party to the deliberations shall not be diminished' and 'the territory of the five most powerful Sovereigns shall not be increased', Saint-Pierre feels very confident that his system will be perfectly acceptable and workable. Once current treaties are accepted 'future differences can never be anything but unimportant', while 'Differences over some little frontier Village, about some difficulty of Merchants, are of no great importance.' And in any case the princes can be assured that problems which do crop up 'will never be regulated in a way far removed from justice.'

The operation of the system is spelt out in rather more detail in the full work. All members shall send one delegate, two substitutes and two agents to form the 'Perpetual Congress' or 'Senate of Peace'. The presidency of this assembly shall be held in turn by each member on a weekly rota. Commissioners would be dispatched to investigate any outbreak of violence or disputes arising over commercial practices. If mediation in a dispute is unsuccessful then the litigant states are obliged to accept the findings of the arbitration undertaken by the Senate. This body would make a provisional award by a plurality of votes. Five years later a three-quarters majority would make the arbitrative decision binding. All states have one vote irrespective of size.

But the force of the law may be insufficient. The fourth article (Castel de Saint-Pierre, pp.28–9) makes provision for the use of armed force within the alliance both to avert any threat by a member-state to its peace and also to exact reparations from that delinquent state. Saint-Pierre recognises the need for both the carrot of the advantages of peace and the stick of firm discipline for disturbing that condition. Foolish princes, he explains, are like children: 'they need the prospect of punishment, certain, near, and sufficient, awaiting anyone who shall violate the fundamental laws.' In Volume I of the *Projet* he describes the procedure to be adopted:

The Sovereign who shall take up Arms before the Union has declared War, or who shall refuse to execute a Regulation of the Society, or a Judgment of the Senate, shall be declared an Enemy to the Society, and It shall make War upon him, 'till he be disarmed, and 'till the Judgment and Regulations be executed; and he shall even pay the Charges of the War, and the Country that shall be conquered from him at the time of the Suspension of Arms, shall be for ever separated from his Dominions (English trans., quoted, Hemleben, pp.61–2).

The fifth fundamental article (Castel de Saint-Pierre, pp.29–31) recognises that many miscellaneous matters will remain to be decided after the inauguration of the union. These, especially procedural questions, should be postponed for the sake of getting the enterprise under way with the minimum of delay and objections. Saint-Pierre even seeks to reassure the princes of Europe that the prescribed method of reaching decisions, namely 'by a plurality provisionally and by three-quarters of the votes finally, shall never be regarded as insurmountable obstacles'. And anyhow, only a unanimous vote can change the fundamental articles.

Satisfied that he has proved his first proposition, Saint-Pierre proceeds to his second (Castel de Saint-Pierre, pp.31–3), namely that 'These five articles are sufficient to give full security for the execution of treaties, made or to be made, and to produce a lasting peace'. Here Saint-Pierre envisages the system, once started, being developed and consolidated by the momentum of its own logic. The advantages of involvement and the disadvantages of remaining aloof will be irresistible binding-forces. Moreover, the union must be permanent. He is indeed extraordinarily fierce with those who would resign their membership:

So long as the Allies can secede from the alliance with impunity it cannot be regarded as a permanent society, but from this no confederate can hope to secede with impunity, or without being regarded and treated as the common enemy of all the Allies. So that . . . the wholesome fear of punishment, adequate and inevitable, will always restrain those Sovereigns who are exceedingly unwise and are drunk with foolish ambition.

Saint-Pierre now passes to a consideration of the particular responsibilities of the European rulers (Castel de Saint-Pierre, pp.34–6). The third, fourth and fifth propositions state that the most important business for the Emperor, the King of France and the other sovereigns of Europe 'is to secure the signature of the five fundamental articles by the greatest possible number of sovereigns.' Saint-Pierre shows that it is in their interests to promote the scheme. For example,

It is important to the King of England that seditious persons in Parliament should not one day reduce the sovereign rights which he enjoys. It is similarly to the interest of the English Nation that the authority of Parliament and the present constitution of government should always be preserved in the state in which it is now, in spite of the measures of too tyrannical Ministers, and impatient and ill-advised Princes.

This brings us to Part II of Saint-Pierre's *Abrégé*: 'Objections and answers' (Castel de Saint-Pierre, pp.38–47) and the First Supplement which adds to the catechism (Castel de Saint-Pierre, pp.48–52). Much of this material repeats what is in the core texts or refers to specifically current issues. A few points are worth highlighting. One relates to the economy of peace. Saint-Pierre asserts by way of illustration that 'if France had all the money which war has cost her during the last two hundred years she would be worth four times more than she is worth at present'. The second is a calming of fears that might arise from the operation of the system of arbitration. It will behove the princes to make just findings, he declares, for in other circumstances those who give judgment 'may be, both they and their children, both sinners and sinned against'. A third point of interest is Saint-Pierre's case for treating all members of the union alike:

It is because the poorest has as much interest, in proportion to his fortune, that the State should take the best course, as the richest can have. Now as they are both equally interested in the common good, and as they are to be taken as equal in enlightenment, is it not natural, is it not reasonable, that they should have an equal voice in things?

The good abbé knew in his heart that he had thought of everything, answered all objections, drafted a thorough and perfect scheme. Yet his certainty and optimism were not rewarded by actual implementation. His project was widely read, not least because of the publicity afforded it by Rousseau. And Rousseau, among so many others, saw how impractical this most grandiose of schemes for European unity really was.

Rousseau's versions

In his *Confessions* (Rousseau, 1781, pp.379–80, 393–5) Rousseau describes how he came to be involved with the work of Saint-Pierre. After the death of the abbé, Mme Dupin proposed that Rousseau should produce a digest of his works. He starts with some typically acidic comments to the effect that the old Saint-Pierre had been Mme

Dupin's 'spoilt child' and that she 'would have been flattered to see her friend's still-born works brought to life'. He then describes the nature of his task. He explains that 'The works themselves contained some excellent things, but so badly put that they were most tiresome to read'. Rousseau had to read seventeen volumes and six boxes of manuscripts, extract the essence and render it digestible. However, he was given considerable latitude: 'I could give such a shape to my work that many important truths might be slipped in under the cloak of the Abbé de Saint-Pierre much more happily than they could under mine.'

Jean-Jacques developed a love-hate relationship with the shade of the benevolent abbé. They had met at Chenonceaux, Mme Dupin's country house, when Rousseau was a young man and as yet unknown, a year before Saint-Pierre's death. As he worked on the books and papers he came to have a high regard for the character of their author. In his *Confessions* Rousseau refers to him as 'This rare man, an ornament to his age and to his kind.' And he thereafter spoke and wrote warmly of him. (Though George Sand thought that he probably 'blushed for having admired him' (quoted, Drouet, p.330).)

One authority has even suggested that Rousseau's own thinking was in no small measure shaped by his study of Saint-Pierre's work during that period, 1756–58. Thus Sven Stelling-Michaud has written:

In the formation of Rousseau's political thought the writings of the Abbé de Saint-Pierre play a role whose importance has been generally misunderstood. By analysing and refuting the theories of the old utopian, Jean-Jacques was led to making comparisons which enabled him to give greater precision to his own thought, at the very moment when he was conceiving and elaborating [various political works including] *The Social Contract*. All that Rousseau wrote about the foundations of the social order, political sovereignty and the nature of government, on inter-state relations, the problem of war and peace must be related to his posthumous and fond dialogue with the author of the *Project for Perpetual Peace* (Rousseau, 1969, p.cxx).

On the other hand, their personalities and assumptions about human nature and political processes were diametrically opposed. Saint-Pierre was the utopian optimist; Rousseau, the worried pessimist. Saint-Pierre believed in the beneficent potential of human reason. Rousseau quarrelled bitterly with the Encyclopedists who built upon this premise; and he argued, on the contrary, that emotions are the cardinal influences in human affairs. Rousseau could not fail therefore to judge the abbé's plans as 'impracticable owing to one idea from which the author could never escape, that men are motivated by their intelligence rather than by their passions.' (Rousseau, 1781, p.393). This put Rousseau into a quandary – how to edit the material honestly. He decided on a double-track: to reproduce Saint-Pierre's thoughts as accurately as possible and then compose his own commentary upon them. He finished two of the projects in this way when he was overcome by one of his attacks of paranoia. Saint-Pierre had been free with his criticisms of aspects of French government. Rousseau was now afraid for himself if he should be accused of being the agent for their repetition. Or perhaps he geared up his persecution complex as an excuse to wriggle out of a tedious undertaking? However, one of the completed pairs of essays was on the project for perpetual peace.

Rousseau was born more than half a century after Saint-Pierre, in Geneva, in 1712. His life was as extraordinary as his genius. He left home at the age of fifteen and was soon befriended by Mme de Warens, an attractive woman twice his age. She provided the young Jean-Jacques with a thorough grounding in music and, in due course, with sexual favours.

Rousseau then decided he wished to be a writer. In Paris he became private secretary to that same Mme Dupin who befriended Saint-Pierre. Through her agency Rousseau spent a year as secretary to the French ambassador in Venice, thus acquiring a modicum of political and diplomatic understanding. In so far as he was known before 1750 it was as a composer and musicologist. The turning-point came when he wrote a prize essay, which became his first Discourse, *On the Sciences and the Arts*. It won the Dijon essay prize, and his argument that man has been corrupted by so-called civilisation also won him considerable fame.

The next twelve years were crammed with literary creativity and controversy. The originality and force of his writing reached their zenith in 1761–62 with the publication of the novel *La nouvelle Héloise*; the study of educational theory, *Émile*; and his crowning work, *Contrat social*. The thesis of his first Discourse cut right across the grain of the prevailing Enlightenment conviction that human progress was under way through the application of rational thought to the resolution of whatever problems lay in its path. This led to quarrels with former friends. Indeed, his personal life generally was not all that happy. He was ill-at-ease in the artificial politeness of Parisian intellectual society. He suffered the pain and embarrassment of a constricted bladder. He entered into a strange liaison with an unintelligent and unattractive servant-girl and was guilty of the shocking action of committing all five of their offspring to the orphanage.

There is much in Rousseau's life and work that has led to accusations of inconsistency, hypocrisy indeed. The most famous quotation of all is his statement that 'whoever refuses to obey the general will ... shall be forced to be free.' (Rousseau, 1762, p.64). But Rousseau recognised that life is in fact full of apparently irreconcilable tensions which can only be resolved by a proper understanding of such paradoxical truths. Thus, man needs to live in a political society in order to achieve his true potential, yet the very institutions he has created for that purpose have corrupted his natural innocence and virtue.

In tackling the idea of European unity as presented to him by Saint-

Pierre, Rousseau, it must be remembered, was already under the influence of competing political models. At root he idealised the city-state. He was emotionally attracted to the historical example of Sparta and his own experience of Geneva. Forgetting the tyrannical strictness of the former and the oligarchical corruption of the latter, he focused on the civic virtue that could be nourished in such compact communities. And yet, at the same time, he was the prophet of nationalism. The modern nation-state, of course, presupposes political units constructed from the geographical extent of people with an ethnic identity rather than from the spatial constraints of the *polis*.

But was a state – be it city, kingdom or nation – to be considered in isolation from the others or as part of a broader community? And if there was any reality to the concept of a community above and beyond the state, was this global or continental in scope? One of his editors has noted a distinction between his views as expressed in the second Discourse (*On the Origin of Inequality*) and his work on Perpetual Peace (Rousseau, 1969, p.cxliii). In the former we read of 'great Cosmopolitan Souls who cross the imaginary barriers which separate Peoples, and who, by the example of the sovereign being who created them, embrace all of Humanity in their benevolence.' (Rousseau, 1969, p.178). In the latter, as we shall see below, Rousseau writes of a living and organic Europe, which has an identity distinct from the rest of the world.

We must not forget, however, that these cosmopolitan thoughts, whether universal or European in their compass, preceded the bitterest phase of his quarrel with the cosmopolitan *philosophes*. He published his second Discourse in 1754 and worked on Saint-Pierre's *Project* from 1756. It was in 1758 that he wrote the *Letter to d'Alembert* which signalled the final breach with the Encyclopedist mentality. Thereafter he writes with a vitriolic pen against the cosmopolitan mode of thinking. In 1761–62 in both the *Émile* and the *Social Contract* Rousseau writes of such people using their generous sentiments in order to hide their hatred of their neighbours (see Cobban, 1964, p.106). Ten years later, in *Considerations on the Government of Poland*, he deplores the fact that, 'Today there are no longer Frenchmen, Germans, Spaniards, or even Englishmen, whatever is said; there are only Europeans. All have the same tastes, the same passions, the same customs . . . They are at home wherever there is money to steal and women to seduce.' (Rousseau, 1969, p.960).

Nevertheless, the issue of supra-state institutions was very much in his mind *c*.1760. It can even be argued that the idea of union(s) of states was integral to his whole political philosophy. In *Émile* he announced his intention of undertaking a comprehensive study of states and their relations. In the latter field he proposed to consider how

. . . in this incessant action and counter-action [states have been] causing more misery, and costing the life of more men, than if they had all remained in their primitive liberty. We shall ask ourselves whether . . . the submission of the individual to the authority of the Law and of other men, while at the same time the several communities remain as regards each other in the state of nature, does not leave him exposed to all the evils of both conditions without the advantages of either . . . Is it not this partial and incomplete association which is the cause of tyranny and war? . . .

We shall examine finally the kind of remedy that men have sought against these evils in Leagues and Federations, which, leaving each State master in its own house, arm it against all unjust aggression from without. We shall enquire . . . how far we can extend the rights of the Federation without trenching on those of Sovereignty (quoted, Vaughan, 1915, p.96. For the analysis which follows see pp.97–100).

In the *Social Contract* Rousseau asks 'if [the republic] is very small, will it not be subjugated? No. I shall show later how the external strength of a large people can be combined with the free government and good order of a small state.' In a footnote to this statement he promises a sequel to the *Social Contract* in which he will deal with such matters, including the nature of confederations. 'This subject is entirely new, and its principles have yet to be established.' (Rousseau, 1762, p.143). He wrote a substantial portion of this work, which, tantalisingly, has not survived.

A few guiding principles are none the less clear from the above extracts. One is that Rousseau's conception of the relationship of the individual to the state and of the state to a confederative system are parallel and complementary. In both cases, security and true liberty are enjoyed only through participation in the greater whole. In the words of one commentator,

his system of foreign policy is joined to his theories of internal policy in the most perfect harmony . . . The Confederative Republic of small states rises above the Social Contract like those domes which form the natural culmination of the buildings they rest upon, and which they marvellously protect (J.-L. Windenberger, quoted, Forsyth, 1981, p.92).

The basic argument runs as follows. The evolution of civil society is incomplete all the while that men have renounced their state of nature vis-à-vis the state but states have not renounced *their* state of nature vis-à-vis each other. Tyranny and war will remain endemic until the transition has been completed by bonding states into a confederal system.

The second feature of Rousseau's scheme is that the chief beneficiaries of this arrangement would be the small states which he so admired. Thirdly, the framework he envisaged is clearly a loose confederation rather than a tight federation as the phrases in *Émile* show: 'leaving each State master in its own house' and 'without trenching on those of Sovereignty'. In other words, he does not push the analogy of state and confederation to the ultimate stage. As Forsyth says, 'the power of the whole in the state is called by Rousseau sovereign, whereas in the confederation of states sovereignty is not abandoned by the partners.' (Forsyth, 1981, p.94).

Extremely brief as these references to confederation are, they even so provide a clear picture of Rousseau's views on the subject. It is against this background that we need to read his interpretation of Saint-Pierre's conception of a united Europe. The first of these essays was the *Extrait* or *Abstract*. This was written in 1756. So controversial were some of its contents that his publisher, fearful of the reaction of the censor, had it printed in Amsterdam, a common ruse at the time. It appeared in 1761, and was translated into English in the same year. The second, commentary essay, *Jugement*, was written at the same time, but was published much later, posthumously, in Geneva in 1782.

Although the *Abstract* is ostensibly a précis of Saint-Pierre's work, Rousseau adds not just his own characteristic style of writing, but his own perceptions and interpretations, even whole passages of material which have no equivalent in the original. 'In a word, except as regards the mere kernel of the Project, there is much more of Rousseau than of Saint-Pierre in the whole statement.' (Vaughan, 1915, p.360). The introductory paragraphs clearly reveal the mixture. Thus we hear an echo of the abbé in the statement, 'Resolved as I am to assert nothing which I cannot prove, I have the right to ask the reader in his turn to deny nothing he is unable to refute.' (trans., Forsyth et al., p.131). However, distinctive Rousseauean thoughts follow: 'each one of us [is] in the civil state as regards our fellow citizens, but in the state of nature as regards the rest of the world'; 'a form of federal Government . . . combines the advantages of the small and the large State.' (trans., Forsyth et al., p.132).

After his introductory remarks Rousseau proceeds with his own historical survey of federal or confederal experiments. In passing, he expresses a high regard for the contemporary 'Germanic Body', the Helvetic League and the Dutch States General. For our purposes he also makes an interesting assertion concerning the homogeneity of Europe:

In addition to these formal Confederations, it is possible to frame others, less visible but none the less real, which are silently cemented by community of interests, by conformity of habits and customs, by the acceptance of common principles, by other ties which establish mutual relations between nations politically divided. Thus the Powers of Europe constitute a kind of whole, united by identity of religion, of moral standard, of international law: by letters, by commerce, and finally by a species of balance which is the inevitable result of all these ties and, however little any man may strive consciously to maintain it, is not to be destroyed so easily as many men imagine (trans., Forsyth et al., p.133).

In the light of the quotations from Montesquieu, Voltaire and Vattel above (p.65), it is evident that Rousseau is here reiterating a commonly held view concerning the cohesiveness of Europe.

Rousseau proceeds to survey the integrative force and legacy of the Roman Empire, especially the cohering power of Christianity. He then lists the reasons why Europe 'still retains a sense of fellowship far closer than is to be found elsewhere' – historical, geographical, cultural, dynastic, commercial. Europe, he declares, unlike Asia or Africa, is 'a real community with a religion and a moral code, with customs and even laws of its own, which none of the component nations can renounce without causing a shock to the whole frame.' (trans., Forsyth et al., p.135).

Yet the other side of the European medal shows a scene of perpetual violence. Given the carelessness with which the states system has been allowed to evolve, this constant conflict is inevitable. The very intimacy of the nations invests their quarrels with the savagery of civil discord. And here we are back to Saint-Pierre: treaties 'are in the nature rather of a temporary truce than a real peace' (trans., Forsyth et al., p.136). The frailty of international law leaves self-interest free rein.

Rousseau then shows how neither a single prince nor an alliance of several could substantially alter by force the political map of Europe. The reasons are partly military, partly geographical. Also partly the position of 'the Germanic Body', i.e. the Holy Roman Empire, which 'holds all the other parts in their place, serving still more perhaps for the protection of its neighbours than for that of its members.' Conspicuously advantageous is 'its constitution which, depriving it both of the means and the will to conquer, makes it a rock on which all schemes of conquest are doomed infallibly to break.' (trans., Forsyth et al., p.140).

He concludes that, despite so many obstacles, there are sufficient grounds for at least believing the system created by geographical chance and the diplomatic design of the Treaty of Westphalia to be capable of sufficient improvement as to render Europe a peaceable continent. We come then, at last, to an exposition of Saint-Pierre's treaty of five articles as the means of achieving this desirable end. However, Rousseau cuts through the abbé's lengthy catalogue of objections and responses. Two questions only need to be addressed: Would the proposed confederation provide a condition of peace? Is it in the interests of the sovereigns of Europe to accede to such a treaty?

There follows a list of the nineteen constituent powers of the 'Commonwealth of Europe' as they appeared in Saint-Pierre's Abridgement (see p.71), though in Rousseau's version 'the Emperor of the Romans' has displaced the King of France from first place. It may be noted here that several commentators have misconstrued Rousseau's list, accusing him of altering the component states of Saint-Pierre's catalogue (see, e.g. Vaughan, 1915, p.360; Hinsley, p.46). The changes in fact relate to the altered political geography from 1713 to 1738/56, not to differences between the two authors (see p.72).

In answering his two basic questions, Rousseau follows Saint-Pierre in showing how solidly peace would be maintained once the confederation is created. However, in considering the likely motivation for princes thus to join together, Rousseau cannot stomach the thought of aligning himself with the abbé's naïve simplicities, which have 'covered the author and his projects with ridicule in all the council-chambers of Europe' (trans., Forsyth et al., p.148). This acerbic aside, true as it is, is unfair in its context. For, having rejected Saint-Pierre's argument that princes would gladly join the confederation for the sake of the glory they would gain as peace-makers, Rousseau in fact summarises without objection in the last few pages the abbé's other arguments based upon self-interest, namely the uncertainty and cost of war, and the benefits of the five articles.

It is none the less true that, whereas Saint-Pierre confidently expects the rational judgment of princes to lead to their acceptance of the inexorable conclusion of his own logic, Rousseau reveals his surer understanding of human nature. He concludes his *Abstract* with the cautionary paradox that

If, in spite of all this, the project remains unrealized, that is not because it is utopian; it is because men are crazy, and because to be sane in a world of madmen is in itself a kind of madness (trans., Forsyth et al., p.165).

Let us now turn to the *Judgment*, a briefer essay and one in which Rousseau is openly displaying his own views. He starts by asserting the infuriating impossibility of achieving this most obviously desirable plan. For 'the very Princes who would defend it with all their might, if it once existed, would resist with all their might any proposal for its creation.' He nevertheless does not dismiss it out of hand: 'it is a work of solid judgment,' he declares, 'and it is of great importance for us to possess it' (trans., Forsyth et al., p.157).

Rousseau launches into his argument with a vituperative attack on the monarchical form of government. Of course princes would not accept Saint-Pierre's scheme because they are incapable of perceiving their real as opposed to their apparent interest. 'They are ceaselessly deluded by appearances.' (trans., Forsyth et al., p.160). 'The whole life of Kings,' he categorically affirms, 'is devoted to two objects: to extend their rule beyond their frontiers and to make it more absolute within them.' (trans., Forsyth et al., p.158). Yet Saint-Pierre's *Project* would make fast the established frontiers and consitutional arrangements, thus blocking any further pursuit of these two ambitions. In any event, every monarch would rather risk the chance of war than the humiliation of judicial arbitration. Nor are ministers likely to be more sympathetic. Yet the essence of the inauguration of the abbé's plan is that not even just a few should come to see the light and renounce these old ways. It is rather that all European governments should simultaneously recognise the wisdom of the scheme and validity of the general interest: a pipe-dream.

Rousseau, then, like so many others, Saint-Pierre included, summons the revered name of Henry IV to show how reasonable is the basic idea. Rousseau, accepting at face value Sully's falsehoods about the French King's authorship of the Grand Design (see Chapter 2), contrasts Saint-Pierre's tactics most unfavourably with Henry's. Henry prepared for the execution of the Grand Design over many years, says Rousseau; planned a *casus belli* to launch the enterprise; and had ensured that all the private, immediate interests of the several princes of Europe would be satisfied. 'Such were the means prepared by Henry IV for founding the Federation which the Abbé de Saint-Pierre proposed to set up by a book.' (trans., Forsyth et al., p.165).

Rousseau concludes with comforting gloom. A plan for perpetual peace in Europe 'could only have been carried out by violent means from which humanity must needs shrink.' He continues:

No Confederation could ever be established except by a revolution. That being so, which of us would dare to say whether a League of Europe is a thing more to be desired or feared? It would perhaps do more harm in a moment than it would guard against for ages (trans., Forsyth et al., p.166).

Assessments and influence

Whereas the Grand Design became famous for being praised, Saint-Pierre's Project became notorious for being mocked. One may take leave to wonder how far these contrary responses were due to the personal reputations of their authors, supposed and real respectively, rather than to the relative merits of the two plans. Saint-Pierre's pestering protestations of the practicability of his scheme merely met with the amused response that it was in truth utterly chimerical.

The most often cited quip was made by Leibniz, who himself in fact produced some similar stillborn schemes (see p.65). He confided to a friend, 'I have seen something of the plan of M. de Saint-Pierre for the maintenance of an everlasting peace in Europe. It reminds me of a motto on a grave, *pax perpetua*; for the dead fight not; but the living are of another temper, and the most powerful have little respect for the courts.' (quoted, Castel de Saint-Pierre, pp.7–8). Kant repeated it, without acknowledgment, in a footnote to his own essay, *Perpetual Peace*. Voltaire, Montesquieu, even Rousseau as we have seen, chided the abbé for his lack of a sense of the possible. So too did Frederick the Great, who wrote sarcastically to Voltaire that 'The Abbé de Saint-Pierre . . . has sent me a fine work on how to re-establish peace in

Europe. The thing is very practicable: all it lacks to be successful is the consent of all Europe and a few other such small details.' (quoted, de Rougemont, p.119).

Yet for all the derision Saint-Pierre's Project did exercise a positive influence. Admittedly Hinsley has stated that 'Imitations and copies of Saint-Pierre's project ceased to achieve the dignity of publication after the middle of the century.' (Hinsley, p.82). This is, however, slightly misleading. His influence can at least be traced into the middle of the nineteenth century. Alberoni's plan (see p.65) owed something to the French abbé's scheme. The Marquis d'Argenson, later to become French Foreign Minister, produced a plan in 1737 in which he openly acknowledged his debt to the work of his friend Saint-Pierre. Also, several minor works followed throughout the century directly inspired by Saint-Pierre. As we shall see in Chapter 5 Kant, Napoleon, Saint-Simon and Tsar Alexander I all knew of the Project. Hinsley is indeed at pains to emphasise 'the similarity of the Holy Alliance to the federal ideas of the first half of the eighteenth century, to the plans of Saint-Pierre and his several successors for a league of European sovereigns' (Hinsley, p.201).

Into the nineteenth century, the American specialist in international law, Henry Wheaton, took a positive interest in Saint-Pierre, even claiming to see his influence in the German Confederation as set up in 1815. The Belgian, Molinari, published a biography of Saint-Pierre in 1857, to which he appended his own much watered-down scheme. The federalist scholars of the 1870s, Lorimer and Bluntschli (see pp.114–5), at least took the trouble to criticise Saint-Pierre. After the First World War, the French abbé's work was viewed as a forerunner of the League of Nations. One French Professor of Law went so far as to declare that his 'system is, more or less completely, the basis of the Covenant.' (P. Collinet, in Castel de Saint-Pierre, p.9). Similarly, E.H. Carr stated that he 'propounded one of the earliest schemes for a League of Nations.' (Carr, 1940, p.34).

Symbolically, if somewhat tenuously, Saint-Pierre's influence stretches down to our own day. In 1970 the Council of Europe and in 1986 the European Community adopted a European anthem, namely the 'Ode to Joy' from Beethoven's Ninth Symphony. Now Beethoven took the words from Schiller, who was inspired to write them by reading Rousseau's Abstract of Saint-Pierre's Project.

Leaving aside his irritating personal manner and 'the morass of verbosity' (Stawell, p.140) of his writing, how are we to assess Saint-Pierre's Project? From the copious criticisms that have been expressed over the past century and a half or so we may identify five main arguments. First, several commentators have pointed out that treating all members equally by giving all states just one vote in the Senate flew against the reality of power. It was self-evident that France, say, was a so much greater power than Florence. To set aside the discrepancies of population, wealth and military might as of no moment on the grounds that all states have an equal interest in the maintenance of peace, was to reveal himself a simpleton compared with his immediate predecessors, Sully, Penn and Bellers. He seemed not to have appreciated how unlikely it was that the handful of major powers would place themselves in a position of being outvoted by the larger number of small states. Yet there is a sense in which justice demands equality of voice: might should not be institutionalised as right. It is a principle enshrined, in however diluted a form, in the articles of the Charter of the United Nations governing the composition and procedures of the General Assembly. And within the European Community a German recommendation was tabled in 1991 to abolish the national weighting in the membership of the Commission.

The second criticism of Saint-Pierre has been concerned with his insistence on petrifying the European political scene both in terms of regimes and frontiers. Most critics have focused on the understanding that change can never be prevented: wisdom lies in managing it. Goumy specifically paints a 'worst case scenario' from Saint-Pierre's principle:

... by fixing governments completely in their current power as well as states in their current frontiers, it follows that ... this excellent man proposes nothing other than a means of perpetuating wrong (Goumy, p.85).

Goumy was writing ten years after the revolutions of 1848. We can share his worry today. Other commentators have also noticed that Saint-Pierre's freezing of frontiers was, given the state boundaries of the time, a denial of the principle of nationality.

Defenders of Saint-Pierre's reputation have tried to counter such arguments by suggesting that characteristically nineteenth- or twentieth-century preoccupations are unfair criteria for judging the abbé. It is a weak defence. Sully, whose text Saint-Pierre claimed to be explicating, made specific provision for the principle of nationality in his redrawing of frontiers. And as for consolidating established regimes, Saint-Pierre was himself inconsistent. For instance he had to shift his position smartly with regard to England. At the start of his work he pronounced that the House of Stuart would reign in perpetuity. After 1714 he conceded the right of the Hanoverians against the claims of the Pretenders.

Two stronger arguments can, in fact, be marshalled in defence of the Project. On the issue of frontiers, the wars being fought in the abbé's lifetime did involve an inordinate expenditure of lives and wealth often for trivial adjustments of territory. Whether on the theological grounds of the just war or the rational grounds of utility, the use of such violence for these relocations of frontiers could hardly be condoned. Secondly, Saint-Pierre's linkage of domestic politics and foreign policy, though novel in schemes for European union until then, has certainly been recognised from Rousseau down to our own day.

Saint-Pierre may have drawn inappropriate inferences from his insight; it was a shrewd insight none the less.

The third element in the case against Saint-Pierre concerns his naïvety, and, for all the detail he does burden the reader with, the casualness with which he delineates the procedures for creating and operating his league. His bland assumption that rulers will flock to sign his treaty without the necessity of vigorous diplomatic preparation has attracted particular scorn – as if pure reason and not murky horse-trading were the stuff of inter-state relations. Saint-Pierre's correspondence with Frederick the Great is particularly revealing. Immediately after his accession to the throne, Frederick launched, in December 1740, an unprovoked invasion of the Habsburg province of Silesia and started the War of the Austrian Succession. The 'enlightened' Crown Prince of Prussia had become an unscrupulous king. European opinion was shocked by the blatant aggression. In letters written in the following spring Saint-Pierre described this evidence of Frederick's apparent Jekyll and Hyde character as a 'political enigma'. He chided the king for his wrongdoing and counselled him, 'in order to recover his good reputation, to rely on the judgment of arbiters such as the Dutch and the English.' (see Drouet, p.136). Saint-Pierre continued to write in this vein until just three weeks before his death. One can imagine Frederick's reaction!

Critics have also commented adversely on his failure to provide a detailed code of international law or detailed arrangements for the enforcement of the Senate's decisions, or for unrealistically requiring decisions by unanimity.

And yet no other scheme has provided for every 'i' to be dotted or 't' to be crossed before its implementation. As we shall see in Chapter 7 the founding documents of the European Community were left deliberately vague in some matters in order to secure agreement on the essentials. As for international law, Saint-Pierre wrote a small, separate work on this: *Rule for distinguishing right from wrong, justice and injustice, between nations* (see Drouet, pp.129–32). But as this rule was the simple catechismal promise 'to do to all men, as I would they should do unto me', perhaps we still cannot absolve the abbé from the charge of over-simplicity.

Many a distinguished commentator on Saint-Pierre has fourthly, in one form or another, echoed the Psalmist: 'O put not your trust in princes . . . : for there is no help in them.' We have already noted Rousseau's opinion. It was to be repeated in less measured tones half a century later by Auguste Comte who wrote: ' . . . he proposed a coalition of kings . . . to maintain peace. He might as well have proposed that wolves should guard the sheep.' (quoted, Hinsley, p.106). On the other hand, it is unreasonable, given the political circumstances of the time in which he wrote to expect the abbé could have conceived of an assembly or tribunal representative of the peoples as opposed to the princes of Europe.

A more pertinent criticism was the comparison Leibniz made to the current German Imperial system. Now it is important to stress that Saint-Pierre himself consciously modelled his own Project on this arrangement (see above p.71). The French historian Sorel even dismissively summarised the abbé's work by stating that 'The abbé de Saint-Pierre looked to the Holy Roman Empire, and his perpetual peace is only a reformed and developed version of its constitution.' (Sorel, p.214). Yet, as Leibniz indicated in a letter to Saint-Pierre, where the abbé's system allowed only for the handling of disputes between rulers, the Imperial Chamber was empowered to receive complaints from subjects. It was a telling point, even if the administration of the Imperial tribunal was so inefficient that by 1772 there were 20,000 pending cases unresolved!

Finally, Saint-Pierre is anything but lucid on the issue of sovereignty. On the one hand, he argues that untrammelled sovereignty has been the cause of wars and must be restrained. On the other, he claims that arbitration is not an infringement of sovereignty because it is less debilitating than war. But then Saint-Pierre has not by any means been alone in his failure to resolve the problem. None of the plans surveyed in the present volume managed to devise a definitive, efficient and acceptable constitutional framework for relating state and union power in a united Europe.

We have perhaps managed to counter some of the criticisms levelled at Saint-Pierre's Project. Most of his supporters, however, ultimately fall back on the argument that he was 'before his time'. We can be fairer to the good abbé even than that. Certainly in old age he did not hold to the simple-minded belief that his Project would, once read and appreciated, produce a sudden Pauline kind of conversion on the princes of Europe. When he wrote the First Supplement for the second edition of his *Abrégé*, he surveyed an international scene in which he cautiously judged that 'Their interest in preserving peace makes itself felt more and more to all Sovereigns.' He nevertheless continues: 'But there is still a long stride to take to preserve their union itself.' He consequently resignedly concludes that,

We must endure more than a hundred years yet of war in Europe, and in consequence more than two hundred years of Sovereignty, before all rulers become fully convinced that no League, no Alliance, can be lasting without a permanent [system of] arbitration, and that therefore no power can have any security . . . unless the general Association of the Sovereigns of Europe guarantees it (Castel de Saint-Pierre, p.49).

This was not a bad forecast. It was two hundred and twelve years later that six European governments signed the Treaty of Paris to start the 'pooling' of that sovereignty which had prevented peaceful collaboration for so many centuries.

We must not, however, forget that the most distinguished critic of

Saint-Pierre's Project was Rousseau. What then of commentaries on his commentary? The Genevan philosopher has had, it must be said, a better press than the French *philosophe*. His greater fame and lucidity as a writer often ensured that his versions rather than the originals have been the conduit for the transmission of Saint-Pierre's proposals. We may thus read such complimentary views of some of his modern editors as the following: 'In his writings on international relations there is clarity and incisiveness of a very high order' (Forsyth et al., p.129); and 'throughout [the *Extrait* and *Jugement*] he has translated the barren details and endless repetitions of Saint-Pierre into broad principles of political prudence.' (Vaughan, 1915, p.360).

It can also be demonstrated that Rousseau was far shrewder than the abbé. Forsyth has pointed to the contrast between Saint-Pierre's faith in identifying a general interest in security and prosperity shared by all states and Rousseau's recognition that the task is infinitely more complex, namely, to harmonise recognisably different and divergent interests (Forsyth, 1981, p.90). Moreover, it was precisely the violent upheavals and threats which Rousseau feared as the generative conditions for European union which did come to pass in the era of the Second World War and the Cold War (see Chapter 7).

On the other hand, Rousseau has not been without his own severe critics. On the publication of the *Extrait*, Grimm wrote, 'This Project has become under his pen more absurd than it is in the author's own work. No profound insight, no political understanding, not even an idea which could at least enable one to ponder on the illusion in an agreeable and moving manner.' (quoted, Drouet, p.333). But the chief weakness of Rousseau's versions is the inconsistency between his apparent enthusiasm for the principles and his scornful rejection of their practicability. Many have seen this as a function of the task he had been set: it was impossible to square the idealism of the one author with the realism of the other. However, Hinsley is not so indulgent (see Hinsley, pp.49–60). He sees the inconsistency as an infection at the very core of Rousseau's own thinking, and his failure openly to denounce Saint-Pierre's utopianism as dishonesty. For did not Rousseau believe that the state, by the very artificiality of its nature, was doomed to engage rather in perpetual conflict than seek perpetual peace with others fashioned in the same mould?

Hinsley denies that the general corpus of Rousseau's political writings adds up to a complementary state-confederal theory as indicated by Windenberger and Vaughan (see pp.79–80). Instead, Rousseau's political theory suggests 'a breakdown of Europe's existing states into federal sub-states on the basis of local rule before the re-association of the sub-states in a confederation of Europe on the model of Switzerland.' (Hinsley, p.55). This would indeed have been a revolutionary reconstruction of the European states system, the violence of which Rousseau trembled to contemplate. And yet in the European Community today the proponents of the principle of subsidiarity have the same kind of vision. Subsidiarity is a concept much favoured by enthusiasts for a federal Europe in the Commission and Parliament. Borrowed from papal political thinking, it propounds the desirability of a pyramidal political structure in which decision-making is delegated to the lowest practicable stratum while reserving matters of only high policy to the central federal government. Such a system could realise Rousseau's desire for a design which 'combines the advantages of the small and the large State.' (see above, p.80).

There were, then, numerous blemishes in the schemes of Saint-Pierre and Rousseau for a united Europe. Yet they measurably advanced the idea. Hay has commented that,

The writers for whom universal peace was a genuine programme also encouraged the further evolution of the consciousness of Europe . . . The chief monument of this attempt by idealists to 'institutionalize' the notion of Europe came, of course, . . . with the Abbé de Saint-Pierre . . . (Hay, p.119).

However, compared with Rousseau Saint-Pierre's Europe is still something of a mechanical construction. It is to Rousseau that we owe the belief that, if ever a political union were brought into being, it would exist in a continent which already enjoyed a cultural homogeneity of sound organic growth.

CHAPTER 5

In Britain's image

Industry and revolution

England was scarcely a byword for political stability in the early eighteenth century. The subjects of one king had severed their monarch's head and their descendants had forced one of his sons to flee the country but three years after his accession. During the century from the 1640s to the 1740s civil war was followed by regicide and republicanism; Restoration was followed by Revolution; then Stuart Pretenders intermittently shook the pretended Hanoverian equilibrium.

Furthermore, as the eighteenth century progressed and gave way to the nineteenth, the defects of the British parliamentary system became increasingly evident. The electoral process was not only rotten with corruption but also socially and geographically quite obsolete. Thus, as the Society of the Friends of the People reported in 1793, patronage was so widespread that a mere 162 individuals returned 303 of the 513 MPs! Moreover, the bulk of all the members had landed backgrounds. As the Birmingham Political Union declared in 1830: 'The great aristocratical interests of all kinds are well represented there. The landed interest, the church, the law, the monied interest . . . *But the interests of Industry and of Trade have scarcely any representatives at all!*' (quoted, Dawson & Wall, pp. 6 & 11).

Yet there was, of course, another, continental, interpretation especially in France of the developments across the Channel. Voltaire eulogised about the freedom and tolerance enjoyed by these off-shore islanders; while Montesquieu sang the praises of their wisely balanced constitutional arrangements. The most influential book on the British constitution during the half century before the Great Reform Bill of 1832 was in fact written by a Genovese, Jean Louis Delolme. This first appeared, in French, in 1771 and was later translated into English. He described the British government as the best in Europe. There was not much competition. For all its faults, the constitutional arrangements did prevent royal autocracy; a representative assembly did meet every year; there was virtually no political persecution or censorship. Such virtues could hardly be found in any mainland European state. If Britain seemed in the vanguard politically so she was also economically. Although European overseas trade generally increased from c.1740, Britain's commercial expansion during the century, and particularly in the last decades, was phenomenal. It rose in value from less than £10 million to £50 million in the period 1700–1800. In the years 1782–88 alone her merchant shipping fleet doubled. At the same time and connected in some measure to this commercial buoyancy was the Industrial Revolution, in which of course Britain led the world. One index of the relative extent of industrialisation is that in 1789 it is reckoned that there were 20,000 spinning jennies in Britain compared with just 900 in France (with about double the population).

If industrialisation is an indicator of modernisation, then England in the early nineteenth century was a modern society. The proportion of the population engaged one way or another in industrial production was rapidly increasing. For example, the population of Manchester more than quadrupled in the half century 1770–1820 under the impact of textile manufacture. Moreover, these developments were having political influences, most notably in the forms of popular protest and reformist legislation. And despite the valid complaint of the Birmingham Political Union quoted above, exceptional men from an industrial background did enter politics. As early as 1834 Britain had a prime minister from such an environment – Peel's family made its fortune from the factories of Bury in Lancashire.

Our central figure in this chapter was a Frenchman who wrote his main work on European unity in 1814. He looked to Britan as a model member for his confederation. Perhaps in the light of these few observations we may on balance agree with him that Britain at that time would have been an asset to any pan-European arrangement.

Certainly anyone looking back over recent history in 1814 would hesitate to use France as a constitutional model. When she tried to create a style of constitutional monarchy à l'anglaise after 1789 the attempt collapsed into Jacobin and Bonapartist dictatorship. The French Revolution nevertheless did change the context of the debate on European union in a number of very dramatic ways. It would perhaps not be too much of an over-simplification to suggest that the various schemes for European union prior to 1789 were based on the principles of princes peacefully agreeing to the geopolitical status quo or its adaptation and eschewing war as a means of any subsequent changes. The emergence of the doctrine of popular sovereignty with the Revolution rendered such an agenda utterly obsolete – and for three reasons.

In the first place, the will of the prince no longer held sway. True, the likes of Metternich tried to restore an international regime based upon monarchical authority in post-Napoleonic Europe. But it could not last. The idea of princes imposing a confederal system of government on Europe without some form of popular consent had become anachronistic. Even the idea of rulers forgoing war was now more difficult to sustain. For warfare too was now revolutionised. No longer was international conflict a murderous game played by princes with their professional and mercenary troops. The French Revolution had introduced conscription, the *levée en masse*, and rendered war total. War was henceforth an even more deadly affair of conflict between peoples mobilised for the sakes of their motherlands.

The style of European wars was being determined by the precepts of nationalism. The concept of the nation-state is, of course, far older than the French Revolution. Indeed, we have already seen (p.32) that Sully's redrawing of the map of Europe took ethnic considerations into account. What the French Revolution did was to give the sense of nationhood immense dynamic force by marrying it to the doctrine of popular sovereignty. In fact, Alfred Cobban went so far as to say that the French Revolution was 'the embodiment of a great idea, the idea of the sovereignty of the people, or nation.' (Cobban, 1960, p.189). The tone was set most strikingly by the Abbé Sieyes in his pamphlet *What is the Third Estate?* In this he firmly asserted: 'The Nation exists before all things and is the origin of all things . . . In whatever manner a Nation wills, it is sufficient that it does will: all forms are good, and its will is always the supreme law.' (quoted, Cobban, 1969, p.189). Once this doctrine became widespread, as it did very rapidly in western and central Europe, no scheme for European union would be valid if it ignored the force of national identity and will as voiced through the mouthpieces of popular opinion.

The force of popular opinion was, if somewhat equivocally, Jeremy Bentham's panacea for European harmony. It is fitting therefore to summarise the position of this English philosopher on the matter of European union. Bentham's output in political theory and jurisprudence was prodigious – some twenty million words (and in atrocious handwriting too!). His reputation in Europe and the Americas in the nineteenth century was unparalleled. The English traveller George Borrow retails a conversation with the mayor of a town in the remote north-eastern corner of Spain, who praised 'The grand Baintham. He who has invented laws for all the world . . . here am I, a simple *alcade* of Galicia, yet I possess all the writings of Baintham on that shelf, and I study them day and night.' (quoted, Everett, pp.7–8).

At a more modest level Bentham also, in 1780, invented the word 'international'. He then set about writing his *Principles of International Law*. The fourth and last essay in this project, and written in 1789, was entitled 'A Plan for an Universal and Perpetual Peace'. He is much concerned to persuade the British and French to relinquish their colonies and reduce their armed forces, but spends only a few pages discussing the issue of supranational control. The essay is divided into a series of propositions. Proposition XIII reads as follows:

That the maintenance of such a pacification might be considerably facilitated, by the establishment of a common court of judicature, for the decision of differences between the several nations, although such a court were not to be armed with any coercive powers. (Reprinted, Everett, p.210).

Bentham suggests that an international force might very occasionally be necessary to enforce the court's arbitrative judgment. However, such recourse to enforcement would, 'in all human probability, be superseded for ever . . . [by] introducing . . . a clause guaranteeing the liberty of the press in each state.' (reprinted, Everett, p.215).

For Bentham a federal structure for Europe was neither necessary nor expedient. Rational public opinion is fully conscious of the inutility of war. Europe but wants an impartial institution to referee disputes and an informed populace to support its judgments.

Just as Bentham, the most esteemed figure in jurisprudence of the age, had tangential comments to make on European harmony, so also did Immanuel Kant, the most distinguished moral philosopher of the time. A citizen of Königsberg in East Prussia, he was a man of meticulous habits. So deeply affected was he by the news of the French Revolution that he altered the direction of the daily walk he had taken at the same time for years. Well before that great turning-point in history Kant had become acquainted with Saint-Pierre and Rousseau on perpetual peace (see p.84). Then, in 1795 he produced his own *Thoughts on Perpetual Peace*. However, in this work, even if he had mainly Europe in mind, he wrote about the pacification of the *world* and not just Europe. Furthermore, in so far as he wrote about a 'union of nations' or 'federal union', he meant by these terms separate, independent states bound only by an improved international law (see Hinsley, p.66).

Indeed, the whole tenor of German political thinking at this time was nationalist. This was especially so in Prussia. There were many complicated strands in early German nationalism. It was part search for a cultural identity, as in the works of Herder. It was part consolidation of the idea of the state, as in the philosophy of Hegel. And it was part a combination of intellectual enquiry and practical anti-French politics as in the famous *Addresses to the German Nation* delivered at Berlin University by Fichte, a pupil of Kant's in 1807–8. One of the most passionate German francophobes was 'Father' Jahn, who declared that any parent who allowed a daughter to learn French was, by that permissiveness, tantamount to delivering her up to prostitution! Such an atmosphere was scarcely conducive to thoughts about European unity.

This German nationalism was targeted against France as a reaction to both her cultural imperialism of the seventeenth and eighteenth centuries and the current military imperialism of Napoleon. Napoleon's place in the history of European unity is extraordinarily ambivalent. On the one hand, his exploits strengthened feelings of separate political or ethnic identity: French armies of occupation, French rulers in some territories and the imposition of French systems of administration stimulated resentment among the politically aware classes. This reaction led to a patriotic rallying to the state as in Prussia; a nationalist search for the bases of ethnic unity for Germany and Italy; even something approaching a popular nationalist movement in Spain.

On the other hand, Europe experienced greater political unity in practice than at any time since the Roman Empire. By c.1810 the French Empire itself stretched from Hamburg to Rome and incorporated the Adriatic coastal province of Illyria. It was flanked by satellite states including the Confederation of the Rhine and the Kingdom of Italy, which provided central Germany and a large portion of the Italian peninsula respectively with a taste of unity. Moreover, the spread of the Napoleonic Code – the renovation of social and legal systems – furnished much of Europe with common quasi-liberal practices. Thus he instructed his brother, Jérôme, King of Westphalia in the Confederation of the Rhine: 'The benefits of the Code, verdicts arrived at in open courts, the creation of juries, must be so many distinguishing marks of your monarchy.' (quoted, Hutt, p.38).

Was Napoleon truly seeking the beneficial unification of Europe rather than just its subjugation to French hegemony and his own will? After defeat, he lived for six years, until he died of cancer, in exile on the remote Atlantic island of St Helena. There, he fell to conversation with his companions, who recorded his thoughts.

We may take as an example of these talks the report of Las Cases that

He would have aimed at the same principles, the same system everywhere. A European code, a European supreme court with full powers to review all wrong decisions . . . ; money of the same value but in different coins; the same weights, the same measures, the same laws, etc., etc.
Thus Europe, he said, would soon have formed actually a single nation, and every traveler would have everywhere found himself in one common homeland (quoted, de Rougemont, p.215).

Another chronicler, Montholon, in his *Memoirs* has the defeated Emperor complaining that he was balked of achieving his splendid vision:

It is wonderful to think what might have been the fortune of France and of Europe if England had listened to the voice of a generous statesmanship and taken the French Revolution for her friend! . . . The plan of St. Pierre might have been realized (quoted, Stawell, pp.214–15).

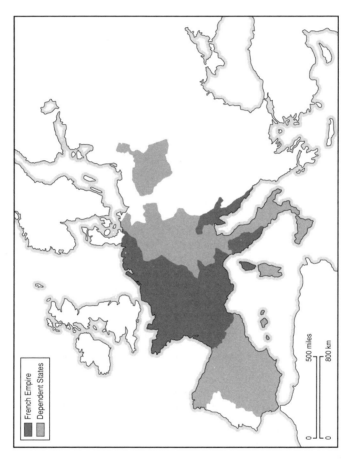

Map 5 Napoleon's Empire

French Empire
Dependent States

Both of these sources represent Napoleon as being none the less confident that the union of Europe would be forthcoming in the foreseeable future – even to be accomplished by his son, the 'King of Rome'. He, according to Montholon's account, would 'reunite Europe in federal links that could never be broken.' (quoted, Stawell, p.213).

We nevertheless have problems about the authenticity of this evidence. Given this opportunity to present his life in the most favourable terms, Napoleon was hardly the kind of man to leave the truth unvarnished. Nor were all his amanuenses entirely faithful in reporting Napoleon's own words. For instance, Las Cases's book was described by one nineteenth-century English commentator as 'the most delicious effusion of sentimental old French twaddle that was ever read.' (quoted, Thompson, p.394). We must consequently treat these versions of Napoleon's motives with some circumspection. Even so, affection for his memory was such that they provided the raw material of a potent posthumous Napoleonic Legend. In particular these memoirs formed the basis for *Napoleonic Ideas* which his nephew, Louis Napoleon, produced in 1839.

The attribution to Napoleon of this keen enthusiasm for European unity (however little truth lay in the reports) harmonised well with the renewed interest in the ideal in the early nineteenth century. Cultural cosmopolitanism and diplomatic balance of power theory had rather outshone the concept of institutional integration for the half-century following Saint-Pierre. However, the revolutionary developments in Europe and the unique position of Britain at the end of the eighteenth century presented inspiring challenges for rethinking the basic objective of European union. The novel context demanded above all freshness of thought.

Saint-Simon's *Reorganisation*

The process of radically rethinking Sully's basic idea of the Grand Design or Saint-Pierre's Perpetual Peace had perforce to involve a clear understanding of the impact on Europe of the dual Industrial and French Revolutions. Their effects had to be fully mirrored in any new scheme of European integration. This task fitted neatly into the analysis of the nature and implications of industrial society as undertaken by Saint-Simon; while the kaleidoscopic shifts in the personal life-style of this eccentric French count matched well the age of deep and rapid change in which he lived.

Claude-Henri de Rouvroy, Comte de Saint-Simon, was born in Paris in 1760, son of a noble family in impoverished circumstances. The family was, however, distantly related to the grand courtier and memorialist, the Duc de Saint-Simon. That proud peer had even claimed Charlemagne as an ancestor. Stuffed with the belief in this ancient lineage, Claude-Henri succumbed while in prison during the Terror to an hallucinatory vision. The Carolingian spectre addressed him thus: 'Since the world began no family has had the honour to produce both a hero and a philosopher of the first rank. This honour has been reserved to my house. My son, your success as a philosopher will equal mine as a soldier and a statesman.' (*Epître dédicatoire à mon neveu Victor de Saint-Simon*, quoted, Manuel, p.40). Never one to doubt his own intellectual powers, Saint-Simon had no hesitation about accepting the authenticity of the message. Furthermore, its relevance to the need to unify (or re-unify) Europe was quite clear.

However, we run ahead of our story. For much of the personal detail of Saint-Simon's early life we are dependent on his autobiographical sketches, which are not always reliable. His formal education was probably perfunctory; and there is no corroboration of his later claim that he was tutored by the great Encyclopedist, d'Alembert. His adult life may be roughly divided into four phases: as soldier (during the American War of Independence), financial speculator, philosopher and political scientist.

Saint-Simon's years as an entrepreneur started in 1788 in Spain where he was involved in a gradiose hare-brained scheme to build a vast canal across the peninsula. There too he met a Prussian diplomat with whom he later shared financial exploits and then quarrelled in most dramatic fashion. Back in France at the start of the Revolution he committed himself to its social objectives. He symbolically renounced his title and even, for a short time, the Christian associations of his name, thus answering simply to Claude-Henri Simon. It was perhaps this republican zeal which led to his arrest in 1793 in the place of a speculator also called Simon. But, then, Saint-Simon himself was no financial innocent. He had amassed a fortune by buying up sequestred *émigré* and former ecclesiastical property. There is even one story of his collaborating with Talleyrand, the ci-devant Bishop of Autun, in an enterprise to buy Notre Dame in order to melt down and sell off the lead roofing! The scheme failed because the cartloads of depreciated *assignat* notes were an inadequate sum.

Released from prison and Midas-rich, he lived the luxurious life of the most famous debauched dandy of the Directory. He also presided over a salon of some intellectual pretension, while he himself strove to acquire a knowledge of the physical sciences. He was married briefly, in 1801–2. He started his life of prolific writing in 1802. But he was rapidly exhausting his financial resources. By 1806 he was penniless. He chanced upon a former manservant, Diard, who gave him not only bed and board but also the means for subsidising his publications.

Thereafter, in various ways, Saint-Simon secured a reasonable income, which for a time stretched to the employment of secretaries to give some semblance of order to the ideas which tumbled from his fertile mind. Meanwhile, in 1812, he had a nervous breakdown. His erratic, eccentric personality could not bear the strain of the extended financial quarrels with his former Prussian associate and the ridicule with which his half-baked musings on the philosophy of science were received by the Napoleonic scientific establishment.

During the first decade of the Restoration, which was the last decade of his life, Saint-Simon sustained himself haphazardly on subscriptions from bankers, merchants and industrialists for his various literary activities and by borrowing from friends. He built up a body of 'disciples', who, both during his lifetime and subsequently, propagated and developed his ideas. One of the most distinguished and highly educated of these, Auguste Comte, revealed in letters written in 1818 something of the quality of the man who inspired discipleship in the young (Comte was twenty at the time): He declared, ' . . . my mind has made more progress in the last six months of our relationship than I would have made if I had been alone . . . He is the most estimable and the most amiable man I have ever known in my life.' (*Lettres à M. Valat, 1815–44*, quoted, Manuel, p.206).

To his very last years Saint-Simon remained extraordinarily energetic. Yet the widespread recognition and acceptance of his ideas for which he craved eluded him. After his death one of his devoted followers vividly described this apparent failure: 'Saint-Simon was not even heard by his contemporaries . . . Disdain, mockery, oblivion, and poverty were the reward for his labors. He ardently loved glory and humanity. Humanity turned a deaf ear to him. Glory delayed in coming and was to appear only at his grave.' (J.L.E. Lerminier, *Philosophie du droit*, quoted, Manuel, p.329). In 1823 his depression drove him to attempted suicide.

The months from this episode to his death saw the publication of his *New Christianity* and were saddened by a bitter quarrel with Comte. Nevertheless, he gathered younger disciples about him; and when he died, in 1825, it was clear that the Saint-Simonians would thrive to interpret and develop his protean thought along many diverse paths.

Saint-Simon's great ambition had been to produce a synthesis of all human knowledge. His endeavours therefore inevitably took him into many fields. His collected works fill eleven volumes. In focusing here on his plans for European integration we are primarily, of course, interested in his political thought.

His work in this area sprang from his strong positivist views and his philosophy of history. Saint-Simon was convinced that a scientific, value-free analysis of politics was both possible and necessary. He despised what he considered to have been the subjective style of all political writing hitherto and aspired to be the Newton of the social sciences. His analysis of history convinced him that the industrial phase of man's progress was, in his own time, coming to a point of final maturity. He argued that social and political transformations were crucial in order to prevent the stifling of the beneficent potential of industrialisation. The traumata of Jacobinism and Bonapartism were, in this regard, unfortunate missed opportunities. The key industrial-scientific elite were prevented from emerging as the essential dominant force.

A cardinal feature of Saint-Simon's political theory is his class analysis, though in detail he changed this in his various publications. Broadly speaking he claimed that modern industrial society is composed of three classes. One of these, which had heretofore been supreme, was non-productive: the nobility, military and lawyers. The two productive classes are the scientists and the '*industriels*'. Saint-Simon coined this word to refer to all those engaged in manufacture – factory owners clearly, but also at times he embraced workers and bankers in the term.

He believed that, if only this productive technocracy could be given their head, the politics of repressive government and conflict would yield to a politics of ability. Government would then be confined to administration. Corporate bodies such as trade unions and employers' associations assume great significance in this system. So too do the transnational operations of business enterprises. Saint-Simon consequently forecast that the traditional state government apparatuses would atrophy and in this process the sovereign nation-state would wither. Professor Ionescu has described the process succinctly:

The nation-state would dissolve both from within and from without. From within it would dissolve among all the internal groups of abilities which disregard the mechanism of controls of and by the state and prefer self-administration, and which can no longer be coerced lest the industrial (-technological) society should grind to a halt. From without, the nation-state would melt into a European confederative association, because the economy of such a society can prosper only in large territorial units. It cannot survive within areas and with resources of the size of England, France, Germany, etc. All the new institutions and the new processes will be European or nothing (Ionescu, 1976, pp.42–3).

So much in Saint-Simon's experience and intellectual system led him to propound and predict the unification of Europe. He was in fact toying with the idea as early as 1802 – in his *Lettre d'un habitant de Genève à ses contemporains*. Two features of his interpretation of the French Revolution point in the direction of European integration. One was his belief that the scientific-industrial class had allowed the movement to be hijacked by the non-productive lawyers and that the nationalist-aggressive face of the Revolution had overcome the reformist. Secondly, he emphasised that the Revolution was in essence, nevertheless, a European rather than a French phenomenon; for it affected those regions of the continent which were characterised by the common experiences of Roman law, feudalism, the struggle against the Turk and absolute monarchy. The Revolution thus failed to exploit the chance of consolidating the industrial society so that renewed, non-revolutionary, efforts must be made. On the other hand, it succeeded in exposing an underlying commonality of experience in much of the western and central portions of the continent – a region he dubbed 'Franche Europe'.

By 1813 the slaughter of the Revolutionary and Napoleonic Wars provoked him to an agonised appeal for the election of a 'scientific Pope'. He addressed the scientists of Europe as follows: '... since the fifteenth century the institution which had united the European nations ... had grown steadily weaker. It is now so completely destroyed that a general war ... has been in progress for the last twenty years and has already harvested several million men ... Only you can restore peace to Europe. Only you can reorganize European Society.' (*Travail sur la gravitation universelle*, quoted, Manuel, p.111).

Saint-Simon's philosophical positivism also led him to similar conclusions. As scientific political analysis reveals the need for European integration, so that idea will be bound to be achieved in practice. In 1808 he wrote: 'One realizes that national organizations are individual applications of general ideas on the social order and that the reorganization of the general system of European politics will bring in its train the national reorganization of the various peoples who, by their political union, form that great society.' (*Introduction aux travaux scientifiques du XIXe siècle*, quoted, Manuel, p.136).

The concept of European union even fitted in to his bizarre notion of universal gravity. Searching for a principle which would provide a unifying explanation of the totality of human, natural and physical experiences and perceptions, he hit upon the force of gravity, which, through the popularisation of the work of Newton, so fascinated eighteenth-century intellectuals. By way of explanation of his publication on this matter, he declared: 'I have given this first sketch of my project on the reorganization of European society the title of *Travail sur la gravitation universelle* because the idea of universal gravity must serve as a base for the new philosophical theory, and the new political system of Europe must be a consequence of the new philosophy.' (quoted, Manuel, p.120).

From his various allusions to a new unified Europe we may glean a general understanding of certain of its features as Saint-Simon conceived them. We have already seen that he recognised a distinction between the western and eastern halves of the continent. Only the western portion had the advantage of the centripetal influences of so many common historical experiences. Secondly, the sense of a common European identity, he claimed, was already in the 1820s sufficiently powerful to overwhelm narrow patriotic feelings. Thus, in *The Catechism of the Industrialists* he wrote: 'We are convinced that having thought about it, you will agree that philanthropic sentiments, those new family sentiments of *Europeanism*, take precedence today among all Europeans over their national sentiments. You will recognize that what we have just said is true even of the English.' (reprinted, Ionescu, 1976, p.203). And thirdly, with regard to a united Europe's external relations, Saint-Simon envisaged a new crusade to erase the irrational superstitions of Asia and Africa by the abrasive power of European science.

So convinced was Saint-Simon of the validity of these general ideas that he published a pamphlet on European integration in 1814 and followed through some of the recommendations in rather more detail in an unpublished work a few years later. In 1814 Saint-Simon employed the nineteen-year-old historian, Augustin Thierry, as his collaborator. It was the year of Napoleon's initial defeat; and the princes and statesmen of Europe were convened on 1 November in Vienna to reconstruct the continent following a quarter of a century of upheaval. Working swiftly with a view to influencing the Congress, Saint-Simon and Thierry published in October a pamphlet entitled, in full, *The Reorganization of the European Community or the necessity and the means of uniting the peoples of Europe in a single body politic while preserving for each their national independence.*

The pamphlet (some 15,000 words) starts by asserting that European intellectual endeavour in the nineteenth century will be characterised by an emphasis on political thought. This indeed was essential because of the political destruction wrought by the recent revolutionary times. 'Lack of institutions,' Saint-Simon declares, 'leads to the destruction of all society; outworn institutions prolong the ignorance and the prejudices of the times which produced them.' He appeals to writers to initiate the essential reform, for 'you govern opinion, and opinion governs the world.' (reprinted, Markham, p.29). (The title-page gives a dual authorship, and Thierry probably disciplined the Master's unstructured thoughts. However, there is little doubt that the basic ideas are Saint-Simon's and indeed the first person singular is occasionally employed. We shall therefore for simplicity's sake refer to the work as Saint-Simon's.) He offers himself as the self-appointed 'pioneer'. He then expresses the hope that two enlightened monarchs might patronise such endeavours.

These prefatory remarks lead to a section addressed to the parliaments of France and England. Saint-Simon makes the assertion that 'Until the end of the fifteenth century, all the nations formed a single body politic, at peace within, but armed against the enemies of its constitution and its independence.' (reprinted, Markham, p.30. The relative harmony of medieval Europe was a common feature of writing about Europe at the time, a trend set by Schiller (see de Rougemont, p.202)). This coherence was provided by the Roman Catholic religion and church. Luther shattered this unity; the Treaty of Westphalia institutionalised the alternative, the balance of power, and consequently war. The one country to benefit from this international anarchy was England, who cunningly divorced herself from continental ways. She developed a unique constitution based upon 'the liberty and happiness of the people'. She then turned outward, bent on 'universal dominion. She promoted her own sea-power, commerce and industry, while hindering those of other countries. If arbitrary governments weighed on Europe, England supported them and reserved for herself liberty and its blessings.' The lesson to be drawn from these historical developments is that 'There will be no repose or happiness for Europe, as long as there is no political link to attach England again to the continent from which she has been separated.' (reprinted, Markham, pp.31–2).

Europe's salvation lies in the reconstruction, in aptly modern style, of the medieval 'federal community united by common institutions, subject to a common government which was in the same relation to the different peoples as national governments are to individuals.' (reprinted, Markham, p.32). It must also be based on intrinsic truths, free of ephemeral beliefs and opinions. The task of institutional reconstruction (or the reorganisation of European society, as he calls it) will of necessity be a gradual process.

The way forward is clear; for France now, as well as England, has embraced politically liberal principles. These two states must therefore be united to take charge of the process of reorganisation. 'This union is possible,' Saint-Simon logically asserts, 'because France is now free like England; the union is necessary, because it alone can ensure the peace of the two countries and save them from the evils which threaten them; the union can change the state of Europe, because England and France together are stronger than the rest of Europe.' (reprinted, Markham, p.33).

There follows an analysis of the constitutional changes for a united Europe which Saint-Simon recommends. The text is sectionalised into three 'books'. The first is entitled 'The best form of government: proof that the parliamentary form is the best.' Saint-Simon reveals the relevance of the pamphlet to the current condition of Europe: ' . . . the sovereigns of all the European nations are assembled to give her peace . . . yet they will not reach their goal . . . [for] I have perceived that there is no salvation for Europe except through a general reorganization.' (reprinted, Markham, pp.33–4). The reason for the inevitable failure of the Congress is that each delegate will argue that the particular interests of his own country are the interests of the continent as a whole. But the pursuit of peace by these conventional means will lead ineluctably to war yet again.

He then repeats his praise of the relative unity and peace enjoyed in the Middle Ages. Constant wars followed the breakdown of that system; and 'Only two men have seen the evil and come near to the remedy: they were Henry IV and the Abbé St. Pierre. The one died before he could realize his plan, which was forgotten after him; the other was treated as a visionary because he had promised more than he could perform.' (reprinted, Markham, p.36). He then proceeds to subject Saint-Pierre's *Perpetual Peace* to rigorous criticism, of which more below (see p.109). This critique leads him to complain that Saint-Pierre ignored the beneficial features of the medieval papal organisation, namely:

(1) Any political organization founded to link together several different peoples, while preserving their national independence, must be systematically homogeneous – that is to say, all the institutions should be derived from a single conception . . .
(2) The common government must certainly be independent of the national governments.
(3) The members of the common government should . . . consider exclusively the common interest.
(4) They should be endowed with a power which is their own, and does not derive from any outside authority; this power is public opinion.

Saint-Simon then adds three of his own criteria to complete what he considers the necessary conditions for an integrated and peaceful Europe. These are:

(1) The best possible constitution should be applied to the common government and the national governments.
(2) The members of the common government should be compelled by the nature of the organization to work for the common good . . .
(3) The intellectual basis of their power should rest on unshakeable principles valid for all times and places (reprinted, Markham, pp.38–9).

He then proceeds by 'scientific' or logical argument to discover what is the best possible constitution. He argues that 'the first requirement is to establish two distinct authorities, composed in such a way that the one is obliged to consider matters from the point of view of the common interest of the nation, and the other from the point of view of the particular interests of the individual members.' (reprinted, Markham, pp.40–1). Each body – the Authority for Common Interests and the Authority for Particular or Local Interests – would have a power of veto over the legislative proposals of the other. A third, Regulating or Moderating Body would ensure that the first two were kept in balance. Moreover, not only does this style of constitution represent political perfection, wonder of wonders, it actually exists – in England!

There follows a eulogistic summary of the British system of government. He is thus able to conclude that both reason and experience prove that the parliamentary form of government is indeed the best possible constitution.

Book II is entitled: 'All the nations of Europe should be governed by national parliaments, and should combine to form a common parliament to decide on the common interests of the European community.' For it follows from his exposition to this point that Europe's ills can be cured only by the adoption of parliamentary constitutions by the several states and a similar, overarching pan-European constitution. He then outlines the desired European parliamentary system.

His starting point is that, just as national governments depend on the cohesive force of national patriotism, so a European government must be able to rely on 'European patriotism'. In the European parliament the development of this feeling will be a two-way process: the common institutions and policies will shape the attitudes of the representatives; but at the same time the representatives will shape the institutions and policies.

It is therefore essential [declares Saint-Simon] to admit to the House of Commons of the European Parliament . . . only such men as by their wide contacts, emancipation from purely local customs, their occupations which are cosmopolitan in aim rather than national, are better able to arrive quickly at this wider point of view which makes the corporate will, and at the common interest which should also be the corporate interest of the European parliament.

These people are: 'Men of business, scientists, magistrates, and administrators.' (reprinted, Markham, p.47).

These representatives are to be elected by their own professional associations, one from each of these professions for every million literate persons in Europe. They must own substantial property, for only men of that condition can be guaranteed to provide stability. However, some outstanding individuals who would be an asset to the legislature but lacked property would be given that necessary source of wealth and be co-opted. Even wealthier would be the members of the House of Peers, nominated by the King and of no fixed number. Selecting the King of Europe was obviously a tricky and delicate question. Saint-Simon ducked it, promised a second pamphlet on the issue, which he never wrote.

He then lists the topics which he considers would fall within the remit of the European, as opposed to any national, parliament. These include: nationalist secession; transcontinental canals; education; the provision of ethical codes; and the protection of religious toleration. Significantly, he believes aggression to be so ingrained in human nature that 'Without external activity, there is no internal tranquility.' (reprinted, Markham, p.49). But he rationalises the bellicose policy, which in consequence the parliament must pursue, by asserting that the conquest and colonisation of other continents is justified on the grounds that Europeans are 'superior to every other human race.' (reprinted, Markham, p.49).

Book III is entitled 'France and England, which have a parliament empowered to control the interests of both nations. Effect of the Anglo-

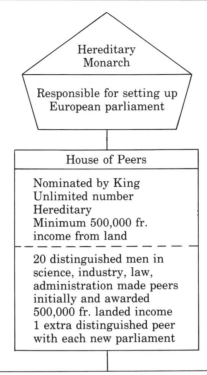

Hereditary
Monarch

Responsible for setting up
European parliament

House of Peers

Nominated by King
Unlimited number
Hereditary
Minimum 500,000 fr.
income from land

20 distinguished men in
science, industry, law,
administration made peers
initially and awarded
500,000 fr. landed income
1 extra distinguished peer
with each new parliament

House of Commons

1 representative from each of 4 professions for every 1 million literate men
($\backsimeq$ 240)
Elected for 10 years
Minimum 25,000 fr. landed income

20 distinguished men in learning, business, law, administration chosen at
every election after the first, and awarded 25,000 fr. landed income

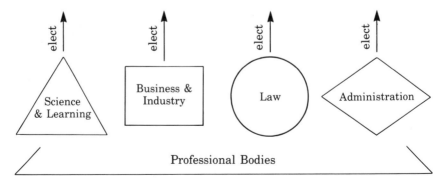

elect · elect · elect · elect

Science & Learning · Business & Industry · Law · Administration

Professional Bodies

Saint-Simon's European Parliament

French parliament on the other European peoples.' Here Saint-Simon reveals his gradualism. France has in fact adopted an English-style parliamentary constitution. Other European states will follow suit. When they have all accomplished this, a European parliament can be established with ease. The problem, therefore, is to damp down war-like tendencies during this lengthy interim phase. This can be done by the immediate conjoining of the powerful parliamentary states, namely, England and France; and 'let the principal aim of this associ-ation be to grow by attracting to it other peoples; consequently, let the Anglo-French government encourage among all the other nations the supporters of a representative constitution.' (reprinted, Markham, p.50).

The Anglo-French parliament should be constructed on the same principles as the proposed European houses. However, because the British are more experienced in these matters and would be making more of a sacrifice in surrendering their sovereignty, they should have twice as many representatives as the French! On the other hand, it is in the interests of both to take this bold step because both are threatened by the plague of revolution still haunting Europe. There follows a substantial analysis of the political conditions in the two countries.

The mutual benefits of an immediate Anglo-French confederation, he concludes, are plain to see. Britain, bled by the financial outlay of the Revolutionary and Napoleonic Wars and alarmed by her massive national debt, reacts, to her shame, by acts of intrigue, oppression and crime. In a confederation, France would share this financial burden, tame Britain's brutality and, in return, be schooled by her partner in the arts of parliamentary government so essential to ward off a renewal of revolutionary chaos.

Saint-Simon then turns to a consideration of Germany, for whom he has a high regard because it is 'infinitely superior in its character, science, and philosophy', and for whom he entertains a deep apprehen-sion because 'it is apparent that a revolution is impending.' (reprinted, Markham, pp.64–5). Accordingly, 'The first undertaking of the Anglo-French parliament should be to promote the reorganisation of Ger-many, by making her revolution shorter and less violent [than the English and French].' (reprinted, Markham, p.66). The accession of Germany to the embryonic European Union would be exceedingly beneficial, because their representatives to the parliament 'will con-tribute in their views that pureness of morality, nobility of sentiments' which are so lacking in the English and French (reprinted, Markham, p.66).

Saint-Simon concludes his pamphlet by drawing the reader's atten-tion to the fact that the desire for a radically different European system is widely desired, yet nothing but tinkering with the old has hitherto been attempted. 'The plan of organization which I have put forward,' he explains not without some degree of immodesty, 'is the first which is new and comprehensive.' The statesmen have failed in their perceptions of what Europe needs. Therefore, 'With great effort and labour I have reached the standpoint of the common interest of the European peoples.' (reprinted, Markham, p.67).

After the publication of this pamphlet Saint-Simon returned to the theme of an Anglo-French union quite quickly, probably the following year, in an unpublished essay entitled *To Englishmen and Frenchmen who are keen to promote the public welfare* (see Manuel, pp.184–8). In working out some of the details of matters which he outlined in the 1814 pamphlet, Saint-Simon was particularly concerned to emphasise the need for 'spiritual' harmony between the two member states. By this he means the supranational encouragement of hard work and of good practice in educational, scientific and religious matters. Separate governmental spiritual institutions are to be created for this purpose. The reform of the national parliaments and their relationship to these spiritual authorities are also dealt with.

Saint-Simon accepts that national differences will prevent exact uniformity of pace in achieving reformed institutions and in their style and composition when achieved. He also accepts that firm pressure might be necessary to effect the changes. Thus he writes: 'The chiefs of industrial enterprises in England and in France should declare to the English and the French governments that if, at a date which they will fix, the governments refuse to consent to the establishment of a scientific and industrial constitution for the two nations, they and their workers will stop paying taxes.' (quoted, Manuel, p.187).

Moreover, in this essay Saint-Simon sees the Anglo-French union not just as the start of a parliamentary-industrial European cluster, but as a confederal snowball that would roll and roll through generations until the whole world had adhered to this modern, beneficient form of human society.

Liberalism, nationalism and federalism

Hitherto the would-be European federalists planned only to adapt the traditional monarchical state system; Saint-Simon's purpose was radically to change it. Whether looking backwards or forwards, commentators on Saint-Simon's contribution are agreed that he occupies a pivotal position. Professor Hinsley describes the *Reorganisation* as 'a more far-reaching proposal for the federal organisation of Europe than anyone had ever proposed.' (Hinsley, p.102). Professor Ionescu in 1976 declared it 'much more advanced and much more in tune with the modern industrial-technological Europe than are, even now, the institutions proposed for the European Community.' (Ionescu, 1976, p.47). While Denis de Rougemont states that 'He broke with the Du

Bois-Sully-Saint-Pierre tradition of alliances among princes . . . He is the true precursor of the institutionalizing tendency which in the twentieth century has produced the Common Market and the O.E.C.D.' (de Rougemont, p.220).

Saint-Simon was himself, as we have seen, very conscious that he was breaking new ground generally in his political works. On the matter of European unity he tended, both in conversation and in writing, to harp on the inadequacy of Saint-Pierre's *Perpetual Peace*. For example, in proposing a merger of English and French industries in his substantial book, *Industry*, Saint-Simon tartly comments that, despite his cogent case, 'we do not fear to forecast with the same confidence that this project will be considered by the majority of people, by the interested parties even, as a dream impossible of realization, as an arrangement analogous to the *impracticable* peace of Saint-Pierre.' (*L'Industrie*, t.II, reprinted, Saint-Simon, pp.61–2).

It was in his *Reorganisation*, naturally, that he subjected the abbé's work to the most detailed criticism. He again uses the word 'impracticable' and states: ' . . . all the weaknesses of a congress remain untouched . . . Can sovereigns negotiating together, or plenipotentiaries . . . revocable by them, have any but particular points of view or any interest but their own?' (reprinted, Markham, p.37). For good measure he also charges the 'noble' Henry IV of naïvety for thinking that princes could be expected to put the interests of the community before their own. Furthermore, Saint-Pierre was culpable of proposing a freezing of the status quo, thus preventing any further erosion of obsolete feudalism or effective resistance to tyranny. 'In a word, this sham organization would be nothing but a mutual guarantee of princes to preserve their arbitrary power.' (reprinted, Markham, p.38).

What were the essential differences between Saint-Simon and his predecessors? His work has in fact been subjected to considerable detailed textual analysis. Was he more interested in industry as a means to a better society than peace itself? Did he really believe that the essence of Anglo-French similarity lay in their level of industrialisation or was it rather their shared civilised values (see Fakkar, pp.77–8)? Despite differing answers to these questions, it is possible to summarise as follows. First, he is properly conscious of *social* change. Where his predecessors envisage the mechanism of change as diplomatic, Saint-Simon sees it in social pressures. Secondly, and closely related to this perception, he recommends unification by gradual evolution and accretion rather than by once-and-for-all treaty. Thirdly, he recognises the necessity of the component members of the federation having compatible social and political systems. Fourthly, those political systems must all be parliamentary. This relates, fifthly, to his most radical view, which he states quite bluntly: '[The European parliament] will decide, not in the interests of the governments, but of the peoples.' (reprinted, Markham, p.49). Indeed, the very wording of the subtitle of the pamphlet about 'uniting the *peoples* of Europe . . . while preserving for each their *national* independence' contrasts sharply with the arrangements of all the previous schemes for harmony among *rulers*. Sixthly, of course, there is the central role he accords to Britain. Not even the English Quakers themselves had believed that European unity depended so vitally on British leadership. Finally, and perhaps most significantly, Saint-Simon was more interested than his predecessors in the unification of Europe for its own political, social and especially economic sake. To the earlier writers, one feels, union was a necessary means to the essential end of peace; and they gave less attention to other benefits accruing from their federal schemes.

These fundamental differences can, of course, be at least partially explained by the extraordinary pace of change in Europe during Saint-Simon's lifetime. Saint-Simon's solution to the unhappy fragmentation of Europe was so materially different from those of his predecessors because the social, economic and political conditions of the continent were so materially different from those in which Dubois, Sully, Penn, Saint-Pierre and even Rousseau lived. In a sense therefore Saint-Simon was guilty of anachronistic thinking in so roundly condemning Saint-Pierre for working within the preconceptions of his own age.

Other thinkers in the field of international affairs were responding to the changes, it is true. Kant appreciated the importance of the homogeneity of regimes for conciliation between them and Bentham was convinced of the importance of public opinion. But no other thinker at the time provided such a comprehensively innovative and far-sighted, yet internally coherent, programme for European union as this ci-devant French count.

Not that Saint-Simon was alone in his concern about European union at this time. Particularly after the defeat of Napoleon the presses poured forth a cascade of proposals, especially in Germany: Arnold Mallinckrodt, Karl Friedrich Krauss, Wilhelm von Gegl, to name a few. Saint-Simon benefited from the general interest: the pamphlet which he and Thierry rushed into print was quickly bought and enjoyed a second edition. Indeed, of all Saint-Simon's publications it was one of the most successful. But with the reading public, not the statesmen. The tsar was likely to be the most receptive of all the leaders at Vienna because he had been introduced by his tutor La Harpe to the projects of Sully and Saint-Pierre. Saint-Simon sent him a copy. But even he ignored the case which its author thought so irrefutable.

However, the interest in Saint-Simon's proposal for European unity was no mere post-war flash-in-the-pan. As Hinsley, summarising the work of A.C.F. Beales, has explained:

It was Saint-Simon who inspired most of the peace plans produced in Europe in the next generation: Pierre Leroux's *Organon des vollkommen Friedens*

(1837); Gustav d'Eichthal's *De l'Unité Européenne* (1840); Victor Considérant's *De la Politique générale et du rôle de la France en Europe* (1840); Constantin Pecqueur's *De la Paix* (1841). All these proposals involved federation – a single government – for Europe (Hinsley, p.103).

All these authors were Saint-Simonians – followers of the Master. Moreover, they not only wrote books developing his thoughts on Europe, they took a variety of opportunities to publicise them. They wrote articles in the magazines, particularly the *Globe*. In the 1850s they campaigned for a European Constituent Assembly. Then, when Napoleon III made a well-publicised speech at Auxerre in 1863, denouncing the 1815 settlement and suggesting a more integrated continent with uniform weights and measures, for instance, the Saint-Simonians were quick to broadcast the view that the essence of the imperial prospectus for European peace had already been set forth by their Master half a century before.

Yet the late Professor Beales's list as cited above does not include the most famous of all the mid-century supporters of European union who recognised their debt to Saint-Simon. Proudhon (see p.114) produced his ideas on federalism a little before the French Emperor's speech. A decade later, in 1872, Lemonnier reflected current terminology by entitling his book quite simply and boldly *Les États Unis d'Europe*. Of all the Saint-Simonians he was perhaps the most dedicated to this ideal. He also started a journal with the same title. The most famous follower of Saint-Simon was that tortured soul, Auguste Comte. He believed that the West Europeans were the *avant-garde* of humanity and would soon be capable of banishing war from their domains. He envisaged a Western Republic centred on France, Germany, Britain, Italy and Spain with the Low Countries, Scandinavia, Greece and Portugal as associates. He specified a joint navy, a common currency (based on 'the Charlemagne') and a common flag. This last would have put Joseph's coat in the shade since it was to be composed of all the member-states' national flags!

Interest in Saint-Simon's proposals for European unity declined somewhat in the 1870s. The First World War restored his relevance. His biographer, Frank Manuel, lists some half-dozen articles published in the 1920s (Manuel, p.401, nn.13 & 15). Also a new edition of the *Reorganisation* appeared in 1925.

On the other hand, if we think ourselves back to 1814, there is much in Saint-Simon's exposition that must surely have struck his readers as either naïve or implausible. Would not his view of the medieval papacy and the pacific nature of international relations during the Middle Ages have worried a medievalist as a vision distorted by rose-tinted spectacles? One wonders what his medievalist associate, Thierry, thought of these passages. Saint-Simon's view of England was similarly roseate. The likelihood of an Anglo-French federation after three-quarters of a millennium of hostility, refreshed by the bitter ideological conflict since 1793, was scarcely an immediate possibility. Furthermore, his idealistic description of the English constitution would have been read with incredulity by those who survived the mass-meeting in St Peter's Fields, Manchester, five years later.

Saint-Simon cursed the lawyer class for seizing the leadership of the French Revolution and thus blocking the emergence of the truly needed technocracy. Yet his vision of a scientific-industrial elite in a commanding political-administrative position scarcely matched reality in early nineteenth-century Europe. For where the landowning aristocracy was effectively challenged at all, the thrust to middle-class power was still exerted by his despised philosophical-legal 'priesthood' in most states.

Nor was his case for the economic obsolescence of the nation-state all that obvious. Indeed, his constant hammering home of the splendid economic achievements of Britain might have been thought an utter contradiction of his own case. The population of the British Isles in the eighteenth century, the period of her commercial and industrial 'take off', was considerably less than the populations of France, the Habsburg dominions and Russia and only a little greater than Spain's. The lesson most observers would have drawn was the advisability of overseas empire rather than continental federation.

A further complaint against Saint-Simon becomes increasingly evident as we elongate our perspective. This relates to his conception of the rights and worth of public opinion. As the nineteenth century progressed, and gave way to the twentieth, xenophobic nationalism grew in power and intensity. The uniting of 'the peoples of Europe in a single body politic while preserving for each their national independence' is presented by Saint-Simon as if it were the solution to the problem. Far from it being a *solution*, the growth of the ideology of nationalism meant that national independence was becoming the most intractable *problem* facing European federalists. The French Revolution had substituted the sovereign people for the sovereign prince. Saint-Simon scorned Henry IV for the ease with which the Grand Design assumed that 'the ambition of temporal power' could be overcome. But Saint-Simon himself underestimated the difficulty of sublimating the temporal ambitions of the European nations seeking self-determination and power. True, nationalism was a mere infant doctrine in 1814; nevertheless it had manifested itself in the German and Spanish resurgence against Napoleon.

And yet, judged from a present-day vantage-point, Saint-Simon's sagacity is thrown into much less doubt. His appeal to the Middle Ages finds an echo in the current search for principles of multiple loyalty, which led the late Professor Hedley Bull to write of the 'new medievalism' (Bull, esp. pp.264–76). Secondly, for all Britain's faults, she nevertheless appeared to many a continental during the period 1815–1945 as a steady beacon of liberty in a Europe intermittently plunged into the gloom of authoritarianism of differing intensities of darkness. Thirdly, technology has become a dominant force requiring considerable political adaptations: Saint-Simon would gladly recognise the technocratic Eurocrats of Brussels. Fourthly, it is almost impossible to read about international economic affairs today without coming across a reference to the imperative of a large domestic market, larger, that is, than the typical European nation-state. Finally, the drive towards European union in the post-1945 period, including the acceleration since the mid-1980s, would scarcely have been conceivable if it had not been congruent with the widespread popular yearning for peace in the post-war years and for closer socio-economic integration more recently.

In spite of his interest in European unity, Saint-Simon paid little attention to the theories of nationalism and federalism or to their practical implementation. By the middle of the nineteenth century, however, it was very evident that they were both highly germane to the problem of European unification. Writers during the period *c.* 1830–80 certainly gave them due attention.

On the face of it, nationalism would seem to be a force utterly antipathetic to European unity. Yet some early nineteenth-century nationalists, notably Italians, on the contrary, believed the two ideals to be not only compatible but even mutually supportive. Cattaneo, the Milanese scholar; Gioberti, briefly Piedmontese prime minister; and, above all, Mazzini advocated Italian national unification as a necessary preliminary to a United States of Europe and indeed to ultimate universal harmony. By the 1840s the term 'United States of Europe' had become common linguistic currency; whilst in 1867 Lemonnier launched his journal with that title (and it continued publication until 1914).

More than anyone else, Mazzini, part mystic, part political activist, was convinced of the extrovert quality of nationalism. He had a vision of Europe as a network of contented, republican nation-states. He wrote that 'the innate spontaneous tendencies of the peoples will replace the arbitrary divisions sanctioned by bad governments. The map of Europe will be remade. The Countries of the People will rise, defined by the voice of the free, upon the ruins of the Countries of the Kings and privileged castes. Between these Countries there will be harmony and brotherhood.' (Mazzini, p.52). Former advocates of union had placed their reliance on the conversion to pacific good sense of the established rulers. Even Saint-Simon posited a King of Europe. Mazzini, in contrast, envisaged the achievement of nationhood and European unity as perforce the outcome of popular pressure.

The corollary was the need for a popular organisation. Mazzini tried to provide this by the creation of the Young Europe movement in 1834. He had already created Young Italy; and there followed Young Germany, Young Poland, Young Switzerland and Young France. Young Europe was to provide the means of fraternal association for these republican and nationalist movements.

Mazzini attended the third Universal Peace Congress in Paris in 1849. So too did Victor Hugo. This famous French literary figure was the most passionate proponent of the idea of a United States of Europe in the mid-nineteenth century. In 1870 he ceremonially planted 'the United States of Europe oak' in the grounds of his home, Hautville House in Guernsey. It was an age of peace congresses, which Hugo most actively supported and whose objectives, he believed, could be most effectively advanced by a united Europe. Although he did not attend the Peace Congress of 1872, in the shadow of the recent Franco-Prussian War, he sent an impassioned message addressed to 'My European fellow countrymen'.

We shall have the great United States of Europe [he declared] . . . The spirit of conquest will be transfigured into the spirit of discovery; the generous brotherhood of nations will replace the ferocious brotherhood of emperors; we shall have a fatherland without boundaries, a budget without parasitism, trade without customs duties, circulation without barriers . . . (reprinted, de Rougemont, pp.279–80).

And he piles benefit upon benefit well beyond this forecast of the Common Market (including somewhat strangely, in his enthusiasm, 'forests without tigers'!).

But eloquence drafts no constitutions. It was left to more hard-headed men to investigate the potential of federal structures for Europe. We have already seen how Rousseau was attracted to the idea (pp.79–81). Nevertheless, it was not until the early 1860s that Proudhon produced the first systematic study of the federal principle – 'the alpha and omega of my politics.' (quoted, de Sainte Lorette, p.37). There were several examples to draw upon, most notably the USA, the German Confederation and Switzerland – at various stages along the tight federal to loose confederal spectrum. The Swiss, Bluntschli, offered his own country as a model for the continent as a whole in a project for a European 'Commonwealth' in which a Council and Senate would have conciliatory functions.

However, it was a Scot, James Lorimer, who, a year before Bluntschli's publication, produced 'the first attempt seriously to define the juridical form of a European federation.' (P. Renouvin, quoted, Hinsley, p.135). The key to his proposal, detailed in an article entitled 'The Final Problem in International Law', is his clear distinction between domestic affairs, the continued responsibility of state governments, and international European affairs, which were to come within the purview of the federal government. This central authority was to comprise executive, bureaucratic, legislative, judicial and military arms, biased in composition to favour the Great Powers. Power would be concentrated in a bicameral Congress with responsibility for defining the extent of federal action at the expense of individual state sovereignty.

Lorimer specifically excludes the colonial exploits of the European powers from the remit of the federal government. Yet within a few years the major European states of France, Germany, Britain and Italy were very fully occupied with imperial expansion and exploitation in Africa and eastern Asia. Perhaps that is why the last two decades of the century reveal so little interest in the possibility and need of reorganising the European continent. Aggression was being externalised. There is an echo here of Saint-Simon. For did he not write as follows in 1814? 'The surest way of maintaining peace in the Confederation will be to keep it constantly occupied beyond its own borders . . . To colonize the world with the human race . . . – such is the sort of enterprise by which the European parliament should continually keep Europe active and healthy.' (reprinted, Markham, p.49).

The issue of European unity remained an interest for academic congresses and papers. One of the most distinguished of these participants, the French professor, Anatole Leroy-Beaulieu, referred to the existence of 'an embryonic Europe which vaguely aspires to be born and which tries in a confused way to live.' (quoted, de Sainte Lorette, p.52). The delivery of this Europe assumed a renewed sense of urgency with the alarums of war which preceded the greatest of all European fratricidal conflicts to date, the Great War.

CHAPTER 6

The Shadow of the Great War

Preoccupations of the 1920s

Europe surpassed herself in concentrated carnage. Within a span of four years the Great War engulfed all but half a dozen European states. The combined populations of those non-belligerents was only some forty millions, while the casualties alone of the European combatant states reached three-quarters of that figure. The shock to the European mind was comparable to the impact of the Thirty Years War.

The shock-waves of the Great War in fact spread much wider. Because of mass mobilisation into the armed forces few families could have been totally unaffected by the war. The mood after 1918 left little doubt that the preservation of peace was a political and popular priority. The atmosphere of anxiety and the feeling of doom in the contemplation of any new major war even pervaded much of the fictional literature of the inter-war period. The development of air-power and chemical warfare in particular generated visions of armageddon. In the words of one authority on war literature, 'The Last Man theme runs through the European fiction of the nineteen-twenties . . . British, French, and German authors made the same points: that the human race must find a way of adapting itself to the new environment created by science or it will perish.' (Clarke, 1966, p.167). 'World War', the conflict might eventually come to be called, but its origins and the ferocity of the fighting were clearly centred in Europe. The mood was propitious for the revival of schemes for European unity. Penn's essay and extracts from Saint-Pierre and Rousseau were published in London at the end of the war (see Hinsley, p.380 n.91).

However, the precise issue of the unification of Europe became absorbed into more detailed discussions. These related to the causes of the continent's pernicious malady of bloody divisiveness and, by extension, various recommended treatments. We may notice four main topics which were widely debated in theory and helped shape policies of international relations in practice. One was the nature of the nation-state. Another was the efficacy of a global League of Nations. The third matter was the specific problem of Germany. And the fourth was the growing recognition of the economic causes of international instability. International peace and security, it was recognised, depended on the positive resolution of these problems. It is clear, therefore, that any realistic new proposal for European integration would perforce need to make satisfactory provision for each of these areas of concern. In order therefore to construe our text for this chapter, namely, Aristide Briand's Memorandum on European Union, it is essential to understand these issues which dominated European international relations in the 1920s. A brief discussion of each is therefore apposite.

The concept and reality of the nation-state grew in importance from the late Middle Ages, toughened and enlivened by the ideology of nationalism from the age of the French Revolution. By the time of the First World War we may discern three attitudes towards the nation-state and nationalism which we may classify as conservative, liberal and radical.

The radical may be quickly mentioned. It is the rejection of the nation-state as either a useful or a desirable political construct, a frame of mind wrought by disillusionment. Thus the English writer, Norman Angell, already famous for his *The Great Illusion* and later to become a Nobel Peace Laureate, wrote in 1914: 'Save only in a juridical sense . . . the nations which form the European community are not sovereign, not independent, not entities.' (Angell, p.xx). In a way, of course, he was right.

Yet those who thought that euthanasia was the most apt way to treat the moribund nation-state had to reckon with its continued vitality in fact. The orgies of nationalist fervour with which the outbreak of the First World War was greeted by the populations of those 'obsolete' nation-states gave the lie to any expectations of their imminent demise. Nor was the emotional appeal of the nation-state by any means exhausted by the dreadful toll it exacted in the war. Popular enthusiasm for the nation-state strengthened the hand of politicians of a conservative spirit adamant to protect the sovereignty, self-interest and glory of their states in classical nineteenth-century style. Not for them any compromise with European integrationist schemes. Fascism, on the extreme right-wing, it goes without saying, was quite incompatible with the ideal of a liberal United States of Europe. It should occasion little surprise therefore to learn that Mussolini supported a journal entitled *Anti-Pan-Europa*.

Yet mid-way between these radical and conservative views of the nation-state flowed the liberal conviction that national self-determination was the panacea for European peace. Shaped from the mid-nineteenth-century equation of nationalism with liberalism, freedom and justice, the principle of self-determination became the theoretical foundation-stone of the post-war peace treaties of Versailles and Saint-Germain with Germany and Austria respectively. That stone was laid by a politician, it must be said, with little understanding of the ethnic complexities of central Europe: Woodrow Wilson. In a speech in February 1918, he declared:

National aspirations must be respected; peoples may now be dominated and governed by their own consent. Self-determination is not a mere phrase, it is an imperative principle of action which statesmen will henceforth ignore at their peril (quoted, Macartney, pp.189–90).

The following January the US president embarked for Paris on the *George Washington*. On the voyage he started to learn from the distinguished geographer, Dr Isaiah Bowman, something of the human geography of the continent whose political boundaries he was about to redraw. That education continued in Paris and sobered his simple enthusiasm. In the event, the not so rock-solid foundation of self-determination had to be supplemented by the buttresses of Minority Treaties and League of Nations arbitration lest the edifice of the new Europe of nation-states prove as prone to damaging stresses as the old.

Thus, because the principle of national self-determination was impossible of exact implementation (let alone its denial to the Austrian, Sudeten and Danzig Germans), greater reliance had to be placed on the League of Nations to defuse international tension caused by nationalist quarrels. True, many continued until the emergence of Hitler to give lip-service to the Mazzinian creed of the compatibility of nationalism and internationalism. For instance, in 1929 the Cambridge historian Melian Stawell could write, 'Underlying this book is the conviction that a sane nationalism, when it understands itself, points the way to internationalism as its completion.' (Stawell, p.7). Those who professed this belief yet put their faith in the League were perhaps rather like the man who crossed his fingers when walking under a ladder, stating, 'I'm not superstitious; but you can't be too careful, can you?' To change the analogy, nations would live in harmony; but the League was necessary to effect constant retuning.

It has often indeed been noticed that the League resembled in both its concept and structure the schemes for European collaboration drafted in times utterly innocent of the principle of national self-determination. The political institutions, the Council and Assembly, were composed of representatives of states, not of peoples. Furthermore, the permanent members of the Council (initially Britain, France, Italy and Japan) were dominating influences. Nevertheless, although the League was a club for member states' governments, a number of its most devoted supporters were keenly aware that the times required the full engagement of public opinion in the enterprise. Most notable

of these advocates was Lord Robert Cecil. He worked most energeti-
cally in Britain to mobilise public opinion for and educate it about the
League by means of the League of Nations Union. At its height *c.*
1930 the LNU boasted a membership of a million. Cecil also attempted
the same work on an international scale through the International
Federation of League of Nations Societies.

However imperfect the League of Nations was in its principles and
operation, it dominated the hopes of the 1920s for the achievement of
conciliatory behaviour among the states of the world and Europe in
particular. Nevertheless, it was not, nor was ever intended to be, a
form of European collaboration. Some early devisers of plans could
write interchangeably about Christendom or the world when, in effect,
they meant Europe. This was no longer so. The League had pretensions of being a global organisation and had to try to act as such.
Indeed, the early illusions about its efficacy were eventually broken
on its abject failure to handle extra-European crises, namely, Manchu-
ria and Abyssinia. Even as a forum for the resolution of European
quarrels it suffered the grave omissions of Germany and the Soviet
Union initially. Germany was in membership in fact for a mere seven
years.

And yet Germany remained, even after defeat and in truth in some
measure because of it, the greatest threat to European peace. The
post-war settlement rankled, partly because of territorial loss and
the prohibition of *Anschluss* with Austria and partly because of the
attribution of blame for the war to 'Germany and her allies' in the so-
called war-guilt clause 231 of the Treaty of Versailles. Hitler latched
on to these causes of national humiliation and exploited them for all
his worth from the very earliest days of his political agitation. He
used the passivity of the government in face of the 'unjust' treaty to
brand them as unpatriotic cowards. He declaimed in *Mein Kampf*:

How much might have been made out of the Treaty of Versailles! Each point
of it might have been burnt into the brains and feelings of the nation, till
finally the common shame and the common hatred would have become a sea
of flaming fire in the minds of sixty millions of men and women (Hitler, p.249).

Much of Germany did become inflamed and Hitler provided most of
the heat for ignition.

Now if Germany was to be bent on a policy of revision (as of course
she was under Hitler), then she would become once again a threat to
the peace and stability of Europe. This threat was felt most keenly by
France. After all, she had suffered bitter defeat at the hands of the
Germans in 1870–71 and five and a half million casualties in 1914–18.
Three options were open to her statesmen. The first was to ensure the
permanent emasculation of Germany. The second was to negotiate
international guarantees of mutual assistance against a resurgent

Germany. The third was to conciliate and tame this seemingly feral nation.

No Frenchman had the two German invasions of his country more deeply etched into his consciousness than Clemenceau. As leader of his country's delegation at the Paris peace negotiations he fought with the ferocity of 'the Tiger', his nickname, to ensure that punitive terms were imposed upon Germany. This was no easy task. Indeed, a fearful crisis occurred in May–June 1919; the British prime minister, Lloyd George, urged a watering down of the terms in case the Germans refused to sign and their country in the ensuing confusion be seized by the forces of Bolshevism. Clemenceau, at the end of his tether, nevertheless tried to stand firm, declaring, 'We know the Germans better than you, our concessions will only encourage their resistance while depriving our own peoples of their rights. We do not have to beg for victory.' (reprinted, Lederer, p.35). During the 1920s this hard policy was pursued by Poincaré, who was prime minister for much of the decade – a man whom Lloyd George described with unfair acidity as 'narrow and vindictive' compared with 'the more sagacious and far-sighted Clemenceau.' (quoted, Hampden Jackson, p.223).

Clemenceau had in fact been forced to make considerable concessions for which many in France never forgave him. Most notable was his retreat on the demand that the Rhineland should be permanently separated from Germany. Wilson and Lloyd George wrung from him this reluctant acquiescence in return for a guarantee. This was the promise of immediate military assistance from the USA and Britain in the event of any future German attack on France. But the Americans did not ratify the treaty and reneged on the commitment made by their president. The British consequently felt released from their obligation. As a result all that was left to the French of their policy of mutual guarantee was the generalised League policy of 'collective security', that is, the altruistic idea that all members would come to the aid of any victim of aggression.

The third option was conciliation or appeasement in the pre-Munich sense of the term. Germany had been made a pariah nation, forced to wear the badge of war-guilt in the form of reparations and exclusion from the comity of nations. Perhaps this was an unrealistic, even counter-productive policy? Perhaps it was impossible to keep Germany in a permanent condition of suppression and perhaps any attempt would only lead to a festering determination for revenge? It was Aristide Briand, French Foreign Minister for most of the 1920s, who came to express these concerns most eloquently and to attempt the alternative policy of reintegrating Germany into the international system (see pp.130–1).

The priorities of Poincaré and Briand were thus at opposite ends of the German-policy spectrum. Policy, in consequence, oscillated between the wielding of the stick and the proffering of the carrot.

Two notable events within the space of just over two years exemplify these different approaches: the French occupation of the Ruhr in January 1923 and the signature of the Locarno Agreements in October 1925. The occasion of the first event was the declaration by the Reparations Commission that Germany had defaulted on her coal deliveries. The Commission recommended occupation of the Ruhr. French right-wing opinion clamoured for such action; and a somewhat uncharacteristically reluctant Plaza Toro Poincaré led from behind to implement the occupation. The action aroused passionate resentment in the Ruhr valley and in Germany generally.

In 1925, with Poincaré temporarily out of office, the evacuation of French troops from the Ruhr began. Briand had become Foreign Minister and the policy of 'movement' replaced the policy of 'the established order'. Briand's friendly and patient diplomacy was rewarded by the conclusion of a treaty at the small Swiss town of Locarno. In fact the treaty contained few really concrete achievements and Briand was criticised for lowering France's guard. Its importance lay in 'the spirit of Locarno', the mood of reconciliation which Briand created with his German like-minded opposite number, Stresemann. (They shared the 1926 Nobel Peace Prize.) To seal the détente Germany was admitted to the League of Nations the following year. Briand summed up this new policy by urging, 'Away with rifles, machine guns and cannons. Make way for conciliation, arbitration and peace.' (quoted, Albrecht-Carrié, p.220). Four years later, in 1930, the Young Plan finally resolved the vexed problem of reparations and French troops evacuated the Rhineland, which they had occupied since 1919. In the words of Alfred Cobban, 'The greatest difficulty [in the way of a peaceful international order], the fog of reparations which had spread like a miasma over the international scene, seemed at last to be dissipated.' (Cobban, 1957–65, vol.3, p.136).

Although historians are now fully alert to the significance of economic factors in explaining international relations, probably at no period before the 1920s were statesmen completely aware of their impact.

The decision to demand reparations from Germany in compensation for the effects of the war suffered by the Allies had considerable international ramifications. It led to the absurd monetary merry-go-round whereby the USA lent funds to Germany so that she could pay her reparations to the west European allies so that they could pay back to the USA the debts they had run up to her during the war. Scarcely a recipe for a sound international economic system. Secondly, many came to believe that Germany would never pay the required amount, especially as the peace treaties inhibited rather than fostered the economic rehabilitation of Central Europe. It was a view given considerable publicity and cogency by John Maynard Keynes in a brilliant and controversial book. One authority on inter-war Europe has described its importance in the following terms: 'Perhaps no book since the Koran had had a greater influence than *The Economic Conse-quences of the Peace*' (Robertson, p.8).

Apart from the distorting effects of the reparations payments on the German and international economies, about which there is still interpretive controversy, there also developed the psychological prob-lem of a guilt complex regarding the treatment of Germany, about which there can be no doubt. This complex arose from the conviction that Germany should be treated with more consideration because the Versailles Settlement was, in Keynes's language, a 'Carthaginian' peace. Many totally rejected any notion that, as it were, 'Germania delenda est'.

The issue of reparations certainly dominated French foreign policy in the 1920s. The whole question of reparations was bound up in the eyes of many in France with the security of their own country against possible further Teutonic aggression. The USA was isolationist; Brit-ain was uncertain if not downright perfidious. Treaties with the Little Entente of Central European states in the mid-1920s provided some safety in the east; André Maginot's line, more concrete defence in the west. But the transfer of German wealth to France was considered at least by the nationalist right, to be the most secure form of insurance in the circumstances.

International economic relations, not just German reparations, gen-erated worry and continual meetings of statesmen. Attempts to lower tariff barriers were constant agenda items. The massive inflation in Germany in 1923 and the Great Crash of 1929 punctuated the regular business with the drama of crisis.

The dominance of economic problems may be illustrated by the World Economic Conference of 1927 – an event then without pre-cedent. The League of Nations convened this three-week gathering. One thousand businessmen and economists journeyed from fifty coun-tries to Geneva.

Rising Nazism in Germany, the virtually universal mounting unem-ployment of the depression and the general gloom of despondency rendered 1931, in Arnold Toynbee's judgment, '*annus terribilis*' (see Marks, p.114). The following year Briand died – the man who more than any other statesman passionately believed in the imperative need for pan-European co-operation for peace. The 1920s, the age of eager hope, or naïve illusion if you wish, were at an end.

The federal and pan-European movements

Although the First World War was a clear watershed in European history, there had been premonitions of conflict, forebodings of arma-geddon, in the late nineteenth century. These fears served to give a fillip to the desire for a federal framework for Europe.

Imaginative writers caught the mood. Nietzsche, who died at the very turn of the century, wrote of the trends to European integration with prophetic lucidity:

What matters is the One Europe, and I see it being prepared slowly and hesitantly. All the vast and profound minds of this century were engaged in the work of preparing, working out and anticipating a new synthesis: the European of the future . . . the small states of Europe – I mean all our present empires and states – will become economically untenable, within a short time, by reason of the absolute tendency of industry and commerce to become bigger and bigger, crossing natural boundaries and becoming world wide (quoted, de Rougemont, pp.329–30n).

Of a younger generation, Jules Romains, French poet, dramatist and novelist, remained a convinced European from the time of the First World War to that of the Common Market. 'Europe, my country of which I wished to sing', he wrote in 1915 (quoted, de Rougemont, p.336).

In terms of political thinking and pressure groups the early years of the century witnessed a resuscitation of federal schemes for Europe in Britain. By 1910 the Quakers were supporting the idea of a United States of Europe and, prompted by them, the British National Peace League adopted the same stance in the following year. Then in 1913 Sir Max Waechter founded the European Unity League. However, in Britain, as on the continent, the war itself strengthened the alternative idea of a looser, world organisation rather than a tightly federal continent.

By the early 1920s the concept of European unity seemed dead in the face of new political ideologies and principles of international security. In the words of that great European federalist, Count Coudenhove-Kalergi, 'The old dream of a federation of European States seemed to have disappeared and to be forgotten. The pacifists of the League of Nations were as foreign to this dream as were the fascists and communists.' (Coudenhove-Kalergi, 1962, p.6).

Yet as the 1920s wore on so the evidence accumulated that the Treaties of Versailles and Saint-Germain had by no means eased Europe's problems; nor was the League the powerful arbitrator and sustainer of peace its supporters had hoped. Both Europe's economic problems and her political difficulties consequently led to a revival of thoughts concerning European integration.

The structural economic problems related particularly to the rise of overseas competitors such as the USA, Japan and Argentina and the break-up of the coherent economy of the Danube basin. The perceived need for better industrial and commercial co-operation in the face of these problems led to a number of responses (see Brugmans, pp.43–9).

The felt need for more international economic co-operation led as early as 1922 to the creation in Paris of an Economic and Customs Action Committee. Four years later a European Economic and Customs Union was also set up in Paris to study technical economic problems. It was copied in many other European cities. The slogan at the time was 'customs disarmament'. Industrialists also organised themselves into cartels to co-ordinate the production and pricing of their products. The most remarkable of these was the steel cartel, which by 1927 embraced the industries of Austria, Belgium, Czechoslovakia, France, Germany, Hungary, Luxembourg and the Saar. Its headquarters was in Luxembourg, run by Emil Mayrisch. Although the prime objective of the cartel was the maximisation of profit, some of its personnel had more idealistic intentions. These included Mayrisch himself, a convinced European. He and those of like mind started to contemplate the advantages of continent-wide mass-production, mass-markets and tariff-free trade – in short, a European Economic Community.

In the meantime there had been created the Pan-European Movement (see pp.125–9). As well as being a political movement, it established Economic Councils in Paris and Berlin. The leading light in this activity was Louis Loucheur, described by Sir Denis Brogan as 'the most eminent and richest of businessmen-politicians in France' (Brogan, p.593). In 1926 he published *Problèmes de la Co-opération economique internationale*, in which in the words of one authority, he formulated 'the proposal for European cartels for coal, steel and wheat "organised by governments in the light of the common interest and not just for the selfishness of the producers", the first forerunner of what would become, much later, the Schuman Plan and the Green Plan.' (Voyenne, p.172). Also in France Francis Delaisi published a book in 1932 entitled *Les Contradictions du Monde Moderne*, in which, by means of statistical evidence, he demonstrated the inutility of economic nationalism. Industrialists and financiers welcomed these arguments. The workers' movements, by and large, did not. For example, when the Dutchman Edo Fimmen of the International Federation of Transport Workers wrote *Labour's Alternative: The United States of Europe or Europe Limited* in 1934, it was received with little enthusiasm by trade unionists.

A veritable torrent of publications advocating European political union poured from the presses at this time, both journal articles and books. To give a few examples: Gaston Riou, active in the European Economic and Customs Union, wrote, *Europe, Ma Patrie* (1928) and *S'unir ou mourir* (1929); Count Sforza, *Les Etats-Unis d'Europe* (1929); Bertrand de Jouvenel, *Vers les Etats-Unis d'Europe* (1930); Edouard Herriot, *Europe* (1930).

The problem was to harness all this interest in a movement to exert leverage on governments. 'The most spectacular [organisation] in favour of united Europe' (Brugmans, p.49) was Count Richard Coudenhove-Kalergi's Pan-European Movement. This extraordinarily cosmopolitan individual devoted his adult life zealously to the cause of European union. His father, a count and diplomat of the Austro-

Hungarian Empire, was descended from a family which had intermarried across the length and breadth of Europe; but he went one better and married a Japanese girl. The founder of the Pan-European Movement spent his childhood in his father's Bohemian castle in a most international social milieu. Even the Armenian butler spoke Turkish to his master, Japanese to his mistress and a faulty German to the children!

The problems facing Europe immediately after the First World War and the evident weakness of the League of Nations convinced the young Coudenhove-Kalergi that a form of European unity was essential. In 1921, by now a twenty-six-year-old Czech citizen, he secured an interview with his President, Thomas Masaryk. He was interested and encouraging, but refused to lead a political movement to this end. The following year, resolved to act on his own initiative, Coudenhove-Kalergi published his programme as a newspaper article in Vienna and Berlin. (The text may be found in Coudenhove-Kalergi, 1962, pp.31–5.) He chose the term 'Pan-European Union' so as deliberately to avoid giving the impression that he wished to promote a tight federal structure.

In 1923 he wrote a book entitled *Paneuropa*, expanding his ideas. It was translated into numerous languages and became the main vehicle for propagating the message. In the Foreword to this work he defined his concept as 'self-help through the consolidation of Europe into an ad hoc politico-economic federation.' (Coudenhove-Kalergi, 1926, p.xv). (He thus incidentally used the very term 'federation' which he eschewed in the name of his movement.) The two main influences on the shaping of the proposals in the book seem to be his admiration for the currently evolving Pan-American Union and his own fascination with geographical and historical patterns, analogies and classifications. For example, central to his analysis is the proposition that the world is divided into 'five planetary fields of force', namely, the American, British, Russian, Eastern Asiatic and European (Coudenhove-Kalergi, 1926, pp.14–16). By 'British' he means, naturally, the British Empire, then at its height in terms of size and economic collaboration.

However, whereas he perceives steady progress towards tighter integration in the Americas, in the USSR and in the British Empire, he foresees in contrast a cataclysmic renewal of fratricidal war in Europe – unless a pan-European union is achieved. The composition of such a union is a matter which he tackles early on. The two problem European states are Russia and Britain. Both are excluded. The grounds for excluding the Soviet Union are readily presented: she is demographically too large and diverse, and ideologically too antipathetic to the democratic foundations upon which Pan-Europe must be built. But if the USSR was the 'northern' federal empire in its own right because of its size and heterogeneity, so much more separate from Europe was the British Empire. The focal-point of this 'southern'

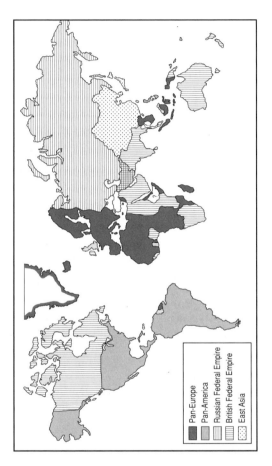

Map 6   Coudenhove-Kalergi's Scheme

empire was the Indian Ocean, around which clustered the imperial possessions of South Africa, Australia and the culturally non-European Indian subcontinent. Yet Coudenhove-Kalergi was uncomfortable about Britain's exclusion, since she has clear historical and cultural ties with Europe and has certainly been committed to the pan-European ideals of democracy and peace. He therefore makes a suggestion, interesting in the light of events in the 1960s and 1970s, that 'As soon as England and Ireland feel themselves drawn to Europe more strongly than to their overseas dominions, the way to Pan-Europe must lie open to them . . . ' (Coudenhove-Kalergi, 1926, p.42). In the meantime 'Pan-Europe must constitute itself *without* England, but not *against* England.' (Coudenhove-Kalergi, 1926, p.41). He looked forward to an entente between the two closely related groupings. Certainly Britain posed no military threat to Pan-Europe, unlike the Soviet Union, from which direction Coudenhove-Kalergi feared an imminent onslaught.

The book, indeed, contains much commentary on the inter-war international scene. What, however, is of primary interest for us is Coudenhove-Kalergi's programme for the achievement of Pan-European union. He recommends a four-stage process: the calling of a Pan-European Conference of the representatives of the twenty-six European states; the conclusion of treaties for the compulsory settlement of intra-European disputes by arbitration; the construction of a customs union; and, finally, the drafting of a federal constitution, about which crucial matter the Count is exceedingly vague. Practicalities no doubt bored the weaver of neat patterns. He was more interested, for example, in proposing the exchange of British West African colonies for the Italian and Portuguese possessions on the Indian Ocean littoral for the sake of less messy cartography and more efficient exploitation of the African continent.

The book ends with a rallying-cry. All who accept his message must assist in creating the appropriate atmosphere for its realisation:

Bridges of understanding, of common interest, and of friendship must be thrown from people to people, from industry to industry, from guild to guild, from literature to literature. The Pan-European sense of solidarity, the European sense of patriotism must establish itself as the crown and complement of the national sentiment (Coudenhove-Kalergi, 1926, p.190–1).

Coudenhove-Kalergi worked hard to expand his movement. He failed to create a mass following. Nevertheless, he was exceptionally successful in recruiting men of influence, both politicians and leading figures in the European economy. Churchill was impressed and later wrote:

So when the idea of the United States of Europe drifted off upon the wind and came in contact with the immense accumulation of muddle, waste, particularism and prejudice which had long lain piled up in the European garden, it became quite evident that a new series of events had opened.

The resuscitation of the Pan-European idea is largely identified with Count Coudenhove-Kalergi (reprinted, Coudenhove-Kalergi, 1943, p.197).

Distinguished figures in the arts lent their support, for example, Thomas Mann, Richard Strauss, Ortega y Gasset, Paul Valéry. Of the politicians in the 1920s, the Germans Stresemann and Schacht were impressed. Stresemann noted in his diary, 'Whatever one may think of him, in any case he is a man of extraordinary knowledge and great energy. I am convinced that he is going to play a great role.' (quoted, Coudenhove-Kalergi, 1943, p.94). Schacht, the financial expert, was keen on the idea of what we would today term European Monetary Union. Also, the young Burgomaster of Cologne was an enthusiastic adherent. This was Dr Konrad Adenauer, who thus provides an interesting link across the years with the creation of the Common Market. In Britain, Leo Amery, the Colonial Secretary, was conspicuous for his enthusiasm in an insular atmosphere of suspicious apathy. In France, Caillaux and Herriot were early supporters. In January 1925, addressing the Chamber of Deputies, Edouard Herriot, now briefly prime minister, declared:

My greatest wish is to see one day the United States of Europe become a reality. And if I have been working with so much courage – I am entitled to say so, – for the League of Nations, I have done so because I have considered this great institution a rough draft of the United States of Europe (quoted, Coudenhove-Kalergi, 1943, p.100).

In Italy the movement had the support of Count Sforza. The Austrian Chancellor, Dr Seipel was also keen and provided the movement with a headquarters in the Hofburg, the former imperial palace in Vienna. And by no means least significantly the movement was underpinned financially by banker friends of Rothschild, most notably Max Warburg of Hamburg.

The first Pan-European Congress, held in 1926, revealed Coudenhove-Kalergi's consciousness of the tradition in which he was working; the hall was decked with large portraits of Comenius, Saint-Pierre, Kant, Nietzsche, Mazzini, Napoleon and Victor Hugo. It must be said, however, that his knowledge of some of his precursors was a little shaky. In his autobiography he describes Penn as having 'given years of his life to the idea of a United States of Europe' (Coudenhove-Kalergi, 1943, p.71); while in a later essay he states that Saint-Pierre worked 'the whole of his life for the realisation of European unity.' (Coudenhove-Kalergi, 1962, p.4). Readers who have assiduously perused Chapters 3 and 4 of the present work will recognise how misleadingly exaggerated those statements are.

Our primary interest in this chapter is in the initiative Aristide

1920 Briand who try to act

Briand took in 1929–30 to try to achieve a European union. It is therefore relevant to ask what his relationship was with the Pan-European Movement. Coudenhove-Kalergi first met the French Foreign Minister early in 1926, a few months after Briand's popular conclusion of the Locarno agreements. In his characteristically effusive way Coudenhove-Kalergi recorded that 'When I met him in his elegant study in the Quai d'Orsay I had the immediate conviction that here was the man I had been seeking for years' (Coudenhove-Kalergi, 1943, p.116): that is, the statesman to effect the Pan-European ideal. The count records that when he took his leave Briand urged him, 'Go ahead, quick, quick, quick.' (Coudenhove-Kalergi, 1943, p.117).

The following year the Central Council of the Pan-European Union met in Paris. Briand was friendly and encouraging and accepted the honorary presidency of the Central Council. The count seems to have had high hopes of the effect this would have for his movement, but was disappointed by what he considered the Frenchman's dilatoriness in pressing forward with specific proposals. In turn, as Briand tentatively prepared his ground, Coudenhove-Kalergi claims that his movement gave crucial assistance by helping to swing business and industry in favour of continental integration. As a result, so he argued,

a number of nationalist papers, in Germany and France, owned or controlled by industrial groups, suddenly favored the idea of Pan-European union; thus they paved the way towards Briand's political initiative which would have been impossible in the face of their combined opposition (Coudenhove-Kalergi, 1943, p.124).

We must, of course, recognise that Coudenhove-Kalergi's purpose in his writings was to publicise his ideas and movement and show them in the best light. Perhaps a more balanced view may be derived from a reading of the American scholar, Albrecht-Carrié. Referring to the exclusion of Britain and Ireland from the Pan-Europe scheme, he has written:

But another body, also private, that called itself European Co-operation, would have brought in the British Isles; this second organization had the endorsement of the French Foreign Minister, Briand.

He sums up Coudenhove-Kalergi's importance by asserting simply that he 'served the function of keeping the idea [of Pan-Europe] alive and of carrying on educative propaganda.' (Albrecht-Carrié, p.222).

But if anyone had both the inclination and opportunity to present and secure acceptance of a scheme for European integration it was Aristide Briand. In 1929 he judged the moment ripe for his Project for European Union.

Briand's Memorandum

A stocky, hunched figure with a generously proportioned walrus moustache, below which often depended a limp cigarette: such is the image of Aristide Briand at the height of his fame in the 1920s. In the long history of schemes for European union he was the first man in a position to ensure that his plan was officially considered by representatives of the states involved. Who was this man?

Aristide Briand was a Vendéean, born in Nantes, raised in Saint-Nazaire, of a family which claimed descent from the famous peasant guerrilla leader of the 1790s, Jean Chouan. At school he was not an assiduous scholar; and a reputation for improvising on an insecure base of shallow knowledge dogged him into adult life, encapsulated by the bitter oxymoronic quip of Jean Jaurès: 'He has an encyclopedic ignorance.' (quoted, Oudin, p.23). Political wits compared him to his rival by putting it about that Poincaré knew everything and understood nothing and Briand knew nothing and understood everything. Yet, after brief careers in journalism and law, he made a great success of his life in politics. Epitomising the stable instability of the Third Republic (if one may continue the oxymoron style), he was a minister twenty-five times and formed eleven ministries himself as prime minister. He was Foreign Minister twelve times including the solid period 1925–32.

The interpretation of Briand's character is clouded by the verbal acidity of his numerous political enemies. How much credence should one give to this precipitation of hatred? He was loathed by many Socialists as a renegade from their party – hence the comment already quoted from Jaurès. He was despised by the nationalists both during the First World War and after for commending an accommodation with Germany. Maurras called him a guttersnipe; and when he offered Clemenceau a place in his cabinet in 1915, the invitation was rejected with the scornful question, 'Do you think that a thoroughbred can go into harness with a toad?' (quoted, Hampden Jackson, p.231). It is particularly difficult to know whether his failure to take decisive actions on occasion was the result of culpable laxness or a subtle biding of his time. Naturally his opponents favoured the first of these explanations.

What is clear is that his desire for European peace was genuine and that he brought to the task of trying to consolidate this a conciliatory personality, a persuasive conversational style and formidable oratorical powers. The diplomat Wladimir d'Ormesson described him as 'of the people and of the élite. He is aristocratic and bohemian, but he is not bourgeois.' (quoted, Oudin, p.14). He thus had great flexibility in both social contacts and negotiations. More poetically Coudenhove-Kalergi saw him as 'a highbred Persian cat, graceful, keen, and shrewd.' (Coudenhove-Kalergi, 1943, p.116). Briand's fame as an orator was universal. A recent biographer has described this talent in the following way: 'His voice, at the same time strong and pleasing, with the modulations of a cello, it was said, fascinated his audiences.' (Oudin, p.17).

The carnage of the First World War sickened Briand, who had borne the burdens of premiership from 1915 to 1917. Gradually he became determined to devote his energies to the preservation of peace in Europe so that a renewal of such senseless slaughter might be avoided. Louise Weiss, who much later became a member of the European Parliament, said in 1922, 'I saw Aristide Briand form his character as a pilgrim of Peace,' (quoted, Oudin, p.442). Moreover, he soon grasped the idea that if further European wars were to be avoided, then some form of union was essential.

Throughout the decade 1921–30 Briand tried with persistent flexibility to consolidate the peace of Europe, engineering so many diplomatic agreements that the distinguished French jurist Renée Cassin has dubbed him a 'pactomaniac' (Elisha, p.15)! He sought to use every opportunity to collaborate with Britain, restore Germany to the community of nations and strengthen the League of Nations. Alternatively, one may conceive his policy as a concentric structure: to ensure French security, European peace and world harmony.

The story of Briand's evolving ambition for a European union may be conveniently started in November 1921 when he discussed with the British prime minister, Lloyd George, the agenda for the forthcoming conference at Cannes. Each agreed to consider the other's priorities. In the words of Briand's biographer, Suarez,

Thus was born the idea of a vast system of European economic agreement which would have as its principal goal the maintenance of peace, the reconstruction of Europe and the limitation of national armaments (quoted, Hermans, p.13).

But Briand had little parliamentary support for his scheme and he was forced to resign. At the same time he let fall a remark which showed that his concern for European integration was also born of broad geopolitical worries: 'We are soon going to find ourselves hemmed in by two formidable powers, the United States and Russia. You see that the making of a United States of Europe is indispensible.' (quoted, Hermans, p.31).

From 1924 Briand pursued his policy of international conciliation at Geneva where, in that year, he became his country's representative at the League. In 1925 he achieved his great triumph of the Locarno agreements. He spoke with optimism and confidence about the new international regime they betokened. 'We spoke European,' he said. 'It is a language that must be learned well.' (quoted, Oudin, p.439). All were negotiating, he declared, with the interests of Europe, not just their own countries, at heart.

One of the results of Locarno was the admission of Germany to the League of Nations. Speaking on that occasion in the Assembly, Briand suggested that international society was moving away from the path of conflict and dared to look to a more peaceful future. He predicted that:

. . . if Europe recovers its economic and moral equilibrium, if the people are aware that they have security, they will be able to shake off from their shoulders the heavy burdens which worrying about war imposes; they will be able to collaborate for the betterment of their conditions; they will at last create a European spirit (quoted, Hermans, pp.32–3).

Plenty of people were worried about war, economic problems and the German question. What Briand was trying to devise was a coherent pattern embracing all these concerns by a concept of European integration in the place of inflamed national passions and *amour-propre*.

Nevertheless, was he naïve in placing his reliance on pacts? None of his achievements has been more criticised in this respect than the Treaty of Paris of 1928, the Briand-Kellogg Pact, jointly produced with the American Secretary of State. In effect, the signatories committed themselves to the proposition that war is evil. For Briand, however, there was a more prosaic motive – the engagement of the USA in the peace-keeping system. A fortnight after its signature he made a speech at the League of Nations in which he declared that the League had been essential for creating the atmosphere that had made Locarno and the Treaty of Paris possible. He was a staunch believer in the League. He would work whenever possible through its agency. But of course, the USA was not a member.

Indeed, the more Briand contemplated the League, for all his deep commitment to it, the more he was conscious of its weaknesses. At the same time, the amelioration of Franco-German relations was proceeding apace with agreements on reparations and the evacuation of the Rhineland. By 1929 he had therefore come to the conclusions that the need to strengthen the League was urgent while the atmosphere of amity in Europe rendered further collaboration possible. The two considerations converged in his proposal for a European regional union within the framework of the League of Nations. In the words of his biographer, Georges Suarez:

Briand had understood that a certain paralysis was born of the very universality of the assembly: that specific attention given to European questions, and essential and limited action concentrated on the spot could lead to a revival of the League of Nations, and with it hopes of peace (Suarez, p.325).

It should be noted that the League context for his scheme was not only consistent with his faith in the quasi-world body, it was also specifically provided for in the Covenant: Article 21 declared that

nothing in its terms should 'impair the validity of regional understandings for the maintenance of peace.'

It is evident that, after the conclusion of the Briand-Kellogg Pact,
Briand's mind was concentrating on the idea of European union. It
may well be that he was influenced in these thoughts by enthusiasts
such as his friend Louis Loucheur and Coudenhove-Kalergi. However,
we must remember that on the significant issue of Britain's role the
French minister and the Czech count drew utterly opposing conclusions. However, it is useful to record Coudenhove-Kalergi's report
of a conversation in the autumn of 1928: 'He told me that he intended
before long to submit to the League of Nations a suggestion concerning
Pan-Europe . . . Nobody knew of his plans except his closest friend
and collaborator Alexis Léger.' (Coudenhove-Kalergi, 1943, p.127. For
Léger, see p.134). Then, that winter, while journeying through Switzerland, Briand spoke to his travelling-companion, the journalist, Jules
Sauerwein:

These are the old Swiss cantons . . . which are the pillars of the Helvetic
Confederation. Confederation! That is the word that must serve as our beacon.
A European confederation would be the true way of assuring peace. The
League of Nations is too vast and feeble. The Locarno treaties are too restricted
and directly linked to the bad peace treaties of 1919. But Europe! The 27
European States united in the economic, customs and military spheres, that
is where there would be safety (quoted, Brugmans, pp.53–4).

The following June finds Briand in Madrid at a meeting of the League
Council. There he sounded out some of his colleagues, especially Stresemann, about the desirability of going public on the issue. The next
month the European press commented on the news that Briand had
the intention of raising the matter at the next session of the League
Assembly. At the same time, Briand became Prime Minister,
announced in the Chamber of Deputies that he had been considering
taking the initiative on the question of European union for four years,
and asked for their support.

On Thursday 5 September 1929 Briand made his statement in the
League Assembly. He incorporated his proposal in a response to the
Belgian delegate's speech on economic disarmament. Briand argued
that, for all their importance, economic technicalities were insufficient
to ensure economic peace. He continued by alluding to the tradition
of hopes for European unity and his own commitment to the ideals,
despite the undoubted problems union would present. Then, after a
passing reference to the League's acceptance of regional unions, he
expressed the core of his message as follows:

I think that among the peoples constituting geographical groups, like the
peoples of Europe, there should be some kind of federal union. It should be
possible for them to get in touch at any time, to confer about their interests,
to agree on joint resolutions, and to establish among themselves a bond of

solidarity which will enable them, if need be, to meet any grave emergency that may arise. That is the link, gentlemen, I want to forge (quoted, Wheeler-Bennett, p.61, incorrectly dated, 1927).

Briand foresaw the most urgent tasks for such a union to be in the economic sphere. However, he insisted that 'from the political or social point of view, the federal bond, without touching the sovereignty of any of the nations which would be able to take part in such an association, can be beneficial.' (reprinted, Suarez, p.327). He explained that he would be calling upon the representatives of the European parliaments to pursue the matter further.

Four days later, Briand invited the representatives of the other twenty-six European states to lunch with him at the Hotel des Bergues. At the end of this working lunch several decisions were made: Briand was to draw up a detailed proposal; the League representatives would commend this to their governments for study; Briand would amend his paper in the light of the consequent responses and present the revised document to the League Assembly the following year. Briand's initiative stimulated immense interest in the press and among various voluntary associations. Herriot and Coudenhove-Kalergi worked hard to ensure the maximum support for Briand.

The actual text was in fact written by Briand's *chef de cabinet*, Léger. Indeed, in Léger's collected works the document is annotated 'conceived and drafted for the French Government by Alexis Léger' (Perse, p.583. For the English text see Wheeler-Bennett, pp.61–73). It is dated 1 May 1930. It was circulated to the chancelleries of Europe on 17 May and came to be known as the Briand Memorandum. There is no doubt that the inspiration, initiative and political drive behind the Memorandum was Briand's. However, since the text and even some of the structural detail was Léger's work, it is important that we pause here to take notice of this man who was so much more than his minister's amanuensis.

Alexis Saint-Léger Léger was born in 1887 in Guadaloupe from whence his family fled to metropolitan France when that Caribbean island was devastated by an earthquake. The young Alexis showed early talent as a poet; but he studied law quite conventionally and entered the diplomatic service. Although he served his country in many distinguished appointments, he is much better known to posterity as a poet under the *nom-de-plume* of Saint-John Perse, a pseudonym he adopted while in exile in the USA in 1940. He travelled extensively throughout his life and developed an exceptionally wide range of interests.

In 1921 Léger was sent to Washington as a member of the French team attending the international Conference there. It was at this conference that Léger struck up a friendship with Briand which was to last until the latter's death. From 1925 to 1932 he was head of Briand's ministerial cabinet. In that capacity he made the detailed arrangements for both the Locarno and Paris Treaties. It was natural, therefore, that Briand should rely on Léger also for drawing up the plans for a European Union.

It is a brief document – a little over 5,000 words – and consists of an introduction and four substantive parts, each carefully divided and subdivided. The Memorandum starts by recapitulating the background events of September 1929. It then rehearses the arguments in favour of union, relating to security, the international economy, the League of Nations and cultural homogeneity. Some excerpts may help to convey the tone:

No one to-day doubts that the lack of cohesion in the grouping of the material and moral forces of Europe does in fact constitute the most serious obstacle to the development and efficiency of all political and judicial institutions on which the foundations of any universal organization of peace tend to be based . . .

Moreover, the danger of such division is still further increased by the extent of the new frontiers (more than 20,000 kilometres of Customs barriers) which the peace treaties have had to create, in order to satisfy national aspirations in Europe . . .

[It is proposed] to bring European interests into harmony under the control of, and in conformity with, the spirit of the League of Nations . . .

There are, in fact, certain questions . . . with which [the European states] are, moreover, specially competent to deal, because of their racial affinities and their common ideals of civilization.

The text is then at pains to emphasise the innocuousness of the project. It would not harm the League because it would operate within its framework. It would not harm the trade of non-members as there was no intention of erecting 'on the boundary of the whole community a stiffer [Customs] barrier' than those of the constituent states. And the adverbial phrases are piled one upon the other to emphasise the integrity of national sovereignty (emphasis added):

Lastly, it is necessary to make the proposed study *very clearly* subject to the general principle, that *in no case* and *in no degree* may the formation of the Federal Union desired by the European Governments affect *in any way* any of the sovereign rights of the States which are members of such an association.

It is even suggested that 'the very genius of each nation [will] be able to assert itself more consciously in its individual co-operation in the collective work'.

The first substantive section is entitled 'Need for a General Agreement, however Summary it may be, to affirm the Principle of the Moral Union of Europe and to place formally on Record the Existence of the Solidarity established between the States of Europe.' The idea was to start with regular meetings. Then 'the consideration of ways and means would be delegated to the European conference or to the

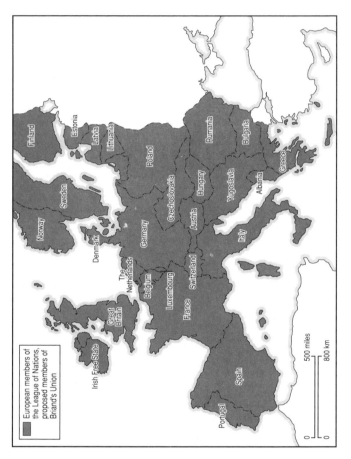

Map 7 Briand's proposed Union

permanent organization which would be called upon to constitute the living link of solidarity between European nations, and thus to incarnate the moral responsibility of the European Union.' A Pact of general principles would be drawn up, leaving detailed powers and procedures for the future. Given the League context, only members of that body would, of course, be eligible for membership.

The second section is entitled: 'Need for Machinery which will secure for the European Union the Organs Essential for the Accomplishment of its Task'. The need for representative, executive and secretarial bodies is outlined. The 'primary directing body' would be the 'European Conference' of member governments' representatives. No details are given except the provision that the chairmanship should rotate annually. A few members of the Conference would constitute the executive 'European Committee'. The Committee would have powers to invite non-members to assist their work on particular issues. The Memorandum recommended that the Committee should investigate the best ways for the Union to achieve its purposes. To economise on bureaucracy, it is suggested that the Chairman's national civil service or the League secretariat might be used.

The third section is entitled: 'Need for laying down in Advance the Essential Principles which shall determine the General Conceptions of the European Committee and guide it in the Inquiries which it makes for the Purpose of preparing the Programme of the European Organization.' Three such principles are outlined. The first is based on the proposition that 'All possibility of progress on the road to economic union [is] strictly governed by the question of security.' Political union must in consequence take precedence over economic union. In any case, so it is argued, the weaker nations need the prior security of political union for fear that the economically powerful states might wield that power for political dominance.

The second principle was to govern the style of this political co-operation:

a federation based on the idea of union and not of unity – that is to say, a federation elastic enough to respect the independence and national sovereignty of each State while guaranteeing to all the benefits of collective solidarity in the settlement of political questions affecting the destiny of the European commonwealth or that of one of its members.

This arrangement was conceived to embrace treaties of guarantees and systems of arbitration.

The third principle concerns the economic organisation of Europe. The ideal is envisaged as 'the establishment of a common market which shall raise to the maximum the standard of human well-being in all the territories of the European commonwealth.' The document proceeds to refer to 'a rational organization of production and of European exchanges' and 'the progressive liberation and the methodical simplification of the circulation of goods, capital and individuals.' The fourth part of the Memorandum is entitled: 'Advisability of reserving, either for the Next European Conference or for the Future European Committee, the Study of All Questions of Practical Application.' There follows a list of work to be undertaken under the subheadings of general economies, economic equipment, communications and transit, finance, labour, health, intellectual co-operation, inter-parliamentary relations and administration. The paper continues by emphasising the general philosophy which underlies its composition:

There is, in fact, no question of building up an ideal edifice corresponding in the abstract to all the logical needs of a vast framework of European federal machinery. On the contrary, while avoiding all abstract anticipation, it is a question of pursuing, in a practical way, the effective application of a first method of contact . . .

The Memorandum ends with a request for responses from the European governments before 15 July and leaves the reader with a peroration: 'To unite in order to live and prosper; that is the imperious necessity which henceforth confronts the nations of Europe.'

How, we may now ask, was Briand's project received? Immediately after his introductory speech in September 1929, Stresemann of Germany replied with enthusiastic support; Beneš of Czechoslovakia was complimentary with reservations; Scialoja of Italy was baldly complimentary; Henderson of Great Britain stayed silent. At the lunch on 9 September Arthur Henderson remained non-committal. Comment in the press was widespread, ranging from hostile to suspicious to apathetic. Few European newspapers were overtly favourable. The *New York Times* was not entirely opposed. Winston Churchill in the *Saturday Evening Post* gave some lukewarm support. The Beaverbrook-owned imperialist *Daily Express* in Britain surpassed itself by grandly asserting 'we are called to a future more exalted than that'! The idea even had a mixed reception in France. One can perhaps only envy the pen of the *Le Figaro* journalist who wrote, 'M. Briand in his Quai d'Orsay has dreamt all the year of his United States of Europe, hoping against hope that a dream must hatch by virtue of being a dream, as an egg is hatched by virtue of being sat upon.' (quoted, de Sainte Lorette, p.88).

Then, nine months later came the Memorandum with its deadline of two months for all twenty-six governments to commit themselves in official responses. It was the opinion of the distinguished French diplomatic historian, Pierre Rain, that they had not expected Briand to be as good as his word and were embarrassed by the position in which he placed them (see Brugmans, pp.55–6).

The replies trickled in, by no means all meeting the deadline (see Wheeler-Bennett, pp.74–9). The French government co-ordinated them. The responses made polite noises about the usefulness of the general idea, but the reservations were altogether weightier. The particular national interests of a number of states were evident in some of the expressed concerns. However, four general worries were reiterated in a number of the replies. One was the denial of the priority afforded in the Memorandum to matters of political co-operation as a precondition for tackling the economic difficulties of Europe. Secondly, there was a plea for the inclusion of all European states (i.e. the incorporation of Turkey and the Soviet Union, who were not to become members of the League until 1932 and 1934 respectively). Thirdly, worries were expressed about the relationship between the projected European union and the rest of the world. The worries were in the form both of concern that the Union might be perceived as a threat and of the need to protect overseas imperial or quasi-imperial interests. And fourthly, despite the careful wording of the Memorandum with regard to the League of Nations, many governments voiced their belief that the world body might well be impaired rather than strengthened by Briand's project.

For all the disappointment Briand must have felt on reading these documents, when the French government's gloss on them was presented to the meeting of the twenty-seven European states at Geneva on 8 September 1930, it was evident that the Quai d'Orsay had decided to put on a brave face. The French paper commended the European governments for 'their prudence and the number of listed criticisms [which], far from diminishing the confidence of the French in their ideas, prove . . . the interest brought to the problems by all the Governments.' (quoted, de Sainte Lorette, p.97). In tackling all the difficulties raised in the replies the French government were in effect saying, 'Yes, of course, you're right, this and that must be included or guarded against.' Thus was implied opposition translated into putative support.

Coudenhove-Kalergi commented, 'Of all the official answers to Briand's memorandum, Great Britain's was the most disastrous . . . It offered collaboration in such reserved terms that it spelled the complete ruin of Briand's initiative.' (Coudenhove-Kalergi, 1943, p.135). True, the Pan-Europeanist had no love for Britain. On the other hand, the attitude of the United Kingdom was bound to be crucial. She and France were, after all, the irreplaceable supports of both the League in general and Locarno in particular. Moreover, Briand knew this. He had constructed his diplomatic priorities ever since 1921 on the closest possible collaboration with France's Anglo-Saxon neighbour. Let us therefore look a little more closely at the behaviour of the British government in this matter.

We have already seen that the Foreign Secretary, Arthur Henderson, avoided any expression of encouragement at the September 1929 meetings. Then, twelve days before the circulation of the Memorandum he had a conversation with Briand. He asked for an assurance,

which he received, that the proposed union should quite unambigu-
ously not be directed against the USA (for this information and what
follows, see Woodward & Butler, Nos.185–194).

After the Memorandum was published, British ambassadors set
about gleaning the opinions of the governments of the states to which
they were accredited. From Vienna came the message that the Austrian Chancellor 'did not believe in the possibility even of an economic
European union.' Sir Horace Rumbold reported from Berlin the unac-
ceptability of a scheme which froze current frontiers. More pointedly
for British policy and our own concern here, Sir Horace asked the
German Foreign Minister what his government's position would be if
Britain did not join the proposed union. He reported the reply that 'in
that case, M. Briand's proposal would have no interest for the German
Government . . . If the idea was to come to anything England must
join.' The telegraphic note from Rome bore the message that the 'Minister of Foreign Affairs told me . . . that Italy would certainly not
accept it and he had already been authorised by Signor Mussolini to
reject it.'

At the same time a Foreign Office official prepared a memorandum
as a basis for Britain's response. The dismissive tone is registered
straight away:

The Memorandum, for which M. Briand has kept Europe waiting all these
months, is, at least at first sight, a surprising and disappointing work. It is
permeated   by   a   vague   and   puzzling   idealism   expressed   in . . .
phrases . . . which may mean a great deal or may mean nothing at all.

The paper calls the recommendation to give political union priority
over economic co-operation a 'curious proposal . . . in direct contradiction to that made by M. Briand's September speech . . . '. The author
continues by expressing fear of the almost inevitably adverse effect the
proposed union would have on the League. There follows interesting
speculation about Briand's true motive. This is thought likely in fact
to be economic rather than political, namely the protection of the
French and European economies generally against extra-European,
notably American, challenges. The document draws the blunt conclusion that this motive was 'primarily what has always been meant
by the "United States of Europe" or "Pan-Europe" . . . '.

In summary this internal memorandum recommends a sly policy:
to allow other states to take the lead in rejecting Briand's proposal so
as to preserve Britain's amicable relations with him. On 3 July the
Foreign Office armed Henderson with a briefing paper to submit to
the Cabinet. It followed much the same lines as the earlier essay. It
homes in on the economic features of the project for which Britain
had much sympathy. However, it warns that 'M. Briand's proposals
constitute a serious danger to the League. It is, therefore, I submit,

the duty of His Majesty's Government to oppose them in their present form.'

In fact, when Henderson handed Britain's response to the French Ambassador the document expressed general approval for Briand's objectives; but it hid behind the skirts of the Commonwealth excusing the reply as 'preliminary and tentative' because of the need to consult the Dominions.

This record of the formulation and exchange of views behind the scenes is an important corrective to the polite courtesies of Geneva. Briand's scheme had no real chance. Yet Britain's style smacked of the perfidy of which France has traditionally complained. A British scholar has summed up the episode effectively by writing,

But if the British reaction was tepid, that of many other European nations, excluding those in the French camp, was not dissimilar – the only real distinction being that the British gave a particularly skilful demonstration of diplomatic hypocrisy (Carlton, p.86).

In the face of these dispiriting reactions, Briand nearly resigned himself to failure at the meeting on 8 September. However, by agreeing to commend the project to the League Assembly as a scheme for 'close collaboration among European governments' rather than a 'federal bond' or 'European union', the proposal went forward on 13 September.

Briand sought with all his eloquence to salvage something from the wreckage.

This idea of the union of European nations [he said] . . . was already classified among the ideas which have been deposited in museums, before allowing them to circulate in life . . . and when it was shown, people said: That is what the poet acclaims, that is what the philosopher advocates. People will perhaps say: a politician who has lost all sense of caution has associated himself with these high minds. I hope to have a better place than in a museum (quoted, Suarez, pp.340–1).

It was a fighting speech, answering his critics. It was a pleading speech, arguing for support. It was a melancholy speech, for he must have known that his project was effectively doomed.

On 17 September the League Assembly decided to establish a Study Commission for European Union. Briand was its chairman until his death in March 1932; it then in practice soon after became ineffective. During its active life it undertook useful work for agriculture; it advanced not a centimetre the ideal of European political union so dear to Briand's heart.

A little before his death his niece asked him to pose for a famous artist. He refused; but added, 'Ah! When there is disarmament and European union – then, yes!' (quoted, Hermans, p.44).

Judgments on Briand

How, then are we to judge Briand's attempt to realise a European union? It is useful to address three questions. The first is, was the scheme so flawed and/or impractical that failure was virtually inevitable? The second is the mirror image of this, namely, was the scheme basically sound and did it founder on the rocks of unforeseen circumstances? The third question to ask concerns the importance of the Briand initiative despite his failure to secure its implementation.

One may make the compelling case that Briand's scheme was constructed on all too frail foundations. Some of his critics always felt that his policy suffered from the self-deception derived of his undoubted eloquence. Passionate in oratory, seductive in conversation, Briand's tongue tended to be immediately persuasive. But applause and verbal assent perhaps led him to believe that he had more deeply committed support for his policies than was sometimes the case. So it was with his project for European union. When it came to the sticking-point, when governments were required to place on written record precisely their support for or rejection of his memorandum, the weakness of his position became clear.

Not, of course, that he was oblivious of the likely reservations beforehand. Indeed, in trying to forestall criticisms, Briand endowed the document with an air of vagueness and contradiction. It emerged as a set of compromises in order to be all things to all men and consequently ended up being nothing to anyone. So much, as we have seen, was left to future negotiation and definition. Was it essentially a plan for economic or political collaboration? Would it preserve or impair state sovereignty? On each of these crucial issues Briand's oral and written words bore all the hallmarks of ambiguity. Let us look at these questions in turn. In the first place, while he persistently argued the primacy of political union, he knew full well that economic problems were generally considered urgent of resolution. Hence the substantive fourth part of the Memorandum for political union concentrates in fact on issues of economic and social co-operation. Or perhaps this apparent ambiguity over the primacy of political and economic collaboration was a mask for more selfish motives? This suspicion has been alluded to by the historian of the League in the following way:

> . . . it was France, economically and financially the strongest power in Europe, which demanded security before economic co-operation. The memorandum reads as though Briand's plan, conceived for the equal advantage of all, had been twisted to serve the special purposes of French policy; and the impression thus created did much to weaken the constructive impulses which his action at the Tenth Assembly had aroused (Walters, pp.431–2).

In the second place, Briand, the gallant champion of the League of

Nations, produced a scheme which most acute critics considered would have precisely the opposite effect from the vaunted enhancement of that body. The German Foreign Minister, Schubert, was scornful: Rumbold reported him as thinking 'that an organisation such as that proposed by M. Briand sitting side by side with the organisation of the League of Nations at Geneva had an element of absurdity.' (Woodward & Butler, No.188). Schuschnigg, who became Chancellor of Austria four years later, gave the matter a different slant. He subsequently wrote, 'When Briand proposed his European alliance in 1930 it became apparent that the League lacked the necessary strength.' (Schuschnigg, p.119). In other words, the fears that a European union would sap the very vitals of the League would not have been so cogent if the League had not already been so evidently weak.

But of course, the central issue for any scheme of political union is that of sovereignty. This is the third problem of ambiguity. Any effective European union would to some degree undermine national sovereignty; any undermining of national sovereignty was likely to provoke opposition to effective European union. Briand did not square this circle; he danced round it. In his League speech of September 1929 he spoke of 'some kind of federal union' and 'a bond of solidarity'. In the subsequent press conference, the first of these post-prandial formulae was dropped. The Memorandum refers variously to 'the Federal Union', 'the European Union' and 'European association' as well as the 1929 forms. When, later, Briand was taxed about this medley of terminology, this veritable thesaurus of linkages, he explained that he wanted to avoid a single, inflexible formula for fear of dividing opinion and frightening certain governments. By employing so many different terms and giving so many assurances about the rights of states, Briand was contriving to give the impression that he was proposing to make a federal omelette without breaking sovereign eggs. Confusion and suspicion were inevitable.

Finally, Briand's plan was bound to fail, it may be argued, because Britain's participation was a *sine qua non* of success and Britain was quite unprepared to involve herself in such a venture. Of the five European great powers, the Soviet Union was ineligible as outside the League system; Germany was uncertain as only just emerging from her post-war pariah status; Italy's commitment to any association was rendered suspect by Mussolini's bombastic nature. Britain alone remained as a potential buttress for the scheme with France. Yet surely the attitudes of Henderson and the Foreign Office recorded above could have been foreseen. Her continuing pretensions as the world's foremost imperial power and her assumed 'special relationship' with the USA (which Coral Bell dates from c.1895 (Bell, p.105)) meant that a tight commitment to Europe in 1930 was even more inconceivable than it was to be in 1950.

And yet Briand was anything but an utter fool. He must have judged and had some good cause to judge that some benefit could conceivably derive from launching his project at the time he chose. The Memorandum stated categorically that 'The hour has never been more propitious nor the need more urgent for the commencement of constructive effort in Europe.'

There were several very clear reasons for drawing this conclusion. The feeling of revulsion against war was still a powerful sentiment because memories of the Great War had not yet faded. However, problems still noticeably persisted so that an effective political structure within which quarrels might be peacefully resolved would seem to have obvious attractions. And in the Pan-European Movement Briand had a ready-made publicity network. At the same time the major post-war economic problems had been eased and consequent tensions relaxed sufficiently so that collaboration to resolve remaining or future quarrels in this sphere could justifiably be expected to win favour. In addition, the economic challenge of the USA, the potential economic competition from Japan and the possible ideological threat from the USSR all suggested the value of some form of European integration. Finally, Briand's own personal standing, especially after the success of Locarno, gave his proposal not insignificant weight.

Faced with failure against this background of favourable circumstances, supporters of Briand tend to emphasise the negative influences of events which Briand could not have foreseen. If only these had not occurred, his scheme would have had a chance, so the argument runs. Two of these events happened in Germany. One was the death, in October 1929, of Gustav Stresemann, worn out at the age of 51. No other German politician had comparable ability, such a close personal relationship with Briand, or was so firmly committed to pursuing his country's interests through pacific and conciliatory methods. The shift to the very contrary, aggressively nationalistic style of politics was signalled by the 1930 election results. The poll was held a week after the meeting in Geneva to discuss Briand's Memorandum and the European governments' reactions to it. The share of seats taken by the Nationalist and Nazi parties rose to a quarter of the total of the Reichstag (148 out of 577).

The electoral success of the Nazis must be understood against the growing financial nervousness in Germany. This worry was indeed becoming widespread in Europe as the effects of the Wall Street crash of October 1929 took hold and became a depression. Far from prompting a desire for Briandist economic collaboration, the crisis strengthened belief in *sauve qui peut* protectionism.

The mood of the period, 1926–29, conducive to thoughts of peace, collaboration, even federal union was transformed. That mood, whether created out of illusion or benign reality, was displaced by disillusion and a reality of harsh grimness.

But how, then, to summarise the significance of Briand's initiative in the history of schemes for European union? First and foremost it must be noted that the Memorandum broke new ground. No other scheme (with the possible partial exception of George Poděbrad's (see p.13)) had been devised by a leading European statesman in office. (Sully was in retirement when he drafted his, whatever his memoirs might suggest to the contrary.) No other scheme had been officially considered by the governments of the several European states. A number of our previous authors, it is true, had ambitions for their plans to be actively considered by statesmen at the time of their composition, most notably Saint-Simon. But none before Briand had been in a position to ensure that that happened. Briand is therefore important for pushing the idea a measurable distance towards the possibility of actual implementation.

Coudenhove-Kalergi, writing in the middle of the Second World War, declared, with characteristic hyperbole, that 'Had he succeeded, Hitler would never have become Chancellor, and the course of European events would have headed in a very different direction. Mankind owes this bold and generous man one of its greatest debts.' (Coudenhove-Kalergi, 1943, pp.137–8). We shall indeed see in the next chapter how the idea of European unity was soon to be revived during the War.

Moreover, continuity from Briand to the post-war work of constructing European union was emphasised in two key pronouncements. The first was Churchill's at Zürich in 1946, when he advised that 'We must build a kind of United States of Europe' and continued by reminding his audience that it was an idea 'which commanded the services of the famous French patriot and statesman, Aristide Briand.' (reprinted, Kitzinger, p.34). Four years later, when Robert Schuman made his Declaration which heralded the creation of the European Coal and Steel Community, he stated, 'In taking upon herself for more than twenty years the role of champion of a united Europe, France has always had as her essential aim the service of peace. Europe was not built and we had war.' (reprinted, Kitzinger, p.37). Commenting on this portion of the speech, Monnet later wrote in his down-to-earth manner, 'This was a homage to Aristide Briand, but also a farewell to rhetoric.' (Monnet, p.300).

A number of commentators have noticed the close affinity between Briand's project and the Common Market. Even the terms 'Common Market' and 'European Community' are used in the 1930 Memorandum. Jules Hermans, in his study, *L'évolution de la pensée européenne d'Aristide Briand*, has listed the remarkable number of similarities between the Briand Memorandum and the Schuman Declaration (see p.161): the motive of peace; insistence that the proposed union should not be directed against anyone else; an understanding that peoples are interdependent; the belief that national characteristics can flourish best within a union; realisation that tight federal bonding could be achieved only gradually; acceptance that Britain would be a special case; judgment that German involvement was crucial; and recognition that the world organisations (the League and UN respectively) were too weak to ensure the maintenance of peace.

Although the cataclysm of the Second World War intervened and perhaps gives the impression of a great temporal distance between them, in fact only twenty years separated the two documents. Furthermore, the events of the Second World War reinforced the considerations which weighed heavily with Briand as a result of his experience of the First. Facing similar problems, it is not surprising that Briand and Schuman produced similar proposed solutions. In addition, neither man was working in isolation. Their colleagues and Quai d'Orsay officials helped translate the broad principles into detailed proposals. Thus, as we have seen (p.134), Léger composed the Briand Memorandum. It was his successor as *directeur de cabinet* twenty years later, Bernard Clappier, who drafted the sentences which Monnet described as 'a homage to Aristide Briand'.

There can be little doubt that, consciously or subconsciously, the men who laid the foundations of the present European Community were working within the same tradition of concerns and preferred solutions as had been crystallised and broadcast in the Briand Memorandum. In particular, the heavy emphasis placed upon collaborative efforts to resolve economic problems is quintessentially twentieth-century thinking. Briand, primarily influenced by the federal concept of a United States of Europe, none the less appreciated the significance of the movement for 'customs disarmament'. There is thus also a contrast: where Briand hoped to use political union as a means to economic integration, the founding fathers of the European Community reversed the process. And that key transposition of priorities derived as much from the backgrounds and interests of the men of the 1950s as the character of all the other previous schemes reflected the experiences of their authors.

---------------- CHAPTER 7 ----------------

Towards realisation

The totalitarian challenge

There are times when history puts herself on fast forward: a short
period teems with rapidly moving significant events. The decade of
the 1940s was such an age. A mere ten years separated the Dunkirk
evacuation in May 1940 and the Schuman Declaration inaugurating
the European Community in May 1950. Extending the time-scale a
little, only twenty-five years divided the death of the disappointed
Briand in March 1932 from the signature of the Treaty of Rome
setting up the Common Market in March 1957. Because the scene is so
crowded it will not be possible to paint in the background as anything
more than an impressionistic sketch. Nor shall we be able to pick out
the minute detail of the negotiations which transformed basic ideas
into instruments of international law. Even so, the pattern of analysis
adopted in the previous chapters with less rich material is still appropriate. First we shall indicate the contextual events of European history and the factors conducive to some form of union. There will
then follow studies of two particularly crucial documents and their
principal authors. These documents are the Treaties of Paris and
Rome, sometimes referred to collectively as 'the constitution' of the
European Community. Their main authors may be taken to have been
Jean Monnet and Paul-Henri Spaak respectively. Finally, we shall
attempt a brief assessment of the style and significance of the work
of the 1950s, the decade when the two notable documents were drafted.

For the period from the death of Briand to the creation of the
European Communities in the 1950s it is illuminating to relate the
ideal of European unity to the totalitarian political styles of Hitler
and Stalin. Totalitarianism is bloated state sovereignty; federalism is
attenuated state sovereignty. The mainstream advocates of European
union in this period were federalists at heart and gained much of their

strength from their evident antipathy to the ideologically motivated policies of the dictators.

During the 1930s the idea of European unity for peace and democracy seemed impossible of realisation, not least because of the Nazi regime in Germany. Hitler's antipathy to unification by any means other than brutal conquest was confirmed by his speedy banning of Coudenhove-Kalergi's movement and books (see pp.124–9). However, interest revived especially during the period 1938–40, rather surprisingly perhaps in Britain. An organisation called Federal Union was established. Although its interests were by no means confined to Europe, two of its committee produced plans for European unity. These were by Ivor Jennings and R.W.G. Mackay – both published in 1940. The two party leaders spoke in favour. In 1939 Attlee declared, 'Europe must federate or perish' (quoted, Mackay, p.36). Churchill made several references to the idea, most notably in a world-wide broadcast in 1943 when he declared, 'We must try to make the Council of Europe, or whatever it may be called, into a really effective League . . . ' (quoted, Wistrich, p.23).

In fact, British commitment to the ideal was quite shallow. Churchill had several years before made a characteristically epigrammatic distinction: 'We are with Europe, but not of it.' (Saturday Evening Review, quoted, Coudenhove-Kalergi, 1943, p.200). Furthermore, as Professor Watt has pointed out, the federalist 'ideas did not make the crossing from intellectual "think tank" to the policy papers of the senior civil servants.' (Watt, p.393).

Many continentals were more serious, whether in governments in exile in Britain or in Resistance movements. Significantly for post-war events, influential French Socialist politicians, the most distinguished of whom were Léon Blum and André Philip, embraced the cause of European union. Italian political prisoners, most notably Ernesto Rossi and the future European Commissioner, Altiero Spinelli, drew up the Ventotene Manifesto. Their document characterised the war as a struggle between the totalitarians who seek 'the conquest of national power' and those whose aim is 'a solid international state' (quoted, Ionescu, 1972, p.6). In 1944 representatives from nine nations drew up the federalist Draft Declaration of the European Resistance Movements. All these wartime continental activities were, interestingly, much influenced by British federalist writing, a fact firmly acknowledged by Spinelli.

By the following summer the war was over, the Axis powers defeated. Yet the federalists could still not forget the totalitarian threat. European union had to be planned in the light of Stalin's motives in the east and of a possible resurgent militarism in Germany in the heart of the continent.

Not that fear of brutal ideology was the only consideration in the post-war surge of interest in European integration. Many factors, including the pressure of dedicated individuals, interacted to determine the nature of the process which has progressed intermittently since 1950. Above all, however, the coalescence of these several forces provided the necessary weight of historical pressure to undermine the inertia that had blocked the chances of success of all previous schemes.

Before embarking on a brief analysis of these factors it will be useful to provide an outline chronology of the main events as far as the Treaty of Rome of 1957, which established the European Economic Community.

In 1946 Winston Churchill, now out of office, in the course of a speech at Zürich called for the creation of 'a kind of United States of Europe'. In 1947 the economic union of the Low Countries, Benelux, was created. In the same year the US Secretary of State, George Marshall, made his proposal for a European Recovery Programme and the following year the Organisation for European Economic Co-operation (OEEC) was established as a structure within which Marshall Aid was to be administered. A number of pressure groups collaborated to organise a congress at The Hague in 1948. This led directly to the formation of the European Movement and, in the following year, to the creation of the Council of Europe. In the event the Council of Europe concentrated mainly on cultural and human rights issues. Robert Schuman unveiled the plan which came to bear his name in 1950 and the European Coal and Steel Community (ECSC) was consequently launched the next year. The period 1952–54 witnessed the attempt, ultimately abortive, to create a European Defence Community (EDC) of amalgamated armed forces. However, economic integration did move a step further in 1957 with the Treaties of Rome setting up the European Economic Community (EEC) and Euratom. With the creation of ECSC and EEC, the 'Little Europe' of the Six (West Germany, France, Italy and the Benelux countries) was established.

Let us now turn to the various factors which moulded the processes of integration. It is possible to discern some ten of these.

The first was the utter devastation of so many parts of Europe: physical destruction, economic dislocation and human demoralisation. Were the immense tasks of industrial reconstruction and the rehabilitation of homeless and potentially starving men and women to be left to the individual states or be subject to a pooling of effort and resources? United States aid was forthcoming in the form of the Marshall Programme. But it was accompanied by considerable transatlantic pressure for collaboration among the recipient states in order to render its allocation efficient. Under-Secretary of State Will Clayton, appalled by the devastation he saw, was especially persistent in this regard. As a result, OEEC was set up. Paul Hoffman, the American Economic Co-operation Administrator responsible for the scheme, tried to push the Europeans further. In October 1949 he delivered a well-publicised speech in Paris in which he made 'this considered request: That you have ready early in 1950 . . . a programme, which . . . will take Europe well along the road towards economic integration.' (reprinted, Vaughan, 1976, p.48).

This consideration of American influence has brought us to our second factor, namely the attitude of the USA towards European union. From an initial nervousness concerning the anticipated competition from an economically integrated Europe, the Truman administration came to accept its desirability. American encouragement, help, even cajoling then became a significant factor in the development of European union. Particularly famously the objections of France to the European Defence Community treaty spurred Secretary of State Foster Dulles to threaten 'an agonising reappraisal' of his government's policy and to assert 'that United States policy had, since 1946, been based on the hope that one day Western Europe would unite.' (quoted, Spaak, p.177).

One of the potent reasons for American support was the onset of the Cold War, the third factor. The US President announced the 'Truman Doctrine' in March 1947, three months before George Marshall made his speech advocating the European Recovery Programme. As tension increased through the late 1940s, so the Americans became increasingly convinced that western Europe must be transformed into a consolidated bastion against Communism. The threat of Hitlerian totalitarianism, which had concentrated minds on European federation a decade earlier, was now exchanged for the threat of Stalinist totalitarianism. In his forthright manner, the Belgian politician Paul-Henri Spaak wrote in his memoirs, 'In the last twenty years a number of Western statesmen have been dubbed . . . "fathers of European unity" . . . Not one of them deserves this title: it belongs to Stalin.' (Spaak, p.141).

In this matter of the Cold War the question of Germany, the fourth factor, became transformed. The resolution of the problem of how Germany should be reinstated into the international system had to balance three issues. One was to prevent a revival of dangerous military might. Another was to ensure that the restoration of its economy did not endanger the interests of its neighbours. The third was, within the constraints of these safeguards, to strengthen the country as a bulwark against the Communist bloc. The shift of emphasis from suspicion to incorporation was symbolised by the following rapid sequence of events. The Anglo-French Treaty of Dunkirk was signed in 1947 for collaboration against German aggression. Eight years later the Federal Republic became a member of NATO, the western military alliance. In the meantime she had also become a member of the European Coal and Steel Community. The deep sense of guilt in Germany for the Nazi era rendered her humbly co-operative in these integrative endeavours. By the 1950s the German problem, the solution to which was a *sine qua non* of European union, was thus being tackled in a positive way – at least from the West European point of view, if not from the Soviet.

Naturally the west European country which was most nervous of a revived Germany was France. The attitude of France to West European integration is the fifth factor to be considered and can usefully be compared with the attitude of Britain. (For the interpretation which follows, see Young, passim.) With eastern Europe shut out from consideration in such matters by the iron curtain and Germany and Italy still in the somewhat outcast status of defeated Axis powers, any movement towards European union in 1945 obviously depended on Britain and France. Britain's experience of remaining undefeated and unoccupied during the war and her close links with the USA and the Commonwealth predisposed her to be less enthusiastic about continental involvement than France, for whom defeat, occupation and partial collaboration with Nazism had been such traumatic experiences. On the other hand, in the three immediate post-war years Britain seemed, if anything, to be keener than France. Churchill made his speech at Zürich in 1946. The following year the United Europe Movement was launched with a mass rally at the Albert Hall. And the Foreign Secretary, Ernest Bevin, was supportive of the principle. However, from 1948 the British and French started to diverge. The French showed a zeal for union which seemed dangerously impatient and impractical to Bevin's pragmatic *festina lente* mind. Both British parties shared this hesitation. Speaking at the Council of Europe in 1950, Harold Macmillan contrasted continental and British styles of approaching such matters. 'The continental tradition,' he affirmed, 'seeks to reason *a priori* and descends, as it were from the summit to the plain; it proceeds from general principles, which it then applies to practical issues . . . The British, on the other hand, prefer to discuss problems *a posteriori*, ascending from practical experience towards the summit.' (quoted, Spaak, p.212).

Commitment to a process of unification was naturally not lightly to be undertaken. No one quite knew what would be involved. Indeed, Schuman himself said of his own plan, 'It is a leap into the unknown,' (quoted, Brugmans, p.133n). As we shall see later in the chapter, the nature and objectives of the European Community have been much disputed both by those most fully involved in its operation and by outside academic observers. Yet there would have been no point in embarking on the operation at all if it did not involve some transfer of sovereignty by the member nation-states to the central authorities. The seventh factor, then, has been the variable willingness of governments to relinquish some measure of sole control over their policies. This variation may be noted as between countries and at different points in time within any given country. Thus, Britain has been much more reluctant to participate fully in the enterprise than Belgium; and France under Mitterrand has been keener than France under de Gaulle, who wished to halt the process of unification at the stage of a 'Europe des patries'.

However, governments, most obviously in democratic states, do not operate entirely in isolation from their own domestic opinion. And so, the eighth factor was the burgeoning of pressure groups, especially in the years immediately after the Second World War. The efflorescence of such groups was quite remarkable – evidence of the widespread and passionate desire for peace through unity. We have already noticed the creation of the United European Movement as a British initiative. This was quickly followed by the French Council for United Europe. One may mention also the European League for Economic Co-operation; the Socialist Movement for the United States of Europe; the European Union of Federalists; the European Parliamentary Union. Some of these organs provided personal continuity with pre-war movements: thus the honorary president of the French Council for United Europe was Herriot (see p.128) and the European Parliamentary Union was inspired by Coudenhove-Kalergi (see pp.124–9). In the list of founders of other organisations we find the names of those who were to play leading roles in the creation of the ECSC and EEC. As examples we may cite van Zeeland in the European League for Economic Co-operation and signatory of the Treaty of Paris; and Spinelli in the European Union of Federalists and EEC Commissioner.

Apart from the Communist parties, powerful in France and Italy and whose supranational interests were focused on the Moscow-directed Cominform, most political parties contained members enthusiastic for the European ideal. However, the Christian Democratic parties tended to be particularly sympathetic. And this is our ninth factor influencing the evolution of West European unity. There was a remarkable growth of such parties after 1945 – in Holland, Belgium, Luxembourg, Switzerland, Austria, West Germany, Italy and France. In the words of one historian of the movement, 'Parties officially known as Christian Democratic, and grouping both Protestants and Catholics, held in 1955 nearly two-fifths of the seats in lower houses of parliament in these countries.' (Fogarty, p.173). Members from the different countries came to know each other through the annual Congresses of the International Union of Christian Democrats (Nouvelles Équipes Internationales or NEI). They shared a basic philosophy of defending the interests of the individual and the family against excessive interference by the state. By the same token, their reduction of the preferred role of the state rendered them particularly receptive to the idea of the melding of separate states into a larger unity, especially if that unity was informed by Christian principles. Pope Pius XII, pontiff from 1939 to 1958, explicitly supported the movement for unification.

It was no accident, then, that Christian Democrat statesmen played such leading roles in bringing the idea of European unity to at least partial fruition. Which brings us to our final factor. The influence of convinced individuals in the 1950s was so much more powerful and widespread than hitherto. It was highly significant that so many were in positions of power and authority simultaneously in different countries. In this chapter we are looking at Monnet and the drafting of the Treaty of Paris and Spaak and the drafting of the Treaty of Rome as analogous to the other authors and documents reviewed in the present volume. But these authors (if we may so call them) had the support of three particularly well-placed politicians to ensure the practical acceptance of the schemes. These were Robert Schuman, French prime minister, 1947–48 and foreign minister, 1948–52; Alcide De Gasperi, Italian prime minister, 1945–53; and Konrad Adenauer, first Chancellor of the Federal Republic of Germany, 1949–63.

These three men, it has often been noted, had much in common that predisposed them to think in a European rather than in a narrowly nationalist mode. In party terms all were Christian Democrats; and because of their supposed clerical connections they were sometimes referred to as 'the Black Front'. In terms of geographical background all were 'border men', two of them even experiencing a change of nationality status due to the fortunes of war. In their pursuit of their common goal the three became friends, conversing easily in German, their *lingua franca*.

Adenauer was born and lived much of his early life in Cologne. It is significant that the Rhinelanders were, generally, Francophile and anti-Prussian. Reflecting this attitude, in December 1923 Adenauer, by now Chief Burgomaster of Cologne, gave a telling interview to a Paris newspaper. He suggested that the secession of the Rhineland from Prussia (of which it was part in the Weimar federal structure) might be necessary for the sake of peace. Later rumours went as far as to suggest that he harboured the ambition during the Weimar period of leading a separatist West German state. These allegations were never in fact proved even by a Gestapo investigation. Be that as it may, Adenauer was anything but a diehard German nationalist.

One other feature of Adenauer's thinking in the 1920s is especially germane to our interests here. He urged the advantages of linking the coal and steel industries of the region. He went so far as to write to the French prime minister along these lines:

The Rhenish-Westphalian Lorraine and Luxembourg industry has been created and has grown as a united economic organism. If we succeed ... to form common economic interests between the peoples of the federal state [i.e. his proposed state created by seceding from Prussia] and France through a reciprocal interweaving of these industries, this federal state would exercise its influence in Germany even more strongly in the sense of peaceful co-operation with France ... (quoted, Mowat, p.18).

He revived this idea in 1945.

De Gasperi was in his late thirties before he became an Italian citizen. He was born in the Trentino province of the Austro-Hungarian Empire and sat for several years in the Austrian parliament. The transference of this '*Italia irredenta*' after the First World War led him to enter Italian politics. Throughout the whole of his political life De Gasperi espoused the cause of peace and internationalism. During the ascendancy of Mussolini it was difficult, if not positively dangerous, to attempt to advance these ideals. Nevertheless, De Gasperi managed to express his support for the Pan-Europe movement and in 1943 wrote an anonymous article in a Vatican journal advocating European unity.

The third of our trio, Robert Schuman, was still more cosmopolitan. But because he played such a central role in conceiving the Treaty of Paris itself, it will be more convenient to leave consideration of him to the next section of this chapter (see pp.159–60).

All three retained interest and sustained activity in the European ideal to the end of their lives. De Gasperi died in 1954. Schuman was out of government office for the last decade of his life (he died in 1963). He nevertheless retained active involvement in the movement in which he played such a distinctive part. For example, he was President of the European Parliamentary Assembly from 1958 to 1960. Adenauer, of extraordinary longevity, at the age of 81 and six years before his retirement, signed the Rome treaties establishing the EEC and the European Atomic Energy Community in 1957.

We must append to these introductory remarks two addenda relating to the particular backgrounds to our two documents. The first concerns the setting up of the European Coal and Steel Community. The question naturally arises, why were these particular industries selected for the first practical essay in European integration? In the first place, of course, they provided the core of modern heavy industry for some two centuries. Secondly, the Ruhr-Lorraine region has been a natural economic unity partitioned by political boundaries. The idea of bringing together these transnational industries had been dreamed about for many years before 1950. And thirdly, there was the problem of harnessing Germany's reviving strength. By integrating the key war potential of the Ruhr with neighbouring coal and steel production, German industrial reinvigoration could be contemplated without fear. Indeed, the area was placed under temporary Allied international administration in the post-war years and a permanent solution had to be found. Various schemes were formulated for something like a coal and steel community. Two in particular no doubt influenced members of their respective governments. One was produced by the French politician André Philip; the other, by the Minister-President of North Rhine-Westphalia, Karl Arnold. Finally, although commentators disagree in detail about this (see Diebold, p.17 esp. n.2), the steel industries of western Europe and especially the French were by 1950 approaching something of a crisis. The creation of the European Coal and Steel Community resolved all these worries (see below pp.157–60).

And so to our second addendum. The success of the ECSC led to suggestions for further 'sectoral' unions, for example, transport and agriculture. But what seemed more pressing in 1950 was integration of the defence forces of the Six. Consideration of this issue was made urgent by the diversion of US and other western military effort to the Far East, especially for the Korean War. This circumstance led in turn to demands for German rearmament. André Philip produced the idea for integrated units and command. It was taken up by the French economic administrator, Monnet, who persuaded the French prime minister, René Pleven. The plan was for 'the creation, for our common defence, of a European Army tied to political institutions of a united Europe.' (reprinted, Vaughan, 1976, p.56). After nearly four years of negotiations the draft treaty for this European Defence Community (EDC) was rejected by the French National Assembly. This event plunged the advocates of further European union (except the ever-resilient Monnet) into a mood of despondency. For not only had the EDC scheme failed, but a parallel plan for an EPC, European Political Community, was now obviously out of the question. This had been drafted largely by the Belgian statesman Spaak in a moment of federalist optimism. Informal discussions none the less resumed for the *relance européenne*, a relaunching of the unificatory enterprise. Fertile minds generated a number of different options. French opinion, shocked by the humiliation of the Suez episode of 1956 against Nasser, was more receptive now to further integrative schemes. In the event, two were taken up, namely, a European Atomic Energy Community and a European Economic Community. These plans were translated into treaties which were signed in Rome on 25 March 1957.

Monnet and the Treaty of Paris

In 1941 two refugees from occupied Europe met in Washington. Over dinner and during their post-prandial walk they fell to talking about their mutual interest in the condition of their home continent. They could not, of course, have known it at the time, but both were to play the most significant roles in creating the treaties which have been the cornerstones of contemporary European integration, namely the instruments establishing the European Coal and Steel Community and the European Economic Community. The two men were the Frenchman Jean Monnet and his guest, the Belgian Paul-Henri Spaak. Recalling that conversation, Spaak later wrote, 'Monnet . . . explained the rough outlines of what later became known as the Schuman Plan' (Spaak, p.213).

Monnet was the true author of the plan which goes by the name of the French foreign minister who made it a political reality. And as this recollection by Spaak reveals, the embryonic idea was already in Monnet's mind a decade before the Treaty of Paris brought it to birth. We may feel that Monnet pays insufficient tribute in his memoirs to the wide currency of the general notion since at least the 1920s (see pp.123–4). It is none the less difficult to disagree with the judgment of a key French authority on the subject, who has written: 'The coal-steel pool cannot be correctly explained, in its origins or in its characteristics except by the psychology and will of M. Monnet.' (P. Gerbert, quoted, Diebold, p.20).

Monnet's influence extends beyond this particular achievement: he was the *éminence grise* of modern European unity. We therefore need to know something about this remarkable man. He was born in Cognac in 1888 and as an adolescent entered the family brandy firm. Its international trading connections induced in him a natural cosmopolitan mode of thinking. He explains this in his memoirs:

So, from the days of my childhood, while French society stagnated in its own parochialism, . . . it was natural for me to expect to meet people who spoke different languages and had different customs . . . So we avoided the proud or defensive nationalistic reactions that were beginning to permeate French politics. In later years, in my relations with other peoples, I have never had to fight against reflexes that I have never acquired (Monnet, p.44).

Very early in his life he conceived the ambition of working for international, especially intra-European, conciliation. In an extraordinary variety of different contexts he persisted in pursuing this objective. Spaak, commenting on the talk in Washington mentioned above, writes: 'It is this continuity of thought, this perseverance in pursuing his ideas, that I feel is Jean Monnet's most characteristic trait.' (Spaak, p.213).

But Monnet was notable not only for generating and repeating his hypothetical plans; he also felt responsibility for participating in their application. Schuman, one of his closest collaborators in the 1950s, highlighted this aspect of his personality:

What characterises him, what distinguishes him from so many men with inventive minds, is that he does not confine himself to conceiving and throwing out ideas at the risk of afterwards leaving them to their fate; he applies himself to putting them to work, to assuming himself part of the responsibility for the operation of the plans he has drawn up (quoted, Brugmans, p.129).

In all his work Monnet combined a remarkable talent for recognising the essentials with an insatiable appetite for detail. He was never frightened to reiterate the basic aim or method to those who were confused by complexities; nor was he ever embarrassed at demanding of his assistants the same exhaustingly long hours he toiled himself to ensure that the ultimate text of a document was unambiguous and as effective as possible for its designed purpose. Furthermore, he rightly prided himself on his ability to identify the most useful person for ensuring that the job be properly undertaken. Monnet's style and ambition lay in the seeking out of the right indi-

vidual, be he head of government or humble civil servant, to ensure
that action was taken. In a moment of self-assessment at the end of
his memoirs, Monnet wrote:

A very wise man whom I knew in the United States, Dwight Morrow, used
to say: 'There are two kinds of people – those who want to *be someone*, and
those who want to *do something*.'

Monnet believed that the reputations of many in the first category
are hollow, and proudly commented 'My friend Dwight Morrow put
me in this second category of people.' (Monnet, pp.519–20). Even
though his personality suited him to working behind the scenes and
in this modest manner exercising his considerable powers of persuasion, these characteristics did not inhibit the American Secretary
of State, Dean Acheson, from describing him as 'one of the greatest of
Frenchmen.' (Acheson, p.76). An English collaborator summarised
this greatness as his ability to make use of 'chance combined with
alertness, persistence, hard work and charm.' (R. Mayne in Ionescu,
1972, p.33).

To complete this brief sketch it is necessary to indicate some of the
main episodes in Monnet's career down to 1950 where, chronologically,
the story of this section begins. During the First World War he showed
a remarkable flair for ensuring the most effective use of Allied merchant marine capacity. After the war he served the League of Nations
for four years as Deputy Secretary-General. He then returned to private life working in international banking. In this capacity he helped
save the Romanian currency from collapse. With the outbreak of war
in 1939 he returned to activity of national importance for France as
Chairman of the Franco-British Committee for Economic Co-ordination. He was therefore well placed to float the idea of common
citizenship between the two nations, which was accepted by the British
War Cabinet though the fall of France prevented its implementation.
He was then employed by the British government negotiating the
supply of war *matériel* in Washington. It was he who coined the term
'the arsenal of democracy' to describe the key function of American
industry in the conflict. 1943 saw him in Algiers, using his talents in
the Free French cause and thinking ahead to post-war problems. At
the end of the Second World War France was in a condition of physical
devastation and economic dislocation. In 1946 the government set up
a Planning Commissariat for Modernisation and Equipment, whose
work is generally recognised as having been vital to the country's
restoration and renewal. Monnet was its head and driving force. In so
many of these activities Monnet's work, largely unrecorded in the
history textbooks, was often more significant than those to whom the
credit is usually given.

By 1950 Monnet was pondering on the related problems of Germany's position in Europe, particularly its relations with France; the

fear in France of Germany's political and economic resurgence; and the central importance of the coal and steel industries in the economies and political strength of these rival nations. Not that these inter-related problems were new. Indeed, the idea of creating organs for the integration of various economic sectors had already been floated by the European Movement, not to mention the various earlier projects specifically for the coal and steel industries.

Monnet mulled over these questions during an Alpine holiday. On his return to Paris, in April, he committed his thoughts to paper. Out of the complex European condition four guiding considerations appear to have emerged from the crystallisation of his thoughts. One was the need for action, albeit on a limited front, to replace the constant talk and theorising about European unity. The second was the need to integrate Germany into the European community in a way which would not exacerbate France's continuing fears of her neighbour.

The third consideration was closely related. We must not forget that, for all his Europeanness, Monnet was still in charge of the Plan for the revitalisation of the French economy. Nearly three years previously he had discovered that 'The German steel industry would soon be absorbing all the coke produced in the Ruhr, with the result that steel production in France and the rest of Europe would have to be limited . . . [Yet] France's steel production targets . . . were the key to the whole French Plan.' (Monnet, p.274). In April 1950 he noted that 'France's continued recovery will come to a halt unless we rapidly solve the problem of German industrial production and its competitive capacity.' (Monnet, p.292). This national economic worry was in fact part of a serious West European crisis predicted for 1952 because of unco-ordinated overproduction of steel.

The fourth consideration was urgency. On Wednesday-Thursday 10–11 May the French foreign minister, Robert Schuman, was due to meet his American and British opposite numbers, Acheson and Bevin, in London. Schuman was due to take with him proposals for resolving a basic dilemma. The Anglo-Saxon powers wished to strengthen West Germany as a buffer against feared Communist aggression. The French, for obvious historical reasons, were nervous of such a policy. Monnet realised that a scheme to integrate the coal and steel indus-tries of these two major European powers (and perhaps others too) might solve a lot of problems.

On Sunday, 16 April Monnet, with help, produced a first draft of a document outlining such a plan. His co-authors were Paul Reuter, a Professor of Law at the University of Aix-la-Chapelle, and Étienne Hirsch, an engineer by training, whom Monnet had originally met in Algiers and who was now working in the Planning Commissariat. Indeed, Monnet and Hirsch had already discussed the basic idea of a coal and steel pool back in 1943 soon after their first meeting. The following day they were joined by the economist Pierre Uri, of whom more later (see p.166). After numerous reworkings a text was ready.

Monnet sent copies to the prime minister, Georges Bidault; and then, on 28 April, to the foreign minister, Robert Schuman.

Schuman now assumed a crucial role in the story. We therefore need to record something of his character and ideas. The Schuman family were Lorrainers who fled to Luxembourg after the Franco-Prussian War rather than live under German rule. Robert was born a Luxembourgeois while feeling himself a Lorrainer. He was educated at German universities and settled in Metz. On the restoration of Alsace-Lorraine to France after the First World War Schuman became a French citizen and in due course entered French politics. Yet his German connections returned to haunt him in 1947. In that year of terrible Communist-inspired crisis he was prime minister and had to endure the epithet 'Boche' hurled at him by the Communist deputies in the Assembly. He had indeed from his earliest days in politics supported a policy of Franco-German rapprochement. He was in favour of Briand's project. Although by nature remarkably humble, shy and lacking both personal charisma and rousing oratory, Schuman was none the less possessed of great courage and devotion to duty born of deep religious convictions. As a young man he contemplated taking holy orders but instead decided to dedicate himself to a secular life of service to others.

Schuman was the ideal man for pushing through Monnet's plan for the Coal and Steel Community. At the heart of the scheme lay the concept of Franco-German reconciliation by means of yoking together their heavy industries; and eighteen months earlier he had already endorsed the similar scheme put forward by André Philip (see p.154).

The link between Monnet and Schuman was Bernard Clappier, a personal friend of both of the principals and Schuman's *directeur de cabinet* (i.e. head of the foreign minister's group of advisers). Clappier asked his minister to consider the paper drawn up by Monnet and his team. Schuman read it over the weekend at his home near Metz. Clappier, in great anxiety to know his opinion, met him at the Gare de l'Est on his return. During the car journey to the Quai d'Orsay Schuman chatted about the weather. Clappier, unable to contain himself, eventually asked what he thought about the document. 'Well,' replied Schuman, 'it's yes.' The cold, unemotional Clappier embraced him. They were joined shortly by Monnet to discuss details.

Conscious of the extreme sensitivity of the subject they combined tight secrecy with careful sounding out of key individuals. It was arranged that the French cabinet should decide on the 'Schuman Plan', as it came to be called, on Tuesday, 9 May. The Sunday before, the US Secretary of State, Dean Acheson, arrived in Paris. Schuman presented himself and, as Acheson later recorded, 'disclosed to Ambassador Bruce and me his Coal and Steel Plan for Western Europe, which he and Monnet had been developing in such secrecy that they had not yet discussed it with the French Cabinet.' (Acheson, p.382). The following evening Schuman dispatched a colleague with

letters to Adenauer urging his support. The German Chancellor
described the episode:

That morning I was still unaware that the day would bring about a decisive
change in the development of Europe . . .
    Blankenhorn [head of Adenauer's private staff] brought the letters to me
in the Cabinet meeting . . .
    In his personal letter to me, Schuman wrote that the aim of his proposal
was not economic but highly political . . . Rearmament would have to begin
by increasing coal, iron, and steel production. If an organization such as
Schuman envisaged were set up . . . both countries [could] discern the first
signs of any such rearmament . . .
    I immediately informed Robert Schuman that I agreed to his proposal with
all my heart (quoted, Monnet, pp.302–3).

    Meanwhile, in Paris the French cabinet met on that Tuesday morn-
ing too. Schuman dare not raise the matter of his plan until Adenauer's reply came through to Clappier. Clappier took the German
Chancellor's message in to Schuman, who gave a brief outline of the
scheme. The cabinet gave their approval. Most of the ministers learned
of the details from the newspapers the next morning. For, at 6.0 p.m.
on that Tuesday evening Schuman held a press conference. He then
left for his London meeting.
    There followed two years of hard work. This fell into three stages:
first, persuading countries to participate; second, drafting the treaty;
third, securing ratification by the parliaments of the would-be participants. Britain refused to be involved. Therefore representatives from
the six interested states (France, West Germany, Italy and the Benelux countries) met in Paris under Monnet's chairmanship to write the
treaty. The working document was in fact drafted by Étienne Hirsch
and Pierre Uri. There were problems. The Benelux governments
tended to be suspicious; Adenauer was impatient. Eventually, the
treaty was signed in Paris on 18 April 1951. The Community started
work on 10 August 1952 with Monnet as President of the core institution, the High Authority. Europe had taken its first step, in Monnet's words, towards a 'merger of sovereignty' (Monnet, p.333).
Enthusiasts believed that Monnet's Fabian and partial tactics were set
fair to achieve the unified Europe which none of the more ambitious
previous plans had ever come near to constructing.
    Two documents brought about this revolutionary change: the Schu-
man Declaration and the Treaty of Paris, which gave the principles
of the declaration legal effect. The Schuman Declaration is a short
paper of some 1,000 words. (The following excerpts are taken from the
text in Patijn, pp.47, 49, 51, 53). Its second paragraph strikes an
altruistic note:

The contribution which an organised and active Europe can make to civilisation is indispensible for the maintenance of peaceful relations . . . Because Europe was not united, we have had war.

The strategy is then clearly asserted:

A United Europe will not be achieved all at once, nor in a single framework: it will be formed by concrete measures which first of all create a solidarity in fact . . . the action to be taken must first of all concern France and Germany . . . [and] be concentrated on one limited, but decisive point.

The declaration continues by proposing 'that the entire French-German production of coal and steel be placed under a joint high authority, within an organisation open to the participation of other European nations.' One obvious benefit will be 'that any war between France and Germany becomes not only unthinkable but in actual fact impossible.' Another is a general raising of living standards particularly in Africa. The initiative is presented as the initial stage 'which is indispensible for the establishment of an economic community' and will thus 'create the first concrete foundation for a European federation . . . '.

There follows an outline of the changes envisaged in the management of coal and steel production in the participating countries, the words 'improvement' and 'equalisation' predominating. The details, however, were to be worked out later. The Declaration nevertheless made clear that the institutional crux of the proposal was to be the joint high authority. This was from the beginning Monnet's most distinctive contribution. It was to be composed of 'independent personalities chosen by the governments; a president will be chosen by the governments by common agreement; his decisions will be enforceable in France, Germany, and other member countries.'

Monnet has written that the Treaty of Paris, which created the ECSC 'enlarged on the Schuman Declaration and made it operational.' (Monnet, p.322). The relationship was as intimate as that. The preamble to the treaty clearly reveals its parentage. (The following excerpts are taken from the text in Vaughan, 1976, pp.60–73.) This refers to: 'the contribution which an organized and vital Europe can make . . . to the maintenance of peaceful relations'; the recognition that 'Europe can be built only through practical achievements'; and creating, 'by establishing an economic community, the basis for a broader and deeper community among peoples long divided by bloody conflicts.'

The treaty was composed of a hundred articles. The first five, in contradistinction to the preamble, were severely economic in their listing of objectives and methods. The task of the Community, as defined in Article 2, was to 'Contribute . . . to economic expansion, growth of employment and a rising standard of living in the Member

States.' However, Article 6 revealed the political novelty of the ECSC. This provision stated that:

The Community shall have legal personality.
In international relations, the Community shall enjoy the legal capacity it requires to perform its functions and attain its objectives.

There followed a definition of the institutional structure. It will be recalled that the Schuman Declaration referred to 'a high authority' and little more thought was given at that stage to the constitutional machinery. Eventually, the working party devised a quadripartite framework: a High Authority, a Common Assembly (or European Parliament), a Special Council of Ministers (or simply Council) and a Court of Justice (or simply Court).

The High Authority, the policy-making and executive element, was the organ which contained the real supranational potential of the Community. In some measure the extent to which this potential could be developed depended on the behaviour of its personnel. Therefore Article 9 specified that 'In the performance of these duties, they shall neither seek nor take instructions from any Government or from any other body. They shall refrain from any action incompatible with the supranational character of their duties.' Also, reciprocally, 'Each member State undertakes to respect this supranational character . . .'. (Article 9 was changed to Article 10 by the Merger Treaty which brought the ECSC, EEC and Euratom together in 1967. Interestingly, the word 'supranational' was withdrawn in the revised text (see European Communities, 1987, p.30). Because changes have been made to the original text, the past tense has been used in this analysis.)

The High Authority was a small group of 'nine members appointed for six years and chosen on the grounds of their general competence . . . not . . . more than two members having the nationality of the same State' (Article 9). Even if a member was tempted to act on behalf of his own state, his power to do so was heavily circumscribed by investing the decision-making power in the majority (Article 13). Pronouncements could be made in any one of three forms; decisions, recommendations and opinions. Only decisions had binding force (Article 14). The High Authority was assisted by a Consultative Committee (Article 18).

But who was to keep a watchful eye on these custodians of the coal and steel industries? Provision was made for an Assembly 'of delegates who shall be designated by the respective Parliaments once a year from among their members, or who shall be elected by direct universal suffrage . . . ' (Article 21). The numbers were specified, being proportionate to the size of the member states: Germany, France, Italy – 18; Belgium, Netherlands – 10; Luxembourg – 4. The Assembly was equipped only with a massive deterrent weapon, namely a motion of censure. Article 24 stated that, 'If the motion of censure is carried by a two-thirds majority of the votes cast, representing a majority of the Members of the Assembly, the members of the High Authority shall resign as a body.'

Despite the Community's independent legal identity it did not, of course, supersede its constituent nation-states. It was therefore necessary to provide for an institutional connection with them. This was the Council. Its function, as defined in Article 26, was 'to harmonise the action of the High Authority and that of the Governments'. Its membership was arranged in the following manner: 'Each State shall delegate to it one of the members of its Government.' (Article 27). Each member of the Council was to act as President in turn. The authority of the Council vis-à-vis the High Authority was extremely complex. For some matters the Council was required to give a unanimous assent; for others, the assent of a majority – albeit preserving the particular rights of the major coal and steel producers.

Any dispute concerning the interpretation and implementation of the treaty was to be handled by a Court of seven judges (Articles 31–45). There followed a long section, Articles 46–75, on economic and social conditions relating to finance, investment, production, prices, wages, transport, agreements and interference. Most of these provisions were of a technical nature relating to the Community's work. Article 49 is of particular interest here. It provides for the imposition of levies on the production of coal and steel so that the ECSC might have an independent income for its work. It was also empowered to exact fines and surcharges for non-compliance with its requirements. Article 92 confirmed this right and procedure:

Decisions of the High Authority which impose a pecuniary obligation shall be enforceable.

Enforcement in the territory of Member States shall be carried out by means of the legal procedure in force in each State.

The treaty was signed by representatives (heads of government or foreign ministers) of the six states. It is of interest to note that a number of the signatories were distinguished supporters of European union. Schuman himself signed for France; Adenauer, for Germany; van Zeeland, for the Netherlands; Bech, for Luxembourg. And the foreign minister of Italy, who represented his country, was Count Sforza, the author of an inter-war book advocating a United States of Europe (see p.124).

As we conclude our survey of Monnet and the Treaty of Paris, we may add a short postscript. Monnet himself lived for many more active years after the founding of the Coal and Steel Community. He served as the first President of the High Authority from 1952 to 1955. He then launched an Action Committee for the United States of Europe, which became a very effective pressure group. Three years before he died the European Council, by then a twelve-member body of heads of state and government, met in Luxembourg. They passed a resolution. It included these words:

Jean Monnet has resolutely attacked the forces of inertia in Europe's political and economic structure, with the aim of establishing a new type of relationship between States, making apparent their *de facto* solidarity and giving it institutional form ... It is only fitting that Europe should pay him a particular tribute of gratitude and admiration.

That is why the Heads of State and Government of the Community ... have decided to confer on him the title of Honorary Citizen of Europe (quoted, Monnet, p.525).

Spaak and the Treaty of Rome

If Monnet's name is particularly associated with the creation of the ECSC, then the name most associated with the creation of the EEC is Paul-Henri Spaak, 'that outstanding Belgian statesman [in the words of Monnet], who laboured so well in the cause of Europe.' (Monnet, p.404). What kind of man was Spaak? He was decidedly corpulent and virtually monoglot. He expressed himself concerning these characteristics with typical humour, saying, 'I'm often told that I look like Winston Churchill and speak English like Charles Boyer, but I wish it were the other way round.' (quoted, Huizinga, p.75). An English journalist described him as 'a big hectoring man' (Beloff, p.77). A kinder adjective would have been 'forthright'. He could certainly be emotional and hot-tempered. Spaak himself was proud of the effects his oratory and more especially his acts of conciliation had in actually achieving practical results in the cause of European unity.

Spaak was a superb chairman, whose skills were much in demand and were deployed to great effect in the post-war world in the UN, OEEC, the Council of Europe and NATO, as well as in the 'Little Europe' of 'the Six'. This skill was, in truth, an amalgam of qualities: common sense; a sure grasp of technical detail acquired by hard work; and persuasive powers for achieving agreements on contentious issues, born of a personal conviction of the urgency of the work to be done. A number of statesmen have recorded their appreciation. Let us take as examples two British prime ministers. Attlee spoke of his 'specially clear and decisive intelligence' (quoted, Huizinga, p.46); while Eden noted that he was a man 'whose opinions I had so often found penetrating and courageous.' (Eden, p.583). And these accolades came from a country about which Spaak constantly and bitterly complained in frustration for its refusal to commit itself wholeheartedly to the cause of European unity.

For it was a cause in which Spaak himself came passionately to believe. We find him as early as 1941, while in exile in England, writing to the Conservative MP Irene Ward in prophetic tones:

The events of the last twenty months in Europe have shown that its countries must unite . . . After the war Europe will be glad to unite behind Britain's victorious leadership . . .
If Britain fails to recognise her duty to Europe . . . she must expect to be rapidly deprived of the fruits of her present efforts (Spaak, pp.76–7).

Later, European integration was to become for him, on his own admission 'a veritable mania' (quoted, Huizinga, p.239). This dedication was recognised by others too, so that, when he assumed the chairmanship of the OEEC in 1948, he was soon dubbed 'Mr Europe'.

It is time now briefly to sketch in Spaak's career to the point when he came to play such a vital role in the birth of the EEC. He was born in Brussels on 25 January 1899, of a theatrical father and a political mother. After the First World War, during part of which he was a prisoner of war, he qualified as a lawyer. He entered politics – as a left-wing Socialist, because his soul heard the loud cries from the destitute but none from God, the inspiration of the alternative Christian Socialist party. He made rapid strides, becoming Belgium's first Socialist prime minister before the age of forty. In the not-so-merry-go-round of Belgian politics he served his country as prime minister and foreign minister in numerous administrations until his retirement in 1966.

Spaak served the UN with distinction in its early days, but soon became disappointed with its weakness. He consequently directed his considerable energies to the cause of European unity. His first success in this sphere was the conclusion of the Brussels Treaty, a defensive alliance among Britain, France and the Benelux countries in 1948. President Truman was especially appreciative of his work. He judged it 'a notable step in the direction of unity in Europe' (quoted, Spaak, p.149) and later explained, 'I think to Spaak goes the credit for lining up the Europeans for the Treaty.' (Truman, p.280). Spaak welcomed the ECSC with enthusiasm. He heard the news of the final collapse of the European Defence Community scheme (see p.149) with gloomy pessimism. That was in August 1954.

In the meantime, other, less ambitious projects were being devised as a means of 'relaunching' Europe. Some involved further essays in sectoral integration – in transport and energy, for example. This was a tactic much favoured by Monnet. The other approach was to devise a common market of broad economic expanse. The main proponent of this way forward was J.W. Beyen, Dutch foreign minister. In June 1955 representatives of the Six met at Messina. Two papers supported by the Benelux trio were tabled. The one favouring a common market, to everyone's surprise, was accepted and slightly redrafted as a Resolution:

The Governments . . . consider that it is necessary to work for the establishment of a united Europe by the development of common institutions, the progressive fusion of national economies, the creation of a common market and the progressive harmonisation of their social policies.

Such a policy seems to them indispensable if Europe is to maintain her position in the world, regain her influence and achieve a continuing increase in the standard of living of her people (quoted, Mayne, p.236).

In fact, two projects were to be pursued – for an atomic energy community as well as a common market. This double-pronged policy was necessary to secure the agreement of France and Germany. At the time, the French were keen for support in developing nuclear power, the Germans more interested in the common market.

Clearly a huge amount of detailed work had to be accomplished in order to bring this ideal to fruition. A novel method of procedure was adopted. This was to nominate a politician to chair a group of experts from the member countries: the experts to grapple with the formidable technical economic and administrative problems; the politicians to ensure that the process of continued unification was advanced in a politically acceptable manner. Spaak had not expected to undertake the chairmanship himself. But by default it fell to him to guide the Six from the ECSC to the EEC and Euratom.

For two years detailed studies and negotiations were undertaken. These led eventually to recommendations known as the 'Spaak Report', the basis for the Treaties of Rome. Spaak described this work as 'fascinating, arduous and full of incident.' (Spaak, p.230). He had a superb team of assistants. Most notable of these was Pierre Uri. A Parisian by birth, Uri had been trained as a philosopher and had been a Professor of that subject before the war. He then turned to economics. In 1947 Monnet appointed him as Financial Adviser to his Planning Commission. He was Economic Director of the ECSC from 1952 to 1959, then engaged in various consultancies before returning to academic life in 1969. Monnet had a very high regard for his sharp mind and skill in the lucid drafting of official documents, though some found him a somewhat tetchy personality. We have already noticed his contribution to the Schuman Declaration and the Treaty of Paris (see pp.158 & 160). Uri's work in paving the way for the Common Market has been recorded by Spaak in the following way:

The 'Spaak Report', an important document, is largely the fruit of his efforts. Uri was one of the principal architects of the Treaty of Rome. If I may put it somewhat cynically, I believe that my achievement was to get the best out of him . . . He had many more ideas than I, though I may have been better at gaining acceptance for them (Spaak, p.231).

Monnet expressed the same view:

The experts' report on which the Treaties were based was essentially the work of Uri – as Spaak himself always acknowledged. It is nonetheless a fact that the political credit for this vital document is due to [Spaak] (Monnet, p.404).

The Spaak Report transmuted the vague agreement of the Messina Conference to a clear-cut commitment to create a common market. But this, in turn, had to be transformed into detailed, legal and binding terms which took account of the minutiae of the trading and employment interests of the six participants. The Spaak Report was accepted by the six foreign ministers at their conference in Venice in May 1956. A mere ten months elapsed between that meeting and the signing of the treaties in Rome – a further tribute to Spaak's indefatigable efforts. The Dutch Foreign Minister, Beyen, who had been Spaak's close companion in so much of the work for European unity, recognised the decisive contribution the Belgian statesman had made. He wrote that,

His powerful personality dominated the scene. What he undertook and fulfilled is without parallel. It is not too much to say that but for his relentless and powerful leadership the European Treaties would never have been ready for signature within so short a time, perhaps never at all (quoted, Huizinga, p.242).

An analysis of one detailed study of Spaak's work at this time suggests that he personally contributed to the creation of the EEC in a number of different ways (Laurent, passim). In the first place, without his pressure the matter of investigating further modes of economic integration might well not have been so seriously considered at the Messina meeting. Once negotiations and planning were under way, he displayed considerable flexibility. In spite of Monnet's canvassing of a move to truly supranational institutions and Spaak's own predilections for tight union, he realised this was impracticable in face of German and especially French opposition. He consciously settled for a much less ambitious scheme in order to avoid total failure. This policy of compromise included appeasing the French on a number of controversial details about which they felt strongly, especially preferential treatment for their colonies. He believed this worthwhile in order to prevent their sinking the enterprise. (As a consequence the Treaty of Rome has been described by one authority as 'Gallic' (M. Camps, quoted, Laurent, p.381 n.11).) Spaak worked exceedingly hard, reading the transcripts of every committee's planning sessions. He really did personally control the operation: 'Spaak not only gathered the talent and established the rules and pace of work,' writes Laurent, 'but also dictated the overall style – closed diplomacy with little publicity given to the stumbling blocks or the accomplishments.' (Laurent, p.395).
    Finally, alert to national sensitivities, he settled for a transitional scheme. He believed that if controversial issues were faced immediately, they would lead to a fatal loss of pace and patience. Fudge them at the treaty stage, and the momentum of the whole enterprise would enforce solutions later on. The result was an incredible patchwork,

but at least it was a garment of sorts. Laurent shows the extent of this policy of cross-fingered procrastination:

The side-stepping decisions in agriculture, transportation, monetary and fiscal matters, the extent of the involvement of the colonies, the tariff reduction timetable, the external tariff, and even how best to reduce hardships liberaliz-ation would bring were all part of Spaak's strategy for avoiding friction and getting agreement on the positive achievements of the diplomats and experts (Laurent, p.392).

The treaty establishing the European Atomic Energy Community is of mainly technical interest. The other treaty signed at Rome, that establishing the European Economic Community, has, of course had a very significant effect in advancing European integration. It is this document that we must now analyse. It was a longer document than the Treaty of Paris: it contained 248 articles. (Text in English trans-lation published by European Communities, 1958. The past tense has been used because some articles have subsequently been changed.)

The preamble referred, inevitably, to economic co-operation and expansion. In particular, the participants declared themselves 'anxi-ous to strengthen the unity of their economies and to ensure their harmonious development by reducing the differences existing between the various regions . . .'. In addition, and of greater interest here, were the political overtones. For example, the preamble opened with the statement that they were 'determined to establish the foundations of an ever closer union among the European peoples.' And it concluded with an expression of their resolution 'to strengthen the safeguards of peace and liberty by establishing this combination of resources and calling upon the other peoples of Europe who share their ideal to join in their efforts.'

Article 2 revealed the basically economic objective of the Com-munity:

It shall be the aim of the Community, by establishing a Common Market and progressively approximating the economic policies of Member States, to promote throughout the Community a harmonious development of economic activities, a continuous and balanced expansion, an increased stability, an accelerated raising of the standard of living and closer relations between its Member States.

Article 3 listed the specific sectors for attention, for example, the elimination of customs duties, the free movement of persons, services and capital and a common agricultural policy. Article 7 strengthened the second of these provisions by explicitly prohibiting 'any discrimi-nation on the grounds of nationality.'

The bulk of the treaty naturally related to the economic technicalit-ies of these programmes of liberalisation, harmonisation and integra-tion. However, in order to place the treaty in the history of European unity we shall concentrate here on three features. First, we need to outline the institutional structure (Articles 137 to 198). Second, we shall select some evidence of the various ways in which the Community was empowered to interfere with the policies of its member states. And thirdly, some articles will be cited to show how the Community was given its own discrete identity.

The treaty made provision for four main institutions: an Assembly, a Council, a Commission and a Court of Justice.

Initially the Assembly was to consist of 'delegates whom the Parliaments shall be called upon to appoint from among their members', though it was then required to 'draw up proposals for election by direct universal suffrage in accordance with a uniform procedure in all Member States.' The seats were allocated in proportion to the populations of the member states, namely, Germany, France and Italy – 36; Belgium and the Netherlands – 14; Luxembourg – 6 (Article 138). The power of the Assembly lay in the same blunt weapon provided in the ECSC system (see p.162), namely, the requirement that the executive body (in this case, the Commission) resign in the event of a motion of censure.

The link between the EEC and its member states was to be the Council. 'Each government,' Article 146 stated, 'shall delegate to it one of its members.' Each of these was to act as its President for six months by rotation. Now although each member state had one member of the Council, when it came to voting, the votes were to be weighted according to the following multipliers: Germany, France, Italy – 4; Belgium, the Netherlands – 2; Luxembourg – 1 (Article 148). The function of the Council was to:

ensure the co-ordination of the general economic policies of the Member States; and
dispose of a power of decision (Article 145).

This power of decision was to be exercised on measures devised and passed through by the Commission. The Commission was the real heart of the EEC, as the High Authority was of the ECSC. Article 157 defined its composition as 'nine members chosen for their general competence and of indisputable independence.' The requirements for a spread of nationalities and the prohibition of any external, including governmental, influences as laid down in the Treaty of Paris (see p.162) were repeated in this instrument. The Commission was to choose its own President and two Vice-Presidents from among themselves (Article 161). The activities of the Commission were extensive and listed in Article 155:

ensure the application of the provisions of this Treaty and of the provisions enacted by the institutions of the Community in pursuance thereof; formulate recommendations or opinions in matters which are the subject of this Treaty, where the latter expressly so provides or where the Commission considers it necessary;

under the conditions laid down in this Treaty dispose of a power of decision of its own and participate in the preparation of acts of the Council and of the Assembly; and

exercise the competence conferred on it by the Council for the implementation of the rules laid down by the latter.

Articles 166 to 188 defined the competence of the Court of Justice of seven judges.

Let us turn now to some examples of how the treaty gave inter-ventionary powers to the Community. In a sense, the whole agreement was concerned with the surrender of state autonomy over certain sectors of their economies. However, Articles 101, 103 and 117 were interestingly explicit:

Where the Commission finds that a disparity existing between the legislative or administrative provisions of the Member States distorts the conditions of competition in the Common Market and therefore causes a state of affairs which must be eliminated, it shall enter into consultation with the interested Member States.

If such consultation does not result in an agreement . . . the Council . . . shall issue the directives necessary for this purpose (Article 101).

Member States shall consider their policy relating to economic trends as a matter of common interest (Article 103).

Member States hereby agree upon the necessity to promote improvement of the living and working conditions of labour so as to permit the equalisation of such conditions in an upward direction (Article 117).

In taking actions both within the member states and outside their frontiers, the Community was defined as having 'legal personality' (Article 210). Furthermore, it was specified that the Community would 'enjoy in the territories of the Member States the privileges and immunities necessary for the achievement of its aims.' (Article 218). Article 224 was a particularly interesting clause in this regard. It required that:

Member States shall consult one another for the purpose of enacting in common the necessary provisions to prevent the functioning of the Common Market from being affected by measures which a Member State may be called upon to take in case of serious internal disturbances . . . in case of war . . . or in order to carry out undertakings into which it has entered for the purpose of maintaining peace or international security.

Thus even in the most sensitive areas of the exercise of national sovereignty, namely the whole field of security, the Economic Com-munity had perforce to be involved and its needs considered.

Finally, the EEC's enjoyment of distinct identity in external relations is made clear in Article 238:

The Community may conclude with a third country or an international organisation agreements creating an association embodying reciprocal rights and obligations, joint actions and special procedures.

The Treaty of Rome was a more tentative advance on the Treaty of Paris than the ambitious federalists had wanted. 'Spaakistan', as the Common Market was sometimes called, was not the United States of Europe. Yet, in the context of the collapse of the European Defence Community (p.149), the achievement was impressive. The range of economic integration required by the creation of the EEC and the potential for further advance provided by the Treaty of Rome were surely sufficient to confirm Paul-Henri Spaak's sobriquet of 'Mr Europe'.

Assessment of the 1950s

What kind of union was this 'European Community' which the treaties drafted by Monnet and Spaak and their co-workers created? And what was its importance?

We have brought our story of plans and their authors to a halt in 1957 with the Treaties of Rome. There are two reasons for this. One is that, as an historical survey, it is inappropriate for the present work to become involved in issues which are still currently unresolved. The second is that, in any case, the more recent moves towards tighter integration, such as the Parliament's Draft Treaty establishing the European Union of 1984 and the Single European Act of 1986, are in essence interpretations and extensions of the documents of the 1950s we have just surveyed. One can be even more basic than that and echo Monnet, who, from the perspective of the mid-1970s, wrote that the Schuman Declaration was 'the European Community's true founding document.' (Monnet, p.295).

The question we must now address is, in what senses these fundamental documents of the 1950s advanced the centuries-old cause of European political unity. There is no doubt that Monnet saw the High Authority as the heart of the integrative enterprise. Professor Haas expressed this idea well when he wrote that, 'In a sense, Monnet considered the High Authority as the repository of the European General Will, with the evil governments merely spokesmen for the selfish particular wills. The Treaty [of Paris], as administered by the High Authority *is* the basic European consensus for progress, peace and federation.' (Haas, p.456). The Schuman Declaration envisaged no other institutional framework; only later, in the drafting of the treaty, was the Council of Ministers, for example, added to counterbalance with national power the unificatory thrust of the High Authority.

The intention of the Schuman Declaration to restrain the autonomy of the member states was further weakened by the Treaties of Rome. A certain nervousness in some industrial and governmental circles inhibited Spaak and his team. As a consequence, whereas the ECSC High Authority was able to make binding 'decisions' on all matters, the EEC Commission was permitted to make the equivalent binding 'regulations' in only relatively non-controversial areas. In the Treaties of Rome the power of the Council of Ministers is correspondingly enhanced. The Treaty of Paris lays down a partial authority: 'Wherever this Treaty requires the assent of the Council . . . ' (Article 28); the Treaty of Rome is blunt: 'the Council shall . . . have power to take decisions' (Article 145).

But, as the American specialist on the ECSC, William Diebold, has written, 'the character of the supranational power cannot be understood if it is read only in the words of the Treaty.' (Diebold, p.605). We must therefore ask three more questions: What were the objectives of the 'founding fathers'? What style of political system was the European Community which they created? And how far did the documents of the 1950s contain within them potential for further progress along the road to European political unity?

An examination of the statements of the leading personalities and the basic documents reveals what would appear to be a confused medley of objectives. Economic and political ideals, selfish and altruistic motives appear in turn and together. It would be unproductive to try to assess which were the true, fundamental objectives. Indeed, the very diversity of aims succeeded in satisfying so many interests simultaneously that this lack of simple clarity must contribute a great deal to explaining the success of the undertaking.

The economic needs of collaboration in steel production and for 'customs disarmament' reflect the worries expressed in the 1920s (see pp.123–4) and are explicit, of course, in the defined purposes of the ECSC and EEC treaties. Article 2 of the Treaty of Paris is quite unambiguous:

The European Coal and Steel Community shall have as its task to contribute . . . to economic expansion, growth of employment and a rising standard of living in the Member States.
    The Community shall progressively bring about conditions which will of themselves ensure the most rational distribution of production at the highest level of productivity . . . (reprinted, Vaughan, 1976, pp.61–2).

The Treaty of Rome pursued the same kind of objective within its sphere. However, the Spaak Report, on which it was based, was even more frank in asserting the need to create a large domestic market as an essential basis for effectively competing with the powerful US economy.

Such a policy could heighten international tension if it led to a transatlantic economic war. And yet the founding fathers seemed to believe that their economic objectives were part and parcel of their more far-reaching pacific purpose. For example, a few days after the finalisation of the Schuman Declaration, Monnet drafted a background briefing document for Bidault and Schuman. In this he expressed his fears of likely Russian and German warlike actions in most forceful language. 'The cold war,' he wrote, ' . . . is the first phase of real war.' He continued, 'The German situation is rapidly becoming a cancer that will be dangerous to peace in the near future.' (reprinted, Vaughan, 1976, p.52). By incorporating West Germany into the ECSC he believed that he could forestall this grim scenario. As to trans-atlantic strains, some hopes were expressed that the collaborative, peaceful style of the European Communities would in due course extend to a harmonious overarching partnership between the Old World and the New.

The word 'peace' also appears in the preambles of both the ECSC and EEC treaties. The very first clause of the Treaty of Paris states that 'Considering that world peace can be safeguarded only by creative efforts commensurate with the dangers that threaten it . . .' (reprinted, Vaughan, 1976, p.60). The Treaty of Rome contains the following phrase: 'Resolved by thus pooling their resources to preserve and strengthen peace and liberty . . .' (reprinted, Vaughan, 1976, p.74).

The creation of the European Community effectively ended the Franco-German antagonism, which can be traced as a virtually unbroken thread in European history from the conflict between Valois and Habsburg half a millennium ago (see Chapter 2). While not wish-ing to minimise this extraordinary achievement, one must, even so, recognise that national self-interest was an extremely powerful motive in bringing the Community to birth. The benefit to the Benelux coun-tries lay in their defence against economically more powerful neigh-bours, now co-members. The benefit to Germany lay in the unique opportunity to resume a major role in European affairs without arous-ing the fears and antagonism which her behaviour from 1870 to 1945 had engendered.

But it is the behaviour of the French which requires closest atten-tion. As we have seen, Frenchmen, especially Schuman and Monnet, were crucial to the whole venture. And if their altruism was not exactly a mask for their national egoism, at least we must acknowl-edge that the supranational schemes of the ECSC and EEC fitted (or were made to fit) French national needs extraordinarily comfortably. Monnet expressed the position of France with his characteristic verbal economy. In a note written in 1943 he stated, 'France is bound up in Europe. She cannot escape. The solution of the European problem is all-important to the life of France.' (Monnet, p.222). And in his memorandum to Bidault and Schuman, just cited, he drew a gloomy extrapolation of current Cold War trends in the event of continued West European fragmentation. He concluded that, 'France will be

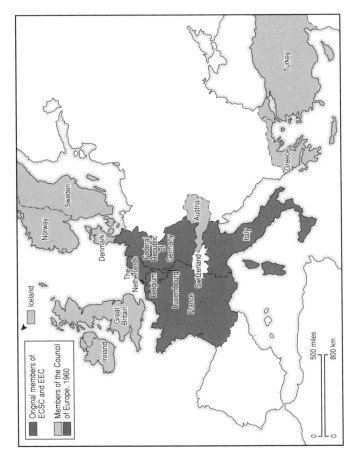

Map 8 Membership of 'West' European organisation *c.* 1960

trapped again in her Malthusianism, and this will lead inevitably to her being effaced.' (reprinted, Vaughan, 1976, p.55). Only incorporation in some form of union could save her. We have, furthermore, already recorded how crucial the Schuman Plan was for the salvation of the French steel industry, which had been built up as the core of Monnet's national modernisation plan (p.158). We have also noticed how Spaak, in the design of the Common Market, had to compromise on any principle of inter-state equity in order to satisfy constant French demands (p.167).

It may also be argued that the Community as a whole was a formula for the exercise of collective self-interest. An objective often mentioned was 'faire l'Europe' as a 'third force' to counterbalance the power of the USA and the USSR on her western and eastern flanks; or, when the Cold War was uppermost in pessimistic commentators' minds, to act as America's powerful ally. For example, to cite Monnet once again, he has reported how he and Adenauer agreed in 1951 that 'Europe seemed to be turning into a pawn in the Soviet-American power struggle.' (Monnet, p.356).

However, as Professor Forsyth has emphasised, this desire for West European integration for greater influence had two aspects: 'The negative feeling is one of European inferiority, of insecurity, of being threatened from outside. The positive one is a desire to influence and improve the world according to European principles' (Forsyth, 1967, p.485). This second, positive feeling may be exemplified by reference to the following passage in the preamble to the Treaty of Paris: 'Convinced that the contribution which an organised and vital Europe can make to civilization is indispensable to the maintenance of peaceful relations . . . ' (reprinted, Vaughan, 1976, p.60).

While it is clear that all these factors played a part in the shaping of the Treaties of Paris and Rome, it is also possible to indicate variations of emphasis. At the personal level, the backgrounds and characters of the main instigators would suggest different priorities. Schuman's deep religious conviction would have placed the ideal of peace in the forefront of his mind. Monnet was no doubt much influenced by his frustration at the sheer inefficiency of non-co-operation in industrial production and supply, as experienced in the two world wars. Spaak was a Socialist who wanted co-operation to raise living standards.

One must also be aware of a slight change of emphasis as between the declared objectives of the ECSC and the EEC. The overtones of political federalism, clearly audible in the Schuman Declaration are softer in the Treaty of Paris and muted in the Treaty of Rome, overlaid by crescendoing economic functionalism. The Schuman Declaration unequivocally stated that its proposal for economic collaboration was 'the first stage for the European federation' (this and the following excerpts, reprinted, Patijn, p.47). The Paris Treaty referred more vaguely to the process as being 'the basis for a broader and deeper community among peoples long divided by bloody conflicts'; and stated that the ECSC would 'lay the foundations for institutions which will give direction to a destiny henceforth shared'. In the Rome Treaty these two ideas are tersely conflated: 'Determined to lay the foundations of an ever closer union among the peoples of Europe.' Already at the Messina Conference in 1955 it was evident that the ambition of the Benelux representatives to revive the supranational dynamic was doomed. Under French and German pressure, Laurent has explained, they 'agreed to strike out from the diplomatic vocabulary of the preparatory talks any mention of a powerful central organization beyond the national governments.' (Laurent, pp.378–9).

The use of the words 'federalism', 'functionalism' and 'supranational' in the last paragraph signals our entry into a semantic forest which has provided the raw material for a whole library of books and articles. It is not our purpose here to penetrate deeply into this forest. It is rather to ask what form or forms of integration the creators of the Communities had in mind and what were provided for in the two treaties we have been considering.

Many nineteenth-century advocates of European unity, as we have seen (pp.113–5) had a clear conception of their desired goal: a federal United States of Europe analogous to the United States of America. In the post-1945 efforts to realise some form of integration, this federal ideal was revived. It is obvious from our survey of the Treaties of Paris and Rome that these documents did not create a federal constitutional structure. Federalists were disappointed that this was not achieved. For example, Spinelli declared that 'Monnet has the great merit of having built Europe and the great responsibility to have built it badly.' In 1983 he expressed his opinion that 'we are still paying for this false departure.' (quoted, Burgess, pp.55–6 & 57).

So if the European Community as created in the 1950s was not a federation, what was it? Some commentators have emphasised the common use of the term 'supranational'. Thus Paul Reuter, whose services were used by Monnet, wrote in 1953 of the sudden popularity of the term in many contexts: 'in the course of the negotiations on the Schuman Plan, in the text of the Treaty (art. 9), in that of the Treaty setting up the European Defence Community (art. 1), and in the language habitually used by statesmen and diplomats.' (Reuter, p.139). But because the term is vague some political scientists have tried a more precise classification, only to conclude that the Community defies such precision. Ernst Haas in his classic study drew the conclusion, with particular reference to the ECSC, that

It is *sui generis* not only in the legal and institutional sense but also in terms of the relationships it sets up among civil servants and ministers, trade unionists and cartel executives, coal consumers and administrative lawyers.

He continued by asserting that 'supranationality in practice has developed into a hybrid in which neither the federal nor the inter-governmental tendency has clearly triumphed.' (Haas, pp.526–7).

However, a new term, 'neo-functionalist' was soon coined to describe both the intention and operation of the European Communities. Functionalism describes the pragmatic and technical co-operation devised to achieve the desired ends of greater administrative and welfare efficiency. In addition, in its developed neo-functionalist form, it emphasises how the very processes of collaboration have 'spill-over' or 'incremental' effects inexorably pushing the Communities to ever tighter integration. Neo-functionalism is creeping federalism.

How do our two main authors and their documents fit these attempted characterisations of the Community they brought into being? There are numerous passing references in the second and third sections of this chapter. An explicit summary will be useful here. Social scientists love to classify. They have consequently expended quantities of ink disputing whether Monnet was a federalist or a functionalist. Burgess, summarising the debate, has written that 'Today we do not regard Monnet as having been a champion of the federal cause in Europe . . . Monnet has been described predominantly as the foremost "functionalist" . . . ' (Burgess, p.44). This verdict is flawed by two weaknesses. It ignores Monnet's flexibility, his lifelong belief in moving to take advantage of beneficial circumstances as they arose. And it assumes that the process of federal construction must be an instantaneous act of creation, a questionably narrow definition. Murray Forsyth has shown how federations have often historically evolved from looser confederal structures (Forsyth, 1981, passim).

There is plenty of evidence that Monnet's ultimate goal was a federal United States of Europe but that he judged a gradualist tactic to be the only practical way of achieving this aim. Let us take as an example of Monnet's federalist convictions his view of the Schuman Plan. The word 'federation' occurs twice in the Declaration. Furthermore, the following month, in a reference to the planned High Authority, he stated, 'Thus we shall lay the concrete foundations of a Federation of Europe.' (Monnet, p.321). When he became the first President of that Authority, he underlined in his inaugural speech the federal character of the Community.

Again, referring in his memoirs to the approach adopted in the ECSC in contrast to de Gaulle's grandiose but distant dreams, he wrote, 'We believed in starting with limited achievements, establishing *de facto* solidarity, from which a federation would gradually emerge.' (Monnet, p.367).

A similar conviction that a frontal assault on state sovereignty would be nugatory in the 1950s led Spaak to trim his federalist ideals. Of a more mercurial personality than Monnet, he expressed his enthusiasms and disappointments more forcefully than the Frenchman. He accepted the presidency of the Council of Europe with high federalist hopes: 'I came to Strasbourg convinced of the need for a

United States of Europe.' (quoted, Mayne, p.169). Frustrated by its impotence, he resigned and channelled his federalist zeal into the abortive scheme for a European Political Community (see p.155). Five years before his death he surveyed a Gaullist Community and voiced his disappointment: 'The Europe that we wanted,' he wrote, ' . . . is no longer realizable . . . My earlier enthusiasms, I can now appreciate, were illusions.' (quoted, Hodges, p.14).

How, then, to place the work of Monnet and Spaak in historical perspective? It has been asserted by one distinguished authority that the post-1945 developments towards European integration 'should not be construed as simply a continuation of earlier European plans for unification.' (Lipgens, quoted, Burgess, p.26). A number of features of the subject-matter dealt with in this chapter, it is true, set this most recent period apart from the schemes discussed in the rest of the book. The widespread public support for European union; the very success of Monnet and Spaak and their colleagues in creating the Communities; and the emphasis on *economic* collaboration render the 1950s distinctive.

Even so, one must not discount the strength of the links of continuity. Several of our earlier authors were alive to the economic advantages of unity. The organisations to promote a federal United States of Europe had their precursors in the nineteenth-century peace congresses, which had at least partial federal inspiration. The focus on economic integration echoed the concerns and ambitions of the 1920s. Moreover, when we read in the Treaty of Rome that its purpose is 'to preserve and strengthen peace and liberty' we may be reminded of Saint-Simon's belief in peace through the spread of constitutional systems of government (see the comment of the keen post-war Swiss federalist, de Rougemont, p.109). Finally, when we notice in the same treaty that the Community should operate 'in accordance with the principles of the Charter of the United Nations' (Preamble, reprinted, Vaughan, 1976, p.74), this requirement is perhaps reminiscent of Briand's use of the League as the basis for his plan.

What, crucially, earlier schemes lacked and what is so characteristic of the European Community launched in the 1950s is the technique of unity on an instalment plan. In 1951 six nations made an initial down-payment of a small portion of their sovereignty to pay for 'a journey to an unknown destination' (this phrase was the title of Andrew Schonfield's 1972 Reith Lectures). Six more have subsequently joined the initial travellers and at least another half-dozen are seeking permission to pursue the same path. In the meantime, the pace of integration has accelerated. What is more, the author-and-document method has persisted. The Belgian prime minister, Leo Tindemans, drafted a report on the concept and shape of European union (1976); Altiero Spinelli produced the Draft Treaty of European Union (1984); Jacques Santer, the prime minister of Luxembourg, provided the basis for the Single European Act (1985); and Jacques

Delors, President of the Commission, drew up a report on Economic and Monetary Union (1989). Monnet, Spaak and their collaborators established a style for the creation of a unified Europe very different from that envisaged by their medieval and early modern predecessors. Yet through all its changing fortunes the idea of European unity has periodically found expression through draft plans designed for its accomplishment. These plans have attempted by methods peculiar to their own times to solve problems which have proved to be of perennial concern over the centuries.

CHAPTER 8

Conclusion: Perennial problems

Cultural, geopolitical and institutional issues

Quot homines tot consilia – So many men, so many schemes, if we may thus adapt Terence. But although each of the authors of the major schemes we have surveyed approached the problem of European unity in characteristic ways, they were all reflecting upon problems that have been constant over the centuries. Our purpose in this concluding chapter therefore is to summarise the ways in which certain crucial issues recurred in the plans and how the individual authors variously responded to these perennial questions.

No project for voluntary political integration would be at all credible unless the putative member states shared some cultural and political traditions and values. This sense of identity necessary for a successful union of states is Janus-faced. In looking inward it must recognise the characteristics which the members have in common and which thus provide at least a modicum of homogeneity. In looking outward it must recognise the distinctiveness, incompatability, even enmity of those outside the union. From c.1300 to c.1800 the consciousness of a European identity grew apace. Voltaire, writing of the seventeenth century in the passage already partially cited (p.65), asserted,

Already for a long time one could regard Christian Europe (except Russia) as a sort of great republic divided into several states . . . all in harmony with each other, all having the same substratum of religion, although divided into various sects; all possessing the same principles of public and political law, unknown in other parts of the world. In obedience to these principles the European nations do not make their prisoners slaves, they respect their enemies' ambassadors . . . and, above all, they are at one on the wise policy of maintaining among themselves so far as possible an equal balance of power, ceaselessly carrying on negotiations, even in wartime . . . (Voltaire, 1756, p.5).

These conditions, which did not obtain in other continents, admirably summarise the foundations upon which plans for political unity could be constructed. Those devisers of plans for European unity could consequently claim to be less utopian in their projects than those who sought to bring conciliation and union to the whole world. Dante, Crucé, Comenius, Bentham and Kant, for example, each in his own way, had this wider, global vision. However, Saint-Pierre spoke on behalf of those who would confine their ambitions to Europe. He explained in the Preface to his Project that he had discarded his original intention of producing a scheme for all the kingdoms of the world as this 'would cast an air of impossibility upon the whole project.' (quoted, Hemleben, p.58).

For the sake of consolidating these feelings of cohesion a number of the schemes specifically restrict the membership of the proposed unions. No state which might be at all antipathetic to the principles of the confederation must be allowed in lest it loosen the bonds of fraternity. Most noticeably, few of our authors would have admitted Russia (see pp.182–3). Saint-Simon and the fathers of the European Community were particularly exclusive because of their insistence on their members' adherence to the practices of parliamentary liberal government. Saint-Pierre is somewhat different in his attitude towards membership. Indeed, he is quite vicious in his proposed treatment of those states which voluntarily excluded themselves: the league thus far created was to exert main force to drag the reluctant ones into the union. He gauged that those unconvinced of the value of the confederation would be more trouble as outside freebooters than as coerced insiders.

With this notable exception, all the members envisaged in these plans were assumed to be willing to collaborate in the operation of two political principles of cardinal importance to the success of the schemes. One was the surrender of some measure of sovereignty (however camouflaged in many of the systems – see p.188); the other was the use of representative institutions. From Dubois to Spaak the plans offered peace or some other common good for the continent in return for the loss of autonomous power and the creation of supranational institutions. Membership was therefore inevitably confined to those states whose princes, governments or peoples agreed to these methods of proceeding.

The common good which was the promised prize for the institutionalisation of Europe's homogeneity was not just to be internal peace and prosperity. In many of the schemes, we find the felt need for collaboration against a common threat or at least the externalisation of European man's aggressive tendencies. The medieval authors and Sully wish to fight the Turks; Saint-Simon advocates colonial conquests; Briand and the founders of the European Community are looking over their shoulders at the economic competitiveness of the

USA. Sully, Saint-Simon, Monnet and Spaak are all, in their own ways, nervous of or hostile to Russia.

Perhaps the most important single element in Europe's distinctive character has been Christianity. This was very obviously so in the Middle Ages, as we saw in Chapter 1, when Christendom and Europe were for long synonymous concepts. Sully, Penn and Bellers are also conscious of the cohesive potential of Christianity despite its violent fragmentation in western and central Europe as a result of the Reformation. Indeed, one of the motives of both Penn and Bellers is to promote the reconciliation of the Christian sects. It is also interesting to note the revival of the Christian motif in the powerful support lent to European integration by Christian Democrat parties after the Second World War.

Christianity has been not only an integrating factor, but a means also of differentiating Europe from Islam, initially as a creed, later as personified by the Turk. One of the main expressed purposes of European union in the plans of Dubois, Poděbrad and Sully was the revival of the crusade. As late as 1300 the Moors still held the European foothold of the Emirate of Granada. The southern and eastern shores of the Mediterranean were for centuries governed by Muslims. In Asia Minor and the Balkans the Turks presented a dynamic threat from the eleventh century: Constantinople fell in 1453; Vienna was besieged in 1529 and in 1683. Little wonder that Turkey was excluded from most schemes for European union. There are few exceptions. Crucé, with a truly cosmopolitan perspective, is not relevant to our case. Penn and Bellers, in characteristically tolerant mood, would accept Turkey if possible even though they are nervous about any continued attacks from that direction. Saint-Pierre wavered over the years, though he had no doctrinal objections. Rousseau, too in his *Extract*, following Saint-Pierre's final position, excluded Turkey. From Saint-Simon onwards Turkey was inevitably excluded because of its lack of a liberal system of government. Coudenhove-Kalergi drew a map of his system of world federations on which he left Turkey ambiguously unshaded (p.126). She was even missing from Briand's scheme – because she had yet to win admission to the League of Nations, not, as Albrecht-Carrié states, because of her 'eccentric geographical location' (Albrecht-Carrié, p.224n).

Russia poses a problem for our writers as well. Of all the plans we have surveyed she is incorporated only by the open-minded generations from Penn to Rousseau. The denial of membership to Russia is harder to explain and justify than the black-balling of Turkey. Even the geographers of the ancient world accepted the River Tanais (the Don) as the eastern boundary of Europe, thus incorporating what we would today regard as European Russia. This was unquestioned until the nineteenth century, when the boundary was sited slightly further east at the Ural river and mountain range. What is more, ever since the baptism of Vladimir, Grand Prince of Kiev, in 988, Russia had been counted a Christian state. Seven hundred years later Peter the Great made strenuous efforts by both practical and symbolic actions to westernise Russian society.

On the other hand, there have been numerous features of Russian experience which have set it apart from mainstream European experience. The population even of European Russia retained Asiatic characteristics as an admixture to their Slav culture. Their Christianity was derived from Byzantium and not Rome. After the Turks overwhelmed Asia Minor and the Balkans, Russia was the sole free personification of eastern Orthodoxy – a schismatic church as viewed from the west. The doctrinal division between Russia and the rest of Europe was revived in secular form in 1917 when Russia embraced Communism (or had it thrust upon her). Moreover, the Russian method of government persisted in an autocratic form from the age of the tsars of Muscovy to that of the Stalinist police-state. It was a style alien to the pluralistic modes of government which evolved in the rest of Europe.

Sully felt so antipathetic towards Muscovy that he even proposed a kind of crusade against her. Penn and Bellers wanted her in their European systems if it could be arranged. Saint-Pierre and Rousseau accepted Russia, Saint-Pierre with interestingly growing enthusiasm. Saint-Simon felt that Russia, along with other east European states, lacked the same historical experiences that would help the rest of the continent to cohere. Morever, although Alexander I was impressed by earlier schemes and produced his own quasi-federal plan in the form of a 'Holy Alliance', the general mood of the nineteenth century was one of fear and suspicion of the Russian bear. As Hinsley reports, 'In the period before 1848 Mazzini and Pecqueur, a Saint-Simonian, explicitly excluded her from their European federation . . . After 1848 . . . Others excluded her . . . by basing their European Federation on historical and ethnical, rather than political uniformity.' (Hinsley, p.105).

In the inter-war period, Coudenhove-Kalergi's world-plan arranged for the Soviet Union to be a federation in its own right alongside his proposed Pan-Europe. Briand excluded her inevitably because, like Turkey, she was not a member of the League. And, finally, it is possible that the European Community might not have been launched in the 1950s had it not been for the Cold War fear of and enmity towards the USSR.

Whereas there has been uncertainty often spilling over into downright hostility towards the incorporation of Turkey and Russia into any European union, there was one state whose role was almost always portrayed as of central importance. This was France. One cogent explanation for this is not far to seek: so many drafters of the major plans were themselves Frenchmen. The nineteenth-century French poet-politician Lamartine declared that 'When Providence desires an idea to influence the world, it kindles it in the soul of a

Frenchman.' (Geyl, p.382). The roll-call of those authors of schemes featured in the present book is predominantly French: Dubois, Crucé, Sully, Saint-Pierre, Napoleon, Saint-Simon, the Saint-Simonians, Briand (and Léger), Schuman, Monnet (and Uri).

Whether the motive was openly admitted or not, many of these projects for European integration were designed to enhance the self-interest of France. In some cases, as in Dubois and Napoleon, this objective is dressed up as France's mission to civilise or liberalise Europe. True, Saint-Simon is reasonably altruistic in recommending that France, with England, should lead Europe to unity. Yet even his message could be distorted into a missionary zeal: for example, his follower Considérant advocated that France should unite Europe by force if necessary – what Napoleon had come near to achieving two decades before. Sully, Briand, Schuman and Monnet were much more concerned with the challenge from Germany – from the Habsburgs and the power of the industrialised Germany of the twentieth century. In the case of Sully he sought French security, domination even, by the emasculation of the Habsburgs in a reconstructed Europe. Briand, Schuman and Monnet pursued an alternative policy of taming Germany by the fusion of its interests with those of France.

The fourth state to be given special consideration in the plans is England. Apart from the work of Penn and Bellers c.1700, the federal enthusiasts immediately prior to the First World War and the members of Federal Union c.1940, there are few examples of Englishmen taking much interest in European unity. Bentham is important, but his perspective was broader than just Europe. The nineteenth-century historian J.R. Seeley supported the idea but wrote nothing of lasting influence about it. Moreover, when concrete proposals were presented in our own century, with the Briand Memorandum, the Schuman Plan and the work of the Spaak committee, the British governments held aloof.

And yet many of the authors of the plans we have surveyed recognised that the success of their schemes could well hinge on England's full-hearted participation. The main exception to this anglophilia is Rousseau. He appended a hostile footnote to his *Extrait* when it was published in 1761, five years after its composition. No doubt reflecting on the contemporary view that England's imperial greed was the cause of wars and on England's victories in the Seven Years War, he made the following forecast:

The situation has changed since I wrote this: but my basic principle holds good. It is, for example, very easy to foresee that, in twenty years from now, England, with all its glory, will be ruined, and, furthermore, will have lost the remainder of her liberty. Everyone ensures that agriculture flourishes on this island; and I myself am willing to bet that it is in decline there. London grows daily; and so the rest of the kingdom is depopulated. The English wish to be conquerors; and so it will not be long before they are slaves (Vaughan, 1915, p.373n).

He later claimed that he had foreseen the American War of Independence. In contrast, Dubois placed Edward I at the head of the list of princes to whom he addressed his tract. Sully even went so far as to fabricate a collaborative conversation with Elizabeth I to 'prove' England's supposed involvement in the Grand Design. In recording his support for Sully's plan, Penn expressed the hope that England would have the honour of actually implementing it. Bellers wrote similarly in addressing his pamphlet to Queen Anne. Most convinced of all of England's indispensability was Saint-Simon, constructing his whole edifice on the English parliamentary system. Just over a century later Coudenhove-Kalergi accepted the practical necessity of excluding England from his Pan-European Union; but it was an arrangement decided upon in a mood of disappointment at England's policy of isolation from the continent. Briand was perhaps less realistic. Although his scheme was primarily prompted by his desire to cement the Franco-German rapprochement, its acceptance was dependent on Britain's support, which fatally it did not enjoy.

When it came to creating a form of European union after the Second World War many enthusiasts on the mainland of Europe were strongly anglophile. At first they looked with eager expectation for British leadership; later, they were depressed by Britain's aloof refusal even to participate. No one regretted that more than Monnet, who knew the country so well. 'The civilization of the West needs Britain,' he wrote in his memoirs; 'and Europe, to continue her unique contribution to that civilization, needs the qualities that reside in the British people . . . The British have a better understanding than the continentals of institutions and how to use them.' (Monnet, p.451).

Let us now turn our attention away from particular states to the question of the boundaries of the states which would compose the variously formulated confederations. These would in most cases remain unaltered. Saint-Pierre has been roundly criticised for adopting this policy. But the Quakers too recommended freezing current boundaries on the argument that all such arrangements were equally arbitrary. Briand was even caricatured for his inflexibility. The English cartoonist Low depicts him sailing a yacht with European colleagues. It carries the notice: 'Danger. Passengers must remain in statu quo' (Low, p.57). Bellers added the refinement of cantonal subdivisions for representational and military recruitment purposes. And Saint-Simon urged the unification of Germany for the sake of progress and peace in that large area of central Europe. Only Sully played cartographer for the purpose of creating continental 'equilibrium' – his diplomatic philosopher's stone, which would turn the dross of bellicosity to a golden peace.

How was a united Europe to be brought into existence? Most of the authors we have surveyed conceived of a diplomatic act of genesis: the states would all adhere to a treaty drafted for the purpose. Indeed, since the prime purpose of creating a union for most of the writers was the achievement of peace, the use of force to bring this about would have smacked of hypocrisy. True, Sully and Saint-Pierre provided for forcible additions to an initial core: by the conversion of Russia to an 'acceptable' form of Christianity in the case of Sully; by the enforced conversion of non-believers to the confederal faith in the case of Saint-Pierre. Both Saint-Simon and the founding fathers of the European Community adopted a policy of voluntary accretion. After the establishment of the Anglo-French union and the 'Little Europe' of the Six respectively, other states would be allowed to join when they were ready to do so. Bellers too recognised the need for a lengthy period for harmonising European states to the underlying principles of his union.

These cultural and geopolitical considerations were but settings for the businesslike building of political machinery. If a union of European states was to be constructed, how was it to operate?

A cardinal feature of all the plans, inevitably, was the provision of central deliberative and arbitrative bodies. Curiously, in the light of his radical move to an effective federal parliamentary system, Saint-Simon alone makes provision for an overall European monarch (that is, if we discount Dante's monarch of the world). All the plans require the constituent states to send representatives to participate in permanent or at least frequent meetings. In some cases great care is exercised to ensure that either the number of representatives or the weighting of their votes is proportionate to the size of their state. This is a notable feature of the Grand Design, Penn's Essay and the European Community. Supplementary bodies were also allowed for in some of the plans. These differ widely in style and function: a Christian Council in Bellers, a House of Lords in Saint-Simon, a European Committee in Briand. Although Dubois envisages some meetings of a Council of sovereigns, only in Poděbrad and the European Community as it evolved is provision made for effective work to be undertaken by heads of government themselves. These bodies were the Council of kings and princes and the European Council respectively. Thus was a recommendation of 1464 implemented in 1974!

In most plans the representative Council has powers of arbitration in disputes as well as policy-making authority. However, here again we hear an interesting echo across the centuries with the device of a separate Court of Justice in Dubois's scheme and in the European Community. The severity of sanctions to be imposed upon offending members varies enormously. Dubois and Saint-Pierre envisage the harshest disciplinary measures. The majority assume that once the system is installed political pressure to conform will be sufficient. Three schemes allow for interesting financial arrangements: Poděbrad and Penn require the victims of aggression to receive compensation; the European Community can exact fines for non-compliance with regulations.

For the sake of internal peace and a common external policy a number of the plans consider military arrangements. Dubois, Poděbrad and Sully are especially interested in the use of union forces for their offensive and crusading strategies. These writers and Saint-Pierre foresee the value of union forces also for federal policing. Sully alone gives precise force strengths, though Bellers has his own exact formula. Penn and Bellers characteristically emphasise disarmament. So too does Saint-Pierre. The attempt to create a European Defence Community in the 1950s failed, though by 1955 all six members of the ECSC/EEC were in any case members of the western NATO military alliance.

Reduction in the incidence of European war is generally viewed as having economic advantages. Sully and Penn particularly emphasise what is today called the 'peace dividend' of diverting monies hitherto used for military expenditure for more productive purpose. Rousseau worries deeply about the costs of war. The authors also consider that international commerce will benefit from the more peaceful conditions. Dubois, Sully and Saint-Pierre especially emphasise this advantage, while Saint-Pierre, Coudenhove-Kalergi, Briand and the founders of the European Community are alert to the advantages of economic co-ordination to improve industrial production, internal confederal trade and standards of living. By the time we reach the twentieth century the issue of economic as distinct from political union has become of signal importance. But an allocation of money to a central, confederal fund as provided for in the Treaties of Paris and Rome is not a specifically twentieth-century device. Poděbrad, Sully and Saint-Pierre allowed for similar arrangements.

No proper federation can, of course, function without its own independent budget. But were these integrative plans federations in any true sense of the word? It must be remembered that many of these authors were writing against a background of political theory and practice which was antipathetic to the adhesion of separate established states into a greater union. The nation-state was the accepted form of polity. Writing about the Middle Ages, Alfred Cobban noted, 'By the twelfth century in Western, and the thirteenth century in Eastern Europe, a considerable number of nation states existed . . . For many nations the fourteenth century is the climax of this age of nation-making.' (Cobban, 1969, p.27). It was in this context that Dubois and Poděbrad canvassed their schemes. In Dubois's native country in particular 'the idea of the king's being an emperor in his realm – *rex in regno suo est imperator* – was voiced several times in thirteenth-century France.' (Ullmann, p.156). Sully composed his Grand Design in the age of 'the new monarchy', a generation or so after his fellow-countryman Bodin published his *Six Books of the*

Republic (1576), containing the classic exposition of the concept of sovereignty. The seventeenth-century style of absolute monarchy, challenged in Stuart England and brought to its apogee in louis-quartorzienne France, found its theoretical justification in Hobbes's *Leviathan* (1651), half a century before the Quakers and Saint-Pierre set to work on their schemes.

The age of the birth of the ideology of nationalism coincided with Saint-Simon's *Reorganisation*. And nationalism in its democratic sophisticated form of national self-determination was sanctified at the Paris peace conference but a decade before Briand circulated his Memorandum.

The strength of the challenge to the prevailing state power and national sentiment – that is, the relative tightness of the federal bonds envisaged in these plans – varied considerably. One might picture a spectrum from the very tentative arrangements of Briand through the wide powers of confederal authority listed by Saint-Pierre to the fully-fledged integrated systems advocated by the nineteenth- and twentieth-century federalists. It is notable, for example, that Saint-Pierre insists on central power to intervene to suppress sedition in a member state and for locally-based federal chambers of commerce to regulate trade. In contrast, some of the authors worry about the problem of state sovereignty. Penn and Briand go out of their way to reassure potential members that their sovereign control over their internal affairs would in no way be infringed. Monnet and Spaak had to rein in their federal enthusiasms for the sake of achieving a modest 'Community' start to the undertaking. Rousseau denied the practicability of any such scheme as Saint-Pierre had devised because of the jealous hold on power which the princes could not be expected voluntarily to loosen.

From Dubois to Bellers the issue was basically very simple. The contracting parties would surrender the freedom to fight each other. Once the union was created the princes of Europe would surrender the 'sovereign right' to territorial aggrandisement in their own continent and transfer the 'sovereign right' of bilateral settlement of quarrels to central arbitration. Saint-Pierre is also primarily concerned to deny individual rulers the right and opportunity to ravage Europe by war. He adds further very specific constraints particularly in the codification and regulation of commercial practice and the express denial of any chance of seceding from his league. The other authors tend, perhaps, to assume that their unions would be equally 'perpetual', so obvious would their advantages be once in operation.

Saint-Pierre was indeed the first to perceive the full potential of a union structure beyond a peace-keeping function. Henceforth, in Saint-Simon, Briand and the European Community treaties the areas of competence of the central authorities are to some extent enumerated. The state's sovereign autonomy to direct its own social and economic affairs now becomes undermined.

Or pooled – to use the term favoured in the European Community. Benefits of extra security and prosperity, it can be argued, are scarcely a reduction in sovereignty. Total, discrete independence involves submission to war and want. As Saint-Pierre wrote, the princes would 'procure to themselves in times of weakness a much greater security . . . of the possession of sovereignty.' (quoted, Hinsley, p.42).

We have used terms such as 'union' and 'federal' somewhat loosely to indicate the co-ordinating and integrative purposes of the plans we have surveyed. But, in truth, almost all were, strictly speaking, confederal in purpose. Even Saint-Pierre, who planned such thorough powers of intervention, has been described by Murray Forsyth as 'an outstanding representative' of 'the universalist or Utopian tendency' of 'thinking about confederation.' (Forsyth, 1981, p.86). For, after all, so many of our authors, Saint-Pierre included, shrank from dissolving the states of Europe as identifiable political units. The existence of princely families would surely in any case have precluded such thoughts. Probably not even Saint-Simon envisaged a state-federal relationship of the kind we now associate with the USA or the Federal Republic of Germany. Not until the mid-nineteenth century, with the developing system of the United States of America as its model, was the possibility of a truly federal United States of Europe really entertained. It is an objective which was then fully embraced at the time of the Second World War and toyed with by the founding fathers of the European Community.

In any case, it would be pointless trying to discern any real exposition of a theory of European federalism in the texts we have examined. For the most part, their authors were practical men bent upon describing pragmatic solutions to Europe's problems as they perceived them. Their motives were utilitarian not moral. Rousseau and Saint-Simon alone of our gallery were theorists of any rank. In Rousseau's case his promised work on federalism was not completed and the fragment he did write was destroyed by a frightened friend during the Revolution. And Saint-Simon's idea of government by technocratic parliamentarians too naïvely underestimated the problem of making *political* choices and institutionalising that process in federal terms. The theoretical problem of the relationship between state sovereignty and federal structure remained unresolved.

Historical and human influences

Real or ostensible, the expressed basic purpose of the schemes for European unity over the centuries was the quest for peace. However, the international circumstances of their composition and the preoccupations of their authors led to variations and additions in detail to this permanent goal.

We may identify five other considerations whose weight in the schemes varies because of the vagaries of circumstance and author. One was the determination to enhance the power or security of one particular constituent state: Bohemia in the case of Poděbrad; France, blatantly in the case of Dubois and Sully, more circumspectly by Briand, Schuman and Monnet. A mirror-image of this purpose was the desire to reduce the power or threat of one particular constituent state: the Habsburg dominions in the case of Sully; Germany in the case of Briand and the founders of the European Community. A third extra motive was increased strength, be it military or economic, against outside powers: the Turk from Dubois to Sully; Russia in Sully and Monnet and Spaak; the USA in Coudenhove-Kalergi, Briand and Monnet. Fourthly, the internal economic advantages of union, either because of reduced expenditure on the military, ending the destructiveness of war or increased trade, was considered by virtually all our authors in their own particular ways. Inevitably, over the centuries the focus of interest shifted from the Mediterranean to the heart of Europe, to transatlantic trade, then to western Europe. Finally, the advantages of stable and efficient government was a factor for Saint-Pierre and Saint-Simon, writing with a vivid awareness of civil upheaval and revolution, in England and France respectively.

The influence of prevailing political practices is especially evident in the styles of the proposed European unions. It has often been remarked that the plans which derived from the pens of all the writers from Dubois to Saint-Pierre were based upon a fatal premiss. This was that they required the surrender of some of their authority by sovereign princes whose very *raison d'être* was the exercise of untrammelled power. The able and experienced chief minister of Louis XV, Cardinal Fleury, put his finger on the problem when he said to Saint-Pierre, 'You must begin by sending a troop of missionaries to prepare the hearts and minds of the contracting sovereigns.' (quoted, Hemleben, p.66). But short of military conquest, which only Napoleon and Hitler attempted, there was no other option. And Rousseau warned that the trauma of going through with the cure of unity might prove more unbearable than the painful disease of disunity itself. To think that any of the writers from the fourteenth to the eighteenth centuries might have proposed achieving union by means of the representative Estates system or popular pressure is to indulge in anachronisms.

Integration by means of like-minded members of parliamentary institutions could not be envisaged until *c*.1800. And in pioneering this approach to the problem Saint-Simon was perfectly justified in his self-assessment of his originality. It was a style of thinking which continued to the age of Briand.

The form of individual state governments through which the process of union would be negotiated was crucially important for most of our authors because they were sketching out merely confederal schemes. The character of the established governments would not be affected, indeed in some of the plans they were to be positively consolidated. Only with the strand of federal thinking from Proudhon to Spinelli is the focus more fully on the character of the constructed United States of Europe than its constituent parts.

By the time we reach the twentieth century we are in the age of public consciousness of and popular movements for European unity. Whether in Coudenhove-Kalergi's Pan-European Movement or the post-war bodies which gave support to the compromise outcome of the European Community, the steady shift of opinion in favour of some integrative solution to Europe's problems was a significant new factor. At the same time the functionalist (or neo-functionalist) and therefore gradualist approach to unification rendered the basic aim more palatable. And although the European Community is not so totally dissimilar from all the previous schemes as is sometimes assumed, it has one vitally different feature from all the rest: it has happened and it works.

Yet, for all the significance of historical context, we must not forget the personal imprint. True, all our authors in one way or another reflected the practices and preconceptions of their times. But they also made their own very individual contributions. Each text is thus an outcome of the interaction of the man and the moment. E.H. Carr, reviewing the problem of the role of the individual in history, has written,

What seems to me essential is to recognise in the great man an outstanding individual who is at once a product and an agent of the historical process, at once the representative and the creator of social forces which change the shape of the world and the thoughts of men (Carr, 1964, p.55).

The great majority of the personalities in the present study are scarcely great men with the influence of an Alexander the Great or a Luther, for instance. They did nevertheless collectively keep alive and develop a dream of a united Europe and they individually contributed certain considerations from their own particular concerns. Carr's guidelines are therefore relevant.

We do not know if the advocates of European union in the seventeenth century inherited any ideas from the Middle Ages across the hiatus of the sixteenth century. We have outlined the reasons for thinking that Sully might have known the work of Dubois (p.14). We can be certain, however, that there is a continuous and conscious building upon and adaptation of plans from Sully onwards. This is not to argue, along with Pascal and the size of Cleopatra's nose, that, without Sully's obsessive hatred of the Habsburgs, we would have no European Community today. Rather to suggest that the writers we have surveyed passed on through the generations an accumulation of ideas and recommendations which had become a rich inheritance by the time some form of union eventually became a practical possibility.

All the writers' plans, in varying degrees, were complex proposals. We may none the less highlight the particularly significant contribution which each introduced to the ideal. Dubois advocated the crystallisation of Europe round the nucleus of a mighty nation-state. Poděbrad introduced the procedure of majority voting. Sully put forward the notion of a continental internal balance of power. Penn ingeniously worked out a system of proportional representation. Both Quakers foresaw the advantages of disarmament. Saint-Pierre showed that outline ideas needed to be worked through in detail. Rousseau laid the foundations for federal political theory. Saint-Simon emphasised the importance of an efficient technocracy to manage such a large undertaking. Coudenhove-Kalergi dreamt of a federal Europe as part of a federalised world system. Briand insisted on an integrated Europe being firmly set in the context of an organised world order. Monnet and Spaak developed in practice the functionalist method of proceeding.

Each of these characteristic contributions were reflections of the experiences of these men in their personal and public lives and of the political priorities that were dearest to their hearts and minds. Furthermore, the core messages of these plans have been of lasting interest.

As Europe looks ahead to a new century it is still faced with the need to resolve many of the same issues which taxed authors of so many essays in the field over the past seven hundred years. The pressure inside the European Community for further economic, monetary and political union, the unification of Germany and the collapse of the Communist system from central Europe to the Soviet Union could not help but stimulate renewed debate c.1990 on the nature of European unity. We may discern some half-dozen models.

The first recognises the European Community as primarily a method of providing nation-states with a useful framework for the collaboration of their capitalist economic systems. Further development would be confined to the accession of additional states as their political styles and economic arrangements allow. A refinement of this strategy is to conceive of a concentric Europe of different collectivities of states engaging in different levels of integration. The second model portrays the European Community itself, while geographically expanding to some degree, moving towards a more clearly federal style of political integration.

The Danish scholar Ole Wæver has identified three 'competing Europes' in the ambitions of the French, Germans and Russians (Wæver, pp.477–93). The French, he argues, seek to make the European Community a nation-state writ large. The Germans are pursuing a *Mitteleuropa* policy emphasising the porousness of national frontiers to the transmission of cultural values and commercial goods. The Russians, or at least those who have welcomed the aims of *perestroika* and the end of the Cold War, wish to be fully accepted as Europeans and be involved in a European security system. Gorbachev voiced the idea of

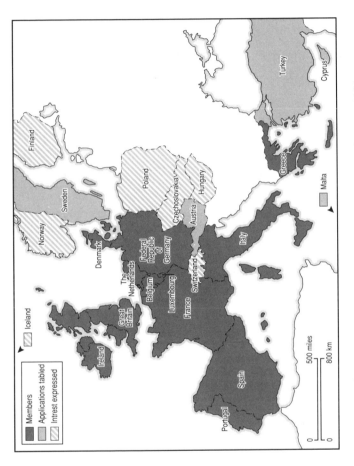

Map 9 The European Community and applicants 1991

a cohesive Europe from the Atlantic to the Urals by means of the metaphor of the 'common European home'. Of this he has written,

... the home is common, that is true, but each family has its own apartment, and there are different entrances too. But it is only together, collectively, and by following the sensible norms of coexistence that the Europeans can save their home, protect it against a conflagration and other calamities, make it better and safer, and maintain it in proper order ... The concept of a 'common European home' combines *necessity with opportunity* (Gorbachev, p.195).

Finally, in April 1990 Pope John Paul II in a speech in Prague reminded the continent of the Christian basis of its unity:

A united Europe [he declared] is no longer only a dream. It is an actual process which cannot be purely political or economic. It has a profound cultural, spiritual and moral dimension. Christianity is at the very roots of European culture (quoted, Kettle, p.14).

It is indeed remarkable how the centuries-old issues surrounding the matter of European unity have persisted to our own day. Let us briefly enumerate them.

The question of eligibility for membership has been radically changed by the events of 1989–91 in central/eastern Europe and the disintegration of the USSR. It has now become possible to envisage an eventual European Union with an eastern boundary along the Finnish and Estonian frontiers with Russia in the north to Bulgaria and Greece in the south. A confederal structure approaching thirty component states seems a not impossible outcome. However, both Turkey and Russia remain problems. Turkey wishes to join the European Community but her poor record in terms of human rights abuses causes embarrassment in Brussels. Russia, however she emerges from the collapse of the Soviet Union, would wish to be accepted as properly European. But her size, economic problems and ethnic complexity make it unthinkable that she could join the 'Europe' of the Community. On the other hand, the demise of Communism in the eastern half of the continent and the revival of both Catholic and Orthodox churches give credence to the Pope's call for a Europe conscious of its common Christian experience, the source of cultural unity in so many of the earlier plans.

The question of the exact quantum of sovereignty to be transferred from the state to the central decision-making bodies is still a contentious issue. This, of course, relates to the age-old problem of the institutional structure: the powers to be accorded to the quasi-federal bodies, the relationship between each of them and between them and the state institutions. For instance, what should be the relative powers of the European Commission and the European Council; or of the European Parliament and the several European state parliaments vis-à-vis the Community executive bodies?

The problems of common defence and security structures and common foreign policy objectives have arisen time and again and remain to be satisfactorily resolved. In particular, has NATO still any role to play in a post-Cold War Europe? Or should the continent-wide CSCE (the Conference on Security and Co-operation in Europe) be developed as a truly pan-European security system? That body is surely more relevant to intra-continental problems like terrorism, drugs and civil conflict.

All these current debates would have been deeply interesting to all our draftsmen of blueprints for European unity. Europe is the smallest of the continents and has the longest tradition of sophisticated government and political thinking. Men have persistently urged the deployment of that political expertise in that relatively small area to achieve a political unity for the greater good of its peoples. Idiosyncratic, wily and not entirely altruistic some of them may have been. They all nevertheless had the insight to understand that the problems with which they wrestled would not disappear by being ignored. Our understanding of European political history is the poorer if we, in turn, ignore those plans and the men who drafted them.

References

Acheson, D., 1970, *Present at the creation*, Hamish Hamilton, London

Acton, Lord, 1906 (1960 ed.), *Lectures on modern history*, Collins, London

Albrecht-Carrié, R., 1966, *The unity of Europe: an historical survey*, Secker & Warburg, London

Angell, N., 1914, *The foundations of international polity*, Heinemann, London

Arendt, H., 1973, *On revolution*, Penguin, Harmondsworth

Ashley, M., 1952, *England in the seventeenth century*, Penguin, Harmondsworth

Barbiche, B., 1978, *Sully*, Albin Michel, Paris

Barraclough, G., 1950, *The medieval empire: idea and reality*, Historical Association, London

Barraclough, G., 1963, *European unity in thought and action*, Blackwell, Oxford

Bell, C., 1972, 'The "special relationship"' in Leifer, M. (ed.), *Constraints and adjustments in British foreign policy*, Allen & Unwin, London

Beloff, N., 1973, *Transit of Britain*, Collins, London

Béthune, M. de (trans. C. Lennox), 1755, (new ed., 1810), *The memoirs of the Duke of Sully, prime minister to Henry the Great*, William Miller, London

Braithwaite, W.C., 1919, *The second period of Quakerism*, Macmillan, London

Brogan, D.W., 1940, *The development of modern France (1870–1939)*, Hamish Hamilton, London

Bromley, J.S. (ed.), 1970, *The New Cambridge Modern History, VI: the rise of Great Britain and Russia 1688–1715/25*, Cambridge University Press, Cambridge

Brugmans, H., 1966, *L'idée européenne 1918–1965*, De Tempel, Bruges

Buisseret, D., 1968, *Sully and the growth of centralized government in France 1598–1610*, Eyre & Spottiswoode, London

Buisseret, D. & Barbiche, B. (eds), 1970, *Les œconomies royales de Sully, I, 1572–1594*, Librairie C. Klincksieck, Paris

Bull, H., 1977, *The anarchical society*, Macmillan, London

Burgess, M., 1989, *Federalism and European union*, Routledge, London

Carlton, D., 1970, *MacDonald versus Henderson: the foreign policy of the second Labour government*, Macmillan, London

Carr, E.H., 1940, *The twenty years' crisis 1919–1939*, Macmillan, London

Carr, E.H., 1964, *What is history?*, Penguin, Harmondsworth

Castel de Saint-Pierre, C.I., 1738 (trans. H. Hale Bellot, 1927), *Selections from the second edition of the Abrégé du projet de paix perpétuelle*, Sweet & Maxwell for Grotius Society, London

Childs, J., 1982, *Armies and warfare in Europe 1648–1789*, Manchester University Press, Manchester

Clark, G.N., 1958, *War and society in the seventeenth century*, Cambridge University Press, Cambridge

Clarke, G. (ed.), 1987, *John Bellers: his life, times and writings*, Routledge & Kegan Paul, London

Clarke, I.F., 1966 (1970 ed.), *Voices prophesying war 1763–1984*, Panther, London

Cobban, A., 1957–65, *A history of modern France*, 3 vols., Penguin, Harmondsworth

Cobban, A., 1960, *In search of humanity*, Cape, London

Cobban, A., 1934, (1964 rev. ed.), *Rousseau and the modern state*, Allen & Unwin, London

Cobban, A., 1969, *The nation-state and national self-determination*, Collins, London

Coudenhove-Kalergi, R.N., 1926, *Pan-Europe*, Knopf, New York

Coudenhove-Kalergi, R.N., 1943, *Crusade for Pan-Europe: autobiography of a man and a movement*, Putnam's, New York

Coudenhove-Kalergi, R.N., 1962, *History of the Paneuropean movement from 1922 to 1962*, Paneuropean Union, Basle & Vienna

Davis, R.H.C., 1957, *A history of medieval Europe: from Constantine to Saint Louis*, Longman, London

Dawson, K. & Wall, P., 1968, *Parliamentary representation*, Oxford University Press, Oxford

de la Mahotière, S., 1970, *Towards one Europe*, Penguin, Harmondsworth

de Rougemont, D., 1966, *The idea of Europe*, Macmillan, New York

de Sainte Lorette, L., 1955, *L'idée d'union fédérale européenne*, Armand Colin, Paris

Diebold, W., 1959, *The Schuman Plan: a study in economic cooperation 1950–1959*, Praeger, New York

Drouet, J., 1912, *L'Abbé de Saint-Pierre: l'homme et l'oeuvre*, Librairie Honoré Champion, Paris

Eden, A., 1960, *Full circle*, Cassell, London

Elisha, A. (ed.), 1965, *Aristide Briand: discours et écrits de politique étrangère*, Plon, Paris

European Communities, 1958, *Treaty establishing the European Economic Community and connected documents*, Publishing Services of the European Communities, Luxembourg

European Communities, 1987, *Treaties establishing the European Communities* (abridged edition), Office for Official Publications of the European Communities, Luxembourg

Everett, C.W., 1966, *Jeremy Bentham*, Weidenfeld & Nicolson, London

Fakkar, R., 1968, *Sociologie, socialisme et internationalisme prémarxiste*, Delachaux & Niestlé, Neuchatel

Fest, J., 1977, *Hitler*, Penguin, Harmondsworth

Fogarty, M.P., 1957, *Christian Democracy in Western Europe*, Routledge, London

Forsyth, M., 1967, 'The political objectives of European integration', *International Affairs*, 43

Forsyth, M., 1981, *Unions of states*, Leicester University Press, Leicester

Forsyth, M.G., Keens-Soper, H.M.A. & Savigear, P. (eds), 1970, *The theory of international relations*, Allen & Unwin, London

Fry, A.R., 1935, *John Bellers 1654–1725, Quaker, economist and social reformer*, Cassell, London

Geyl, P., 1967, *Encounters in history*, Collins, London

Gorbachev, M., 1987, *Perestroika*, Collins, London

Goumy, E., 1859 (repr. 1971), *Étude sur la vie et les écrits de l'Abbé de Saint-Pierre*, Slatkine Reprints, Geneva

Haas, E.B., 1958, *The uniting of Europe: political, social and economic forces 1950–1957*, Stanford University Press, Stanford

Hampden Jackson, J., 1946, *Clemenceau and the Third Republic*, Hodder & Stoughton, London

Hampson, N., 1968, *The Enlightenment*, Penguin, Harmondsworth

Hauser, H., 1948, *La prépondérance espagnole (1559–1660)*, Presses Universitaires de France, Paris

Hay, D., 1957, *Europe: the emergence of an idea*, Edinburgh University Press, Edinburgh

Hazard, P., 1946 (trans. J. Lewis May, 1954), *European thought in the eighteenth century*, Hollis & Carter, London

Heer, F., 1962, *The medieval world*, Mentor, New York

Hemleben, S.J., 1943, *Plans for world peace through six centuries*, University of Chicago Press, Chicago

Hermans, J., 1965, *L'evolution de la pensée européenne d'Aristide Briand*, Université de Nancy, Nancy-Saint-Nicolas-de-Port

Hinsley, F.H., 1967, *Power and the pursuit of peace*, Cambridge University Press, Cambridge

Hitler, A., 1926 (abr. ed., 1933), *My struggle*, Paternoster Library, London

Hodges, M. (ed.), 1972, *European integration*, Penguin, Harmondsworth

Huizinga, J.H., 1961, *Mr Europe: a political biography of Paul Henri Spaak*, Praeger, New York

Hutt, M., 1965, *Napoleon*, Oxford University Press, Oxford

Ionescu, G. (ed.), 1972, *The new politics of European integration*, Macmillan, London

Ionescu, G. (ed.), 1976, *The political thought of Saint-Simon*, Oxford University Press, Oxford

Jones, R.M., 1921 (repr. 1970), *The later periods of Quakerism*, Greenwood Press, Westport, Conn.

Kennedy, P., 1989 *The rise and fall of the great powers*, Collins, London

Kettle, M., 1990, 'John Paul's grand design for Europe', *Guardian*, 27 April

Kitzinger, U., 1967, *The European Common Market and Community*, Routledge & Kegan Paul, London

Laurent, P.-H., 1970, 'Paul-Henri Spaak and the diplomatic origins of the Common Market, 1955–1956', *Political Science Quarterly*, LXXXV

Lederer, I.J. (ed.), 1960, *The Versailles Settlement: was it foredoomed to failure?*, D.C. Heath, Boston

Lindsay, J.O. (ed.), 1957, *The new Cambridge Modern History, VII: the Old Regime*, Cambridge University Press, Cambridge

Linklater, A., 1982, *Men and citizens in the theory of international relations*, Macmillan, London

Low, 1940, *Europe since Versailles: a history in one hundred cartoons with a narrative text*, Penguin, Harmondsworth

Macartney, C.A., 1934, *National states and national minorities*, Oxford University Press, Oxford

Mackay, R.W.G., 1941, *Peace aims and the new order* (new ed. of *Federal Europe*, 1940), Michael Joseph, London

Manuel, F.E., 1956, *The new world of Henri Saint-Simon*, Harvard University Press, Cambridge, Mass.

Markham, F.M.H. (ed. & trans.), 1952, *Henri Comte de Saint-Simon (1760–1825): selected writings*, Blackwell, Oxford

Marks, S., 1976, *The illusion of peace*, Macmillan, London

Marx, K., 1867 (trans. B. Fowkes, 1976), *Capital*, Penguin, Harmondsworth

Mayne, R., 1970, *The recovery of Europe*, Weidenfeld & Nicolson, London

Mayne, R. & Pinder, J., 1990, *Federal union: the pioneers*, Macmillan, London

Mazzini, G., 1907 ed., *The duties of man*, Dent, London

Monnet, J. (trans. R. Mayne), 1978, *Memoirs*, Collins, London

Morrall, J.B., 1960, *Political thought in medieval times*, Hutchinson, London

Mousnier, R. (trans. J.W. Hunt), *Louis XIV*, Historical Association, London

Mowat, R.C., 1973, *Creating the European Community*, Blandford, London

Nye, R.B. & Morpurgo, J.E., 1955, *A history of the United States*, 2 vols., Penguin, Harmondsworth

Oudin, B., 1987, *Aristide Briand: la paix: une idée neuve en Europe*, Éditions Robert Laffont, Paris

Pagès, G., 1946, *La monarchie d'Ancien Régime en France*, Armand Colin

Paine, T., 1791–92 (ed., H. Collins, 1969), *Rights of man*, Penguin, Harmondsworth

Patijn, S. (ed.), 1970, *Landmarks in European unity*, A.W. Sijthoff, Leyden

Peare, C.O., 1956, *William Penn: a biography*, Dobson, London
Penn, W., n.d., *The peace of Europe: the fruits of solitude and other writings*, Dent, London
Perse, Saint-John, 1972, *Œuvres complètes*, Gallimard, Paris
Pfister, C., 1894, 'Les "Économies royales" de Sully et le Grand Dessein de Henri IV', *Revue historique*, LXI
Power, E., 1923, 'Pierre Du Bois and the domination of France' in F.J.C. Hearnshaw (ed.), *The social and political ideas of some great mediaeval thinkers*, Harrap, London
Reuter, P., 1953, *La Communauté Européenne du Charbon et de l'Acier*, Pichon et Durand-Auzias, Paris
Robertson, E.M. (ed.), 1971, *The origins of the Second World War*, Macmillan, London
Rochefort, R., 1968, *Robert Schuman*, Les Éditions du Cerf, Paris
Rousseau, J.-J., 1762 (trans. M. Cranston, 1968), *The social contract*, Penguin, Harmondsworth
Rousseau, J.-J., 1781 (trans. J.M. Cohen, 1953), *The confessions of Jean-Jacques Rousseau*, Penguin, Harmondsworth
Rousseau, J.-J., 1969, *Œuvres complètes*, IV, Gallimard, Dijon
Sabine, G.H., 1951, *A history of political theory*, Harrap, London
Sagnac, P. & de Saint-Léger, A., 1949, *Louis XIV (1661–1715)*, Presses Universitaires de France, Paris
Saint-Simon, C.-H. de, 1966, *Œuvres de Claude-Henri de Saint-Simon*, II, Éditions Anthropos, Paris
Schonfield, A., 1973, *Europe: journey to an unknown destination*, Penguin, Harmondsworth
Schuman, F.L., 1951, 'The European scene: the Council of Europe', *American Political Science Review*, 45
Schuschnigg, K. von, 1947, *Austrian requiem*, Gollancz, London
Seward, D., 1971, *The first Bourbon: Henri IV, King of France and Navarre*, Constable, London
Sorel, A., 1885 (trans. A. Cobban & J.W. Hunt, 1969), *Europe and the French Revolution: the political traditions of the Old Regime*, Collins, London
Spaak, P.-H. (trans. H. Fox), 1971, *The continuing battle: memoirs of a European 1936–1966*, Weidenfeld & Nicolson, London
Stawell, F.M., 1929, *The growth of international thought*, Thornton Butterworth, London
Strachan, H., 1983, *European armies and the conduct of war*, Allen & Unwin, London
Suarez, G., 1952, *Briand: sa vie – son oeuvre: VI: l'artisan de la paix, 1923–1932*, Plon, Paris
Thompson, J.M., 1952, *Napoleon Bonaparte: his rise and fall*, Blackwell, Oxford
Truman, H.S., 1956 (1965 ed.), *Years of trial and hope*, New American Library, New York
Ullmann, W., 1965, *A history of political thought in the Middle Ages*, Penguin, Harmondsworth
Vaucher, P., 1930, 'The Abbé de Saint-Pierre' in F.J.C. Hearnshaw (ed.), *The social and political ideas of some great French thinkers of the Age of Reason*, Harrap, London
Vaughan, C.E. (ed.), 1915, *The political writings of Jean-Jacques Rousseau*, I, Cambridge University Press, Cambridge
Vaughan, R. (ed.), 1976, *Post-war integration in Europe*, Edward Arnold, London
Voltaire n.d. (ed. L. Moland), *La Henriade, poëme de Fontenoy, odes et stances*, Librarie Garnier Frères, Paris
Voltaire, 1756 (trans. M.P. Pollock, 1926), *The age of Louis XIV*, Dent, London
Voltaire, 1764 (trans. T. Besterman, 1971), *Philosophical dictionary*, Penguin, Harmondsworth
Voyenne, B., 1964, *Histoire de l'idée européene*, Petite Bibliothèque Payot, Paris
Walters, F.P., 1952 (1960 ed.), *A history of the League of Nations*, Oxford University Press, Oxford
Wæver, O., 'Three competing Europes: German, French, Russian', *International Affairs*, 66

Watt, D.C., 1990, review article, *International Affairs*, 66

Wheeler-Bennet, J.W. (ed.), 1931, *Documents on international affairs 1930*, Oxford University Press, Oxford

Wistrich, E., 1989, *After 1992: the United States of Europe*, Routledge, London

Woodward, E.L. & Butler, R. (eds), 1946, *Documents on British foreign policy 1919–1939*, Second series, 1, HMSO, London

Young, J.W., 1984, *Britain, France and the unity of Europe 1945–1951*, Leicester University Press, Leicester

Index